GENERAL
CAREER
INTELLIGENCE

RAY BLASING

GENERAL CAREER INTELLIGENCE

Ignite *your* **Potential** *with*
Essential Insights *and*
Expert Advice

RAY BLASING

Foreword by **GUY KAWASAKI**

Copyright © 2024 by Ray Blasing. All Rights Reserved.

Legal Notice:

This book is copyright-protected and is intended solely for personal use.

No portion of this book may be amended, reproduced, duplicated, distributed, sold, quoted, paraphrased, or transmitted in any form or by any means, electronic, mechanical, photocopying, recording, scanning, or otherwise, without direct written permission from the author.

Limit of Liability/Disclaimer of Warranty: Every attempt has been made to provide accurate, up-to-date, reliable, and complete information. No warranties of any kind are expressed or implied. The author makes no representation or warranty concerning the accuracy or completeness of the contents of this book or fitness for a particular purpose. Readers acknowledge that the author does not render legal, financial, medical, or professional advice. The strategies and suggestions contained herein may not be suitable for your situation. You should consult with a licensed professional where appropriate.

The content of this book has been derived from a combination of personal experience and extensive research. The book has drawn insights and advice from hundreds of expert sources, including articles, books, studies, and other publicly available materials. Every effort has been made to cite and acknowledge these sources properly. However, any omissions or errors in attribution will be corrected in subsequent editions or updates. The inclusion of third-party references is for informational purposes only and does not imply endorsement or sponsorship of this book by those authors, publications, or organizations. Readers should be aware that websites and sources listed in this work may have changed or disappeared between when it was written and when it was read. The author and publisher are not responsible for the content or accuracy of any third-party websites or materials referenced in this book.

By reading this document, the reader agrees that under no circumstances will any blame, legal, or financial responsibility be held against the author or publisher for any damages, reparation, or losses of any kind, either direct or indirect, special, incidental, or consequential, which are incurred due to the use of the information contained within this book, including, but not limited to, advice, errors, omissions, or inaccuracies.

Book Layout ©2017 BookDesignTemplates.com

General Career Intelligence/ Ray Blasing. —1st ed.

Published in the United States by WWIT Press.
ISBN 979-8-9918093-0-6

To Cori and Kyler—I wrote this book for you.

And to Elaine—my partner, best friend, and the love of my life. Every day with you is a priceless gift.

Contents

Foreword	xi
Introduction	1
Education and Learning	5
Learning Diversity	6
Arts and Humanities	7
The Importance of STEM	9
Generalists	11
Tradespeople	13
College Education	16
Community College	18
Evolving Education	20
Lifelong Learning	23
Dangerous Undercurrents	25
Foundational Character Traits	27
Confidence	30
Curiosity	34
Humility	36
Kindness	38
Empathy	41
Positivity and Optimism	44
Humanity	47
Ethical Principles and Integrity	49
The "Golden Rule"	51
Integrity and Trust	52
Respect	54
Honesty	56
Truth and Lies	59
Ethics	64
Moral Compass	65
Inner Strength and Personal Growth	69
Courage and Bravery	70
Conquering Fear	72
Persistence	74
Perseverance and Resilience	76
Failure and Risk-Taking	79
Presence	82

Forgiveness	84
Dealing with Unfairness	86
Emotional and Psychological Management	**89**
Managing Your Emotions	90
Pause First	93
Imposter Syndrome	95
Ego and Arrogance	98
Influences and External Factors	**101**
Upbringing and Norms	102
Luck	103
Behavioral Effects of Wealth	106
Image and Reputation	107
Professional Conduct and Behaviors	**109**
Initiative	110
Boundaries	112
"Can-Do" Attitude	115
Office Politics	117
Swearing at Work	119
Chain of Command	121
Skill Building	**125**
Career Diversification	126
Climbing the Ladder	128
Strategy and Execution	130
Communication Skills	131
Deep Listening	134
The Art of Questioning	136
Writing Skills	138
Conversation and Public Speaking	141
PowerPoint Presentations	146
Slide Deck Alternative	149
Executive Presentations	151
Story Telling and Charisma	153
Meetings	156
Unlocking Soft Skills	**161**
IQ and Intelligence	162
EI and EQ	165
Emotional Discipline	167
EQ and Optimism	169
EQ and Leadership	171
Cognition and Bias	**173**
Cognitive Bias	174

Cognitive Dissonance	178
Decisions and Problem-Solving	**181**
Difficult Decisions	184
Problem-Solving	187
Intuition	191
Transitioning Jobs	**195**
Non-Linear Career Path	196
Losing Your Job	199
Greener Pastures	202
Leaving on Good Terms	205
Reinventing Yourself	207
Job Search Strategies	**211**
Selecting Target Companies	212
Networking	214
Your Résumé and Online Profiles	217
Application Timing	221
Recruitment Automation	222
Interview Preparation	223
Rewire Your Brain	225
Keep At It	226
Qualifications	227
Know Your Worth	229
Personal Branding	230
Phone Interviews	232
The 1-on-1 Interview	234
Articulating Creativity	241
Ageism	242
When You Receive an Offer	245
First Weeks on the Job	248
Management and Leadership	**251**
Manager vs. Leader	253
Leadership Styles	256
Leadership Adaptation	261
Servant Leadership	263
Words Matter	265
Empowerment	268
Leadership Growth and Maturity	270
Managing Superstars	273
Micromanagement	276
Delegation	279
Leadership Trust	281
Recognition and Appreciation	283
Accountability and Ownership	288

x • GENERAL CAREER INTELLIGENCE

Motivation and Engagement	292
Fear vs. Inspiration	294
Goals	297
Connect With Your Team	301
Multigenerational Teams	304
A Calming Force	307
Laughter is Healthy	308
Penny-Wise and Pound-Foolish	310
Passion, Strengths, and Superpowers	313
Debate and Groupthink	318
Speaking Truth to Power	320
Managing Up	323
Sleep to Perform	325
Change Management	327
Evolution of Leadership	332
AI and Future Managers	336
Tomorrow's Leaders	339

Conclusion: Embracing the Future — **345**
Looking Ahead: What's Next in Career Intelligence — 350

Acknowledgements — **353**

About the Author — **355**

Foreword

Ray and I have shared a unique journey, one that began with a simple video consultation and evolved into a friendship built on mutual respect and shared passions.

Ray initially contacted me for advice on publishing this book, given my experience in the field and my enthusiasm for helping others become "remarkable." In exchange for a half-hour of my time, he pre-ordered twenty-five copies of my latest book, *Think Remarkable*. That half-hour consultation turned into an hour-long conversation, during which I was struck by Ray's dedication, energy, and commitment to sharing his career-long learnings with others. Ray's devotion to his craft and his desire to make a positive impact on others are qualities that I deeply admire.

One of the highlights of our friendship was the day we spent together building a surfing balance trainer. Ray, who enjoys woodworking as a hobby, patiently coached me through the many operations required to complete the project. It was a day filled with learning, laughter, and a few humorous mishaps, like when I almost sawed off my thumb. But hey, I have another thumb!

Ray's passion for giving back and creating something enduring is evident on every page of this book. He has performed the heavy lifting of research and introspection over a period of years, and his dedication shines through. His book covers foundational concepts such as character, positivity, growth mindset, continuous learning and skill building, humility, empathy, mentoring, leadership, and more—topics that are not only comprehensive but also incredibly timely, given the many challenges we face today.

Ray has created a guide that is both comprehensive and accessible. His insights are not just theoretical; they are practical, actionable, and grounded in real-world experience. Whether you are just starting your career or looking to make a significant change, this book offers valuable insights that can help you achieve your goals.

So, as you dive into *General Career Intelligence*, I encourage you to take your time, absorb the wisdom Ray has to offer, and apply it to your own life. You won't be disappointed. And remember, as Ray and I have both learned, the journey to becoming remarkable is filled with hard work, dedication, and a few humorous events along the way.

Enjoy the read, and here's to your remarkable journey!

Guy Kawasaki.
Chief evangelist of Canva and host of the Remarkable People podcast.

Introduction

Welcome to *General Career Intelligence*. This book is designed to equip you with the knowledge and skills necessary to thrive in your career. Unlike conventional career guides, this book doesn't just offer advice. It equips you with the strategic mindset and tools required to succeed in a world where the only constant is change; it's your roadmap to mastering the complexities of the modern working world.

My journey to writing this book began as I transitioned from a 38-year career in the tech industry to retirement. I looked forward to the freedom that retirement promised—more time for travel, hobbies, and my family. Yet, the words of Robert Harris echoed in my mind: "The true currency of life is time, not money, and we've all got a limited stock of that." With this wisdom in mind, I pondered how to navigate retirement in a way that balanced leisure with a pursuit that would provide a sense of enduring significance.

This led to a moment of reflection as I sorted through a garage filled with work-related books accumulated over the years. Preparing to donate them, I realized the vast collective knowledge these books represented, which had guided me through countless challenges and transitions. Inspired, I decided to distill this knowledge and my own work experiences into a comprehensive career guide.

Initially, this project was meant to be a collection of "dad notes" for my adult children, aimed at nurturing their burgeoning careers. However, it quickly grew into something much more significant. A few weeks of writing turned into years of research and introspection. *General Career Intelligence* combines the latest insights from hundreds of experts across diverse fields with my personal narrative, offering a guide on the skills, behaviors, processes, and techniques needed to navigate a successful modern career.

Throughout the writing process, I was inspired by the profound shifts reshaping our world, particularly the transformative impact of the COVID era. In a few short years, the familiar workplace landscape has been upended, leaving us in a state of constant adaptation. Employers, having navigated the challenges of a remote workforce, now face new demands for corporate responsibility and greater workplace flexibility. Meanwhile, a more diverse and vocal workforce is raising the bar for what they expect from their employers.

Adding to this upheaval, we're experiencing a societal shift toward despair, sadness, and even hostility. Hate crimes are on the rise, and social trust, philanthropy, and confidence in our institutions are cratering. Some people have abandoned their moral upbringings, choosing hatred and tribalism over character and ethics. [1]

Amid these changes, employees are investing more time and effort into their work but often feel adrift in their pursuit of the American dream. Workers face a future defined by their ability to learn, build new skills, and continuously reinvent themselves. The reality is stark: nearly three out of four college graduates work in a field unrelated to their major, and over half of today's students will find jobs that don't yet exist. While many still chase traditional aspirations of status, prestige, and wealth, they are beginning to realize that these goals often fail to provide what matters most. [2]

While employers are vested in a stable workforce, it is crucial to view our careers as dynamic journeys. Embracing change as an opportunity rather than a setback opens the door to unexpected possibilities. Navigating uncertainty becomes a strategic advantage in an ever-evolving professional landscape.

So, how do you navigate a path toward success and fulfillment when your next move could be outdated before you make it?

Achieving success, whether in work or life, requires a disciplined approach—study, effort, persistence, courage, and a willingness to experiment and adapt. Real improvement comes from hard work and dedication. It's about more than just reading a book; it's about committing to the ongoing process of transformation and growth.[3]

General Career Intelligence stands out by celebrating the unique qualities that make us human, qualities that even the most sophisticated algorithms cannot replicate. In an age where *General Artificial Intelligence* (AI) is reshaping industries, this book shifts the focus from the artificial to the authentic. Unlike AI, which relies on data, algorithms, and logical processing, this book emphasizes intuition, empathy, adaptability, and ethical judgment—the hallmarks of human intelligence.

In a world increasingly influenced by technology, we're reminded of humanity's enduring importance in our professional lives. *General Career Intelligence* highlights the significance of character, morality, ethics, and the behaviors that shape our interactions, mold our reputations, and reinforce the essential norms that sustain civil society.

This book explores the nuances of interpersonal relationships, the subtleties of workplace dynamics, and the complexities of personal growth and fulfillment. We examine how the best decisions are rooted not just in efficiency but in values, passions, and a deep understanding of ourselves and others. While AI can provide data-driven insights, it's our human capacity for empathy, creativity, and moral reasoning that genuinely shapes our career paths.

As you embark on this journey, remember that your career is a dynamic and evolving adventure. Embrace its twists and turns and see each challenge as an opportunity for growth and discovery. The wisdom within these pages is here to inspire, guide, and empower you as you navigate your unique path. Whether you're just starting out or looking to advance in your field, *General Career Intelligence* will help you understand the broader landscape of your career, make meaningful connections, and find purpose in your work.

Recognize your uniqueness in all your pursuits, for each of us has something distinct to contribute. Together, our endeavors create a broader human tapestry, like water droplets in a pond creating ripples with the transformative power to carve paths through even the hardest stone.

Just as ripples spread out when a single pebble is dropped into water, the actions of individuals can have far reaching effects. —The Dalai Lama, Tibetan spiritual and temporal ruler, former head of state, speaker, and author.

CHAPTER 1

Education and Learning

The purpose of education is to replace an empty mind with an open one. —Malcolm Forbes, American publisher, and business mogul.

Education, in the most fundamental sense, provides the foundation for almost everything we achieve in life, both personally and as a society. Our first jobs are predicated on our knowledge, combined with attitude. Subsequent roles build upon our earlier accomplishments and the additional expertise we've gained. Similarly, each sequential level of education builds upon the prior in a compounding fashion. Society as a whole represents the culmination of each of our abilities and accomplishments. It stands to reason, therefore, that our competitiveness and leadership are underpinned by the scaffolding provided by education, which has become critically important as we continue to migrate as a global economy.

Education and learning are the keys to solving many of our challenges today. For example, education can reduce crime, poverty, income inequality, homelessness, and much more. Nationwide, hundreds of thousands of jobs in technology go unfilled every day. Fundamentally, whether we want to pursue a blue-collar or white-collar career, education and skill building (hard and soft) are the enablers that can help us to achieve our goals.[4]

At work, we learn through the experiences we're afforded. If we allow ourselves to be pigeonholed, we can expect our learning and, therefore, our advancement to suffer. If we're offered challenging assignments and work alongside knowledgeable and skilled individuals, our learning accelerates. Stagnation inhibits learning, so taking an active role in our careers and seeking stimulating assignments and work environments is crucial.

> *Intellectual growth should commence at birth and cease only at death.* —Albert Einstein, German theoretical physicist, educator, and author.

Learning Diversity

Elon Musk used to read two books daily, Bill Gates reads 50 books per year, Warren Buffett reads 500 pages weekly, and the average CEO reads 60 books yearly. On the other hand, the average American spends more than 2,000 hours every year watching TV or on social media. Given the average reading speed of most readers, almost anyone could instead read hundreds of books each year and, by so doing, improve their mind, their life, and their career.[5]

Science has shown that reading doesn't just fill your brain with valuable information. It changes the way your brain works for the better. When you read, your brain projects itself into the story. If the character in your book is playing golf, the areas of your brain that light up are those exercised when you're out on the course.

When deeply engrossed in a great book for an extended period, we build up our ability to focus and grasp complex ideas. Conversely, the less you read (skimming doesn't count), the more our essential skills wither. Reading rewires your brain. It strengthens your imagination and enhances your memory and ability to solve complex problems. Reading makes you more knowledgeable and transforms you into being functionally *smarter*.[6]

Whether traveling, attending lectures, or trying new activities, each experience is an avenue for learning, challenging our perspectives, and understanding diverse cultures. Beyond a means to an end, education becomes a lifelong habit when actively pursued.

Allocate daily time for learning, be it through books, magazines, or instructional videos. Explore hobbies, plan overdue vacations, and utilize resources like local libraries or apps offering access to numerous books and magazines. For those opposed to reading, apps providing book summaries or audio options offer alternative ways to absorb knowledge efficiently.

Investing in yourself, first and foremost, is the best investment you can make. If you put in the effort, you can learn almost anything. It takes commitment, time, and sometimes money, but it's worth it. It is how you excel, advance, and outperform others.[7]

In the case of good books, the point is not to see how many of them you can get through, but rather how many can get through to you. —Mortimer Adler, American philosopher, and educator.

Arts and Humanities

Studying the arts and humanities is crucial for students because it fosters creativity, critical thinking, and a deeper understanding of the human experience. These disciplines teach students to explore diverse perspectives, question assumptions, and express complex ideas through various forms of art, literature, history, and philosophy. Beyond the development of intellectual skills, the arts and humanities cultivate empathy, cultural awareness, and ethical reasoning—qualities essential for thriving in an interconnected and rapidly changing world. By engaging with these subjects, students gain a well-rounded education that enhances their personal growth and equips them to make meaningful contributions to society.

Unfortunately, a few years ago, we experienced substantial budget cuts for Arts and Humanities endowments, public television and radio, libraries, and museums. Thankfully, in a rare demonstration of bipartisanship within Congress, politicians rallied to keep minimal funding in place. When mired in political arm wrestling and deception, it's easy to lose sight of how the arts contribute to our nation's health by enriching our culture, fostering creativity, driving economic growth, providing vital educational opportunities, and uniting communities across diverse backgrounds.

The arts and humanities belong to everyone and, as such, deserve government funding and support. In the limit, think for just a moment how gray and dull life would be without museums, art, music and musicals, movies, theatre, public television, and all the other enriching offerings that life provides.

Given the societal challenges we face today, it has become even more urgent that we encourage and inspire our youth to pursue education and careers in the humanities. Critical thinking matters. We need young people who can evaluate our behaviors and trends and unpack what's happening now in the context of what has happened before to guide us to a better future. To thrive, we should encourage, inspire, and nurture thinkers who reflect the diversity of our nation. We need people trained in liberal arts who deeply understand history, politics, and the complex mechanics of how our government functions.[8]

More specifically, the arts and humanities teach history, culture, and human behavior as essential lenses for understanding how policy and governance are shaped over time. By studying history, individuals gain insight into the successes, failures, and patterns of past governance, enabling them to make informed decisions and avoid repeating mistakes. Cultural studies provide a deep appreciation for the diversity of human experiences, values, and societal norms, helping leaders craft policies that respect and address the needs of different communities.

The study of human behavior, through disciplines like psychology, philosophy, and sociology, offers a clearer understanding of what motivates individuals and groups, informing more effective policy design and leadership strategies. Together, these fields help policymakers and leaders comprehend the complex interplay of historical context, cultural dynamics, and human nature, leading to more thoughtful, ethical, and sustainable governance.

The arts and humanities teach us who we are and what we can be. They lie at the very core of the culture of which we're a part. —Ronald Reagan, American politician, actor, and 40th president of the United States.

The Importance of STEM

Science, technology, engineering, and mathematics (STEM) workers are critical for sustained growth and stability in the U.S. and elsewhere, and STEM education creates the next generation of innovators and inventors. Innovation leads to new products and processes that grow and sustain our economy.

Think about cellphones, iPods, electric vehicles and bicycles, smart home devices that improve our lives and keep us safe, online gaming, cinematic special effects, and advanced smartphone cameras. Satellites enable global communications and commerce, while GPS enables a multitude of products that we can't imagine living without. The rate of technological advancement is mind-numbing, and the products and markets they affect are too many to list.

Many people don't understand, even in the most basic sense, all that is required to bring new technology to market—the months and years of dedicated design, analysis, prototyping, documentation, destructive and qualification testing, reliability optimization, design for manufacturing, beta trials, iterative optimization, and so forth. Without STEM education and training, none of this would be possible.

Despite the vital role of STEM education, critics question our current focus, raising concerns about potential overemphasis and its impact on workforce balance, diversity, and well-roundedness. They highlight the predominantly male, higher socioeconomic background of STEM workers, emphasizing the underrepresentation of women, minorities, and low-income individuals. Female students are reported to be 50% more likely to leave STEM coursework than their male counterparts. To address these issues, some experts advocate for a more holistic educational approach, encompassing not just STEM but also financial, social, and livelihood education. This broader perspective aims to build a multi-dimensional solution for the diverse needs of the future workforce while promoting economic citizenship, sustainable well-being, poverty reduction, and rights for all.[9]

While a nationwide strategy for STEM education is essential, we must avoid fixating on STEM at the expense of other interests and pursuits. Many students have inclinations toward non-STEM fields, and imposing universal college-readiness math may lead to academic struggles and dropouts. Amidst a polarized society, there's a growing need for extensive political science training to enhance discourse and strengthen democracy, as citizens face challenges in making informed decisions based on history.[10] Education isn't a zero-sum game; focusing on STEM doesn't necessitate neglecting other areas. The challenge lies in the technical nature of STEM occupations, which require a deep and sustained education. Without adapting early education systems to encourage long-term commitment, our ability to nurture the expertise that future business demands remains a struggle.

Compounding the issue, societal perceptions often label STEM-focused students negatively as nerds, geeks, and outcasts. To address this, we must acknowledge, encourage, and celebrate the brilliance of STEM-trained youngsters, ensuring they aren't ostracized. Starting from the formative years, this shift in perspective is crucial for fostering STEM education and facilitating entry into respected technical universities.

Generalists

These days, there's a growing emphasis on hyper-specialization in college education. Particularly in U.S. technical degree programs, the focus on a specific discipline has intensified, often neglecting exposure to other valuable areas of knowledge that contribute to a more holistic mindset.

The world, however, requires generalists, yet their value is not always adequately recognized. Individuals capable of integrating expertise, understanding intersections, and bridging cultures and perspectives are precious assets.

Those with a broader upbringing who have expanded their professional knowledge beyond a single domain tend to be the most curious and profound thinkers. While specific fields like surgery demand specialists, in disciplines like engineering, the most innovative minds often excel as system engineers, adept at handling diverse concepts across multiple disciplines. Workers with a generalist approach often exhibit greater creativity and a propensity to challenge the status quo, which is crucial for companies seeking innovation.[11]

At the college level, we can enhance the preparation of engineering and other students with practical skills that yield immediate impact in the real-world work environment. We can improve students' soft skills, including public speaking, technical writing, interpersonal communications, conflict resolution, and negotiating skills. Courses in program management, covering basic scheduling, program planning, and risk management, lay the foundation for effective team participation and leadership.

While depth of expertise was crucial in the past, the evolving world now places equal importance on breadth of perspective. Those with diverse tools are better equipped to navigate today's business uncertainties. Successful companies leverage cross-discipline thinking, as exemplified by Apple's CEO Steve Jobs, who emphasized the marriage of technology, liberal arts, and humanities for meteoric success. At a time when technology affects every aspect of our lives, workers must think across disciplines, creating collaborative bridges and spanning multiple business units—a philosophy some universities are now incorporating into their curricula.[12]

For instance, the USC Jimmy Lovine and Andre Young Academy aim to impart skills essential for success in a collaborative, complex, and hybridized business world. Their Master of Science in Integrated Design, Business, and Technology equips students to solve intricate problems at the intersections of engineering, business management, and the arts. Emphasizing teamwork as a key pillar, the academy instills empathy-focused problem-solving that prioritizes end users and customer service in product development.

Companies highly value employees with general cognitive abilities, enabling them to seamlessly transition between teams and roles. This agility allows companies to adapt swiftly to changing needs. Individuals with diverse geographic and functional experiences, basic statistical skills, and critical reasoning position themselves competitively in the evolving global marketplace.[13]

> *The bigger the picture, the more unique the potential human contribution. Our greatest strength is the exact opposite of narrow specialization. It is the ability to integrate broadly.*
> —David Epstein, environmental scientist, author, and investigative reporter.

Tradespeople

Often, we emphasize bachelor's degrees as the obvious next step after high school. This results in far too little attention being paid to the importance of other highly valued skills that can be acquired through vocational training.

> *Clearly, apprenticeships are a win-win: They provide workers with sturdy rungs on that ladder of opportunity, and employers with the skilled workers they need to grow their businesses. And yet in America, they've traditionally been an undervalued and underutilized tool in our nation's workforce development arsenal.* —Thomas Perez, American politician, and civil rights lawyer.

The U.S. economy is currently suffering from a significant and sustained skills mismatch. It faces a massive shortage of truck drivers, welders, electricians, construction workers, and other skilled tradespeople. In addition to trade jobs rooted in manufacturing, there are also essential trade jobs in medical, mechanical, industrial, and other areas too many to mention.

Skilled trades offer lifelong careers for people who seek good salaries, employment stability, and job satisfaction for those who are not particularly able or inclined to follow the college degree path. Workers can become trained in various skills and hit the ground running, making great money and enjoying satisfying careers in less than two years without needing a college degree.[14]

In junior high, I could choose between metal, wood, and other shop classes. Opting for wood shop ignited my passion for woodworking, a hobby I continue to enjoy today. In high school, I delved into "auto shop," gaining a foundational understanding of automobile systems. Performing tune-ups for myself and others brought a sense of accomplishment and saved money on professional services. Passing down car basics to our kids has further extended the benefits.

At Cal Poly, their "Learn by doing" philosophy led me to various other shop classes. I acquired skills in welding, machining, and metalforming techniques. These skills became invaluable throughout my career, and any of them could legitimately form the basis for a satisfying and lucrative career.

These days, students can benefit even more broadly than before by learning modern trade skills wherever the will and funding necessary to teach them exists. They can learn the traditional techniques of woodworking, metalworking, leathercraft, weaving, ceramics, and auto shop, just as I did. But now, they can also learn about digital design, engineering fundamentals, 3-D printing, laser cutting and etching, robotics, and more. With this knowledge, people can pull themselves up by their bootstraps on a path toward self-reliance. They can secure high-paying jobs right out of school or start their own businesses. Thankfully, some of the more progressive colleges around the nation offer curricula in the crafts and trades.

Trades also offer an excellent opportunity for industries to collaborate with our educators. When our companies invest in teaching trades, they create an expanded workforce that they can begin to tap into immediately. For example, industrial mills can offer their skills and digital looms to complement hand looms in teaching students to weave. Modern digital tools are the perfect enablers for students to learn online sales and marketing. People skilled in those arts can help other crafts and tradespeople to grow and expand their businesses exponentially when they leverage the power of the Internet.[15]

Our national employment strategy should prioritize the potential of electronic trades in revitalizing high-skilled electronics manufacturing jobs domestically. While the perception is that we've outsourced electronics manufacturing due to low-cost labor in countries like China, the real reason is their emphasis on trades in workforce training. Apple, Microsoft, and Intel manufacture in Asia not just for cheap labor but for their skilled workforce adept at handling complex tooling and exotic materials. Apple's Tim Cook notes Asia's deep expertise in tooling skills, a depth unmatched in the U.S.[16]

Renewed interest in trades is positive, but there's room to better educate and guide workers, particularly in middle-class and less-affluent communities. Financial support from local companies to community colleges can address skills gaps, making vocational education more accessible and eliminating the need for outsourcing.

Serving in the US Military is another excellent path to receiving world-class skills training in a field that suits your aptitude. After your term of service, the GI Bill is still a great way to get a college education for those who otherwise might not be able to afford it.

Progress requires that we come to grips with what's needed, resolve plans for how to get there, and apply our priorities and political might toward accomplishing it. As we contemplate how to up-skill America and train and modernize our workforce, particularly in the

Rust Belt areas that have been left behind, trades can play an important role in re-establishing a robust and upwardly mobile middle class throughout our country. It is certainly within our reach. Crafts and trades are an essential element of the global economy. What better way to unleash one's passion and creativity than to teach them those basic skills?

> *A skilled worker regardless of the job description remains a treasure.* —Madeleine M. Kunin, American diplomat, author, and politician.

College Education

Anyone can read a book and, in so doing, learn a variety of facts. However, attending school, particularly at the college level, teaches us to think uniquely. There, we learn how to break down and untangle complex concepts and solve problems that would otherwise seem impossible. Bloom's Taxonomy teaches us that there are multiple levels of learning. At the bottom are knowledge and facts. The next level is understanding and comprehension. Above that is application, followed by analysis, synthesis, evaluation, and creation. Education is, of course, cumulative.

> *It is not so very important for a person to learn facts. For that, he does not really need a college. He can learn them from books. The value of an education in a liberal arts college is not the learning of many facts but the training of the mind to think something that cannot be learned from textbooks.* —Albert Einstein.

While not essential for success, a college degree significantly impacts earning potential and career advancement. Most Fortune 500 CEOs, members of Congress, presidents, and influential figures hold degrees. However, notable exceptions like Bill Gates, Steve Jobs, and Mark Zuckerberg flourished without them. Pursuing a degree remains an excellent option for academically inclined individuals with means, but alternatives exist, especially in careers that do not mandate a degree. That said, not everyone is interested in or can afford to go to college to make a decent living, and they shouldn't have to.

It should be evident that society benefits from contributions across various jobs, skill levels, and professions. And yet, we're seeing a recent shift by some extremist politicians advocating for less emphasis on college, favoring short-term postsecondary certifications or vocational skills to meet the immediate needs of skilled workers. Critics argue this reflects a bias against liberalism, with an aim to shape a less educated electorate over time.[17]

However, steering students away from college overlooks the future demands on our workforce. Cultivating habits of the mind, fostering deep learning and resilience, transforming information into action, and creatively evaluating complex ideas are indispensable. Rapid technological changes demand workers who can navigate complexity. As workplaces evolve, we need individuals with accumulated wisdom, interpersonal competence, critical thinking, and altruism—underpinned by complex theories taught in college. Downplaying the need for higher education jeopardizes national prosperity and the well-being of a civil, democratic society.[18]

Admittedly, much about higher education is broken and urgently needs fixing. However, those issues can't be solved by adopting an attitude that prioritizes short-term training over comprehensive, deep learning. We should not attempt to shorten a student's college educational experience or encourage motivated, qualified, and aspiring college students to seek an alternative path. Nothing beats college for producing high levels of intellectual, personal, and social development, which is the foundation for continuous life-long learning.

> *The function of education is to teach one to think intensively and to think critically. Intelligence plus character—that is the goal of true education.* —Martin Luther King Jr., American minister, and social activist.

Community College

I grew up in a family that considered a college education a *must-have*—a foregone conclusion. My father advised my brother and me from an early age to plan on going to college. The degree choice was secondary to attaining *any* degree, which he described as a *ticket to success*. And so, as I grew up, I never experienced any doubt as to my inevitable path. I endeavored throughout K-12 to excel academically, knowing that I'd need to *earn* my way into a university.

During the college application process, I realized I could save my parents substantial money by attending a local community college (Junior College or "JC") for the initial two years. After weighing the pros and cons, I chose our local JC, Foothill College. Enrolling there, I completed full course loads for two years, covering general ed, physics, calculus, and various electives, earning an Associate of Science degree. I then applied to Cal Poly at San Luis Obispo and was accepted into their engineering program.

From my own experience and based on discussions with many other co-workers and friends over the years, the community college path remains a fantastic choice for anyone interested in pursuing a post-high school education. Community colleges offer a tremendous education at a small fraction of the cost of attending a four-year institution. Within the community college, you can learn valuable skills, prepare for further educational pursuits, or even dabble in coursework related to your passion.

Unfortunately, community colleges still face the stigma of being perceived as less than traditional four-year institutions. However, my experience at Foothill College contradicts this notion. The courses I took there were as in-depth and demanding as those at Cal Poly or Santa Clara University. When JC course credits transfer to four-year institutions, the curricula and standards align. For credit transfer, community college courses are equivalent to their counterparts at four-year universities. I found my community college professors to be just as knowledgeable, capable and informed as those at Cal Poly, and sometimes even more so. Additionally, class sizes at Foothill rarely exceeded 30 students, fostering direct engagement with professors—an advantage over larger classes at some four-year colleges. From an educational perspective, the stigma around community colleges seems unwarranted; however, it's essential to research and choose wisely when selecting a college to attend.

Statistically, while community colleges offer a tremendously valuable education at an attractive price, most students who enroll never graduate. Over two-thirds of first-time, full-time students don't complete an associate's degree within three years.

A growing body of evidence suggests that there are ways of improving those statistics, such as investing in completion and retention programs. These "wraparound" programs are impactful and cost-effective. They employ mentors or advisors who help students identify challenges that hinder or impact their ability to graduate and provide them with the necessary resources to succeed. Multiple studies have shown that these programs can almost double the graduation rates. And students who received wraparound services went on to earn 20% more on average than those who did not. While these support programs aren't cheap (their costs range from $1,000-$5,700), the price is low compared to the long-term economic benefits of a degree. Usually, the cost of the program can be offset within roughly four years of graduation, assuming that the student secures reasonable employment. The challenge is scaling these programs to impact the greatest number of students and ensure that the community college track achieves maximum success and impact. That investment is worthy of our collective support.[19]

Ultimately, community colleges serve as accessible and affordable educational paths that cater to diverse learners and provide essential skills and credentials for various careers. By offering flexible learning opportunities and fostering local community ties, they play a crucial role in empowering individuals to pursue fulfilling careers and contribute meaningfully to society.

> *Education is the most powerful weapon which you can use to change the world.* —Nelson Mandela, South African anti-apartheid activist, politician, statesman, and philanthropist.

Evolving Education

We're now witnessing a renewed commitment by colleges to revamp and modernize their course and degree offerings to keep pace with our rapidly changing business demands. For example, Cal Poly now offers courses in entrepreneurial studies and training within their Center for Innovation and Entrepreneurship program. Their mission is to expose students to entrepreneurship inside and outside the classroom, regardless of major. Their curricula include events and competitions, including accelerator and incubator programs designed to train, fund, and assist emerging, student-launched businesses.

Likewise, at other colleges, we're seeing a merging of specific curricula to better meet future business needs. For example, technologies such as machine learning, Blockchain, and Python coding language are blurring the lines between finance and computer science. Students studying fintech and fin-analytics enter the workplace with financial knowledge and technical skills, essential for automating and rewriting the financial services industry of tomorrow. Merging industrial technology with art and design has resulted in product-packaging program curricula that leverages cross-discipline learning. This enables students to exploit their comprehensive background, which better prepares them for packaging jobs of the future.

Arizona recently passed a law allowing community colleges to offer bachelor's degrees. Three of the state's public research universities will now offer bachelor's degrees in Arizona, enabling students to avoid the crushing cost of higher education. This is an essential first step in the right direction, and hopefully, it will encourage other states to follow suit.[20]

Colleges are now sprinting to offer MBA programs online to cater to workers who can't afford to commit the time and money for in-person study. Google is working to disrupt the world of education by launching new certificate programs designed to help people bridge skills gaps and acquire qualifications for high-paying, high-growth job fields without a college degree. Google's initiative includes offering several "Career Certificates" in data analytics, project management, and user experience design, over 100,000 scholarships for those in need, partnerships with employers working with Google to hire graduates of its certificate program, and new Google search features that facilitate the job search for people without experience or degrees.[21]

Not everyone can access a four-year degree due to socioeconomic factors, emphasizing the need for inclusive training programs. These programs should pave a clear path to well-paying jobs and stable careers by imparting in-demand, real-world skills and creating pipelines for nontraditional talent in collaboration with forward-thinking employers like Google.

Half of the U.S. workforce comprises STARs (Skilled Through Alternative Routes), including most workers facing barriers to economic advancement. These skilled individuals, such as Hispanic, rural, veteran, and Black workers, possess the potential for higher-paying jobs, but systemic barriers hinder their progress. Policymakers at various levels should remove obstacles, invest in training programs, and support connecting STARs with job opportunities. At the same time, companies should eliminate restrictive automated résumé screens and invest in talent development to unlock the full potential of these non-degreed, skilled workers.[22]

While educators are focused on modernizing their offerings, it's worthwhile to contemplate current trends relating to human culture. Lately, we've found that with the advent of social media and the internet, hostility is at an all-time high, and much of it occurs online. We're inundated daily with abject anger, mistruths, and contorted claims of reality. It's also hard to find examples of industry executives who are outwardly prioritizing humanity over profits.

In focusing on technology, business, and innovation, our educational system may have overlooked essential qualities needed for tomorrow's leaders. While it has never been more important to educate the next generation with a focus on technology, business, and innovation, we should also train tomorrow's leaders to be great inventors who push humanity forward through impactful and benevolent pursuits while advancing how we live and interact with one another. Given the powerful tools currently available to enable, empower, and accelerate corporate success, there's no reason we can't encourage an expansive new generation of American *greats* in the category of

Vanderbilt, Rockefeller, Carnegie, Morgan, and Ford. American ingenuity needs a jump-start and a renewal. We must teach our children the importance of morality, perseverance, humility, ethics, empathy, philanthropy, sustainability, and essential theoretical and liberal studies to achieve sustained greatness as a society.[23]

Successful companies often thrive with diverse workforces that encompass various backgrounds and education levels, including non-STEM roles and individuals without college degrees. When empowered by role models, practical tools, support, and growth opportunities, motivated employees can advance their careers, regardless of their educational background, benefiting themselves and their employers. Encouraging an inclusive and supportive environment allows workers to learn and grow into the roles they aspire to achieve.[24]

If we can learn anything, we can be anything. —Ravi Kumar, nuclear scientist, and business executive.

Lifelong Learning

In the current job market, a job seeker's assets include skills, knowledge, and relevant experience. Post-pandemic, over a third of Americans express the need for additional training or education to secure new jobs, highlighting the increasing necessity for continuous skill development. Most U.S. adults identify as lifelong learners, with over 60% of working adults embracing the mindset of professional learners.

Given the global transition to a digital economy and the rate at which change occurs in the marketplace today, it's wishful thinking to believe that our K-12 and formal college educations are adequate to serve our needs for the remainder of our working lives. Change is inevitable, and continuous learning is necessary for those seeking to remain relevant, current, and marketable throughout their chosen professions.

Colleges are embracing and rallying to the need for lifelong learning by modernizing their online course offerings, certificate programs, and accredited degree programs. While some are ahead of the curve, others will follow. Everything today seems driven by technology, from businesses to personal lifestyles. Universities of the future will offer increasingly flexible, short-term learning opportunities that permeate the learning experience over everyone's lifetime.[25]

The recent pandemic has accelerated corporate trends toward adopting workplace automation, AI, and advanced analytics, as well as focusing on learning and development (L&D) to better handle long-term challenges and short-term crises. Recent studies reveal that few companies had L&D programs before the pandemic.

Research shows that L&D enables companies to equip themselves to take on new challenges by ensuring their workforce has the skills to implement and adopt technologies that enhance productivity and competitiveness. However, this requires investing in L&D with a long-term perspective, a commitment towards establishing a skills baseline and inventory, and designing individual learning pathways that accommodate evolving conditions to equip workers to adapt and remain agile over time.[26]

Embracing lifelong learning enriches our knowledge and skills and enhances career adaptability and resilience in a rapidly evolving job market. By committing to continuous growth and development, individuals can proactively navigate career challenges, seize new opportunities, and achieve sustained professional success.

Dangerous Undercurrents

A notable segment of our population scorns those with knowledge and education. Individuals who harbor aversions towards academics or those engaging in research outside formal education often believe their own common sense is superior. They often disdain knowledge and expertise because they contradict their biases or intuition.

> *Don't hate what you don't understand!* —John Lennon, English singer, songwriter, musician, and peace activist.

Pursuing intellectual knowledge often clashes with and challenges established philosophies, societal structures, and prevailing power dynamics. Those who wish to maintain power and privilege resist advanced learning and education by dismissing new ideas as irrelevant or false (e.g., labeling them as "fake news"). When scientific evidence emerges, especially if it doesn't comprehensively explain every facet of an issue, "anti-elitism" is invoked to discredit scientists, researchers, and experts, portraying existing research as useless, contradictory, and unnecessary.

Isaac Asimov noted in the 1980s that "... anti-intellectualism has been nurtured by the false notion that democracy means that 'my ignorance is just as good as your knowledge.'" With the rise of the internet and social media, people are more prone to sharing information without critically assessing the sources and motives behind it, contributing to the spread of misinformation. Politicians, influencers, corporations, and religious institutions often exploit this trend.

For instance, corporations opposing clean energy policies use strategies reminiscent of the tobacco industry's efforts to sow doubt about the dangers of smoking, as seen in the infamous 1969 memo stating: "'Doubt is our product,' since it is the best means of competing with the body of fact that exists in the minds of the general public."

There are several ways in which we can combat anti-intellectualism. We all must contribute if we are to be successful as a whole:

- Embrace the idea of not knowing everything, and see it as a driving force for continuous growth and learning.

- Practice the willingness to change your mind based on new, truthful, and defendable information, recognizing it as adaptive learning rather than weakness or failure.

- Foster continuous learning by reading broadly, and critically evaluate the arguments presented.

- Initiate challenging conversations with friends, family, and peers, being mindful of emotions during these interactions.

- Actively counter falsehoods and conspiracy theories in public discourse, serving as a voice of reason and encouraging others to emulate such behavior and techniques.[27]

- Leaders, educators, and experts should avoid dictating, and instead focus on educating with facts and details. Initiating respectful dialogues, patiently answering questions, and seeking to understand detractors' perspectives can help build a common understanding. Techniques should be relevant to diverse backgrounds, and acknowledging people's natural distrust for experts is crucial for fostering productive discourse.[28]

Anti-intellectualism significantly challenges societal progress by devaluing expertise, critical thinking, and rigorous inquiry. Overcoming this phenomenon requires a renewed commitment to promoting education, fostering a culture that values knowledge and thoughtful discourse, and encouraging lifelong learning as foundational principles for a thriving and informed society.

> *The secret of freedom lies in educating people, whereas the secret of tyranny is in keeping them ignorant.* —Maximilien Robespierre, French lawyer, and statesman.

CHAPTER 2

Foundational Character Traits

> *The purpose of education is to replace an empty mind with an open one.* —Malcolm Forbes, American publisher, and business mogul.

Foundational character traits are the aspects of our personality and behavior that express who we are. They are a core feature of our underlying values, beliefs, and identities that shape our interactions, decisions, and overall approach to life. They are the building blocks of our personal and professional identity, guiding how we relate to others and navigate our challenges.

In general, *good* character embodies a variety of positive behaviors such as honesty, sincerity, responsibility, integrity, and the like. A person of good character's habits, actions, and emotional responses are all united and directed toward the moral and the good. Character enables us to go beyond simply living a healthy and happy life—it also underpins our desire to help others to be healthy and happy. When we collectively act on our good character, we can improve the world.

> *Inside of me are two dogs. One is mean and evil and the other is good, and they fight each other all the time. When asked which one wins, I answer, the one I feed the most.* — Sitting Bull, Hunkpapa Lakota Native American chief.

While character and personality can describe a person's behavior, our personalities are more immediately visible, while our character becomes apparent over time through varying situations and circumstances. Personality is outwardly apparent and easily read, while character takes longer to discern. Personality can be innate, while character is shaped over time by environment, beliefs, and experiences. As such, one's character can be fluid.[29]

We are who we are, at least when we are not trying to be somebody else. We are all unique and distinct individuals. However, sustaining this uniqueness requires commitment, confidence, and persistence to push against norms and societal pressure. It's easy to succumb to the comfort of surrounding ourselves with *like thinkers*—people who act and think like we do. But that practice creates silos in thinking and behavior, which can lead to tribalism, extremism, and polarization. We see this play out in our daily politics; truths are lies, up is down, and political opponents are no longer simply adversaries—they are now our enemies. In this age of cyber-bullying and political discord, it seems that positive character traits are somehow losing their relevance.

As I reflect on the leaders I've admired most, it's clear that their character consistently surpasses their credentials or intellect. Enlightened leadership embodies vulnerability, empathy, and generosity—traits that define our humanity. While business and leadership classes may not have explicitly taught these concepts, I've encountered them abundantly throughout my career. When you observe enlightened leadership in your management team, it becomes easy to take it for granted until you change jobs and find it lacking or absent. That is when you learn how important it is to your happiness and well-being.

We're witnessing a transition to hybrid workforces post-pandemic in today's landscape. Further, younger workers are drawn to companies that prioritize both profitability *and* social responsibility. They advocate for increased work flexibility, learning opportunities, and growth, often prioritizing them over compensation. Enlightened leadership is not just a preference but a necessity—an attribute desired by employees and essential for organizational success.

Employees respond more positively to empathetic leaders. Conversely, rigid hierarchies, characterized by fear-driven leadership, foster toxic work cultures. These toxic cultures lead to employee health problems, increased absenteeism, errors, disengagement, decreased productivity, and higher turnover rates.

Embracing the principles of enlightened leadership isn't simple; it's more challenging than focusing solely on cerebral pursuits like business plans and strategy execution. It demands emotional intelligence (EQ) and should be a deliberate commitment of every exceptional leadership team. When done correctly, employers, customers, and shareholders will notice, and everyone will reap the rewards of the effort.[30]

Understanding and cultivating our character traits lays a strong foundation for growth and success in our careers and personal lives. Whether you're just starting your career or looking to refine your personal development, these foundational character traits are essential for creating a fulfilling and impactful life.

> *Be more concerned with your character than with your reputation. Your character is what you really are, while your reputation is merely what others think you are.* —John Wooden, American basketball coach and player.

Confidence

Have you ever encountered someone who spoke with such unwavering confidence that you were utterly captivated? Their words felt sacrosanct, and undeniable. These individuals are the visionaries, the ones you'd follow without hesitation. While their knowledge and truthfulness contribute, their confidence and optimism captivate others.

Self-confidence is a common challenge we all face, triggered by various factors to differing degrees. It resides within our brains, specifically in the amygdala, a part of our reptilian brain responsible for the fight-or-flight response. While its primary role is to protect us from harm, it can sometimes go awry, filling us with self-doubt and depleting our confidence. This manifests as an internal voice whispering unhelpful messages that hinder us.

No one can make you feel inferior without your consent. — Eleanor Roosevelt, American first lady, diplomat, and humanitarian.

For instance, chronic discontent stems from a persistent feeling that nothing is going right. Combat this by cultivating gratitude for the positive aspects of life. Similarly, if you find yourself trapped in a cycle of "what-if" scenarios, focus instead on the potential positive outcomes while downplaying negative thoughts or fears of risk.[31]

As epigenetic experts have demonstrated, a toxic environment surrounded by negativity can have severe physiological impacts. Removing or minimizing exposure to such unhealthy relationships or situations is essential. This shift enables you to concentrate on more positive thoughts and pursuits, surrounded by uplifting influences. Dwelling on weaknesses, deficiencies, or past failures fosters self-doubt. Instead, acknowledge mistakes, learn from them, and move forward. Embrace positive thoughts and nurture them into habitual patterns.[32]

> *Some of the best advice I've been given: 'Don't take criticism from people you would never go to for advice.'* —Morgan Freeman, American actor, director, and narrator.

Over the past decade, neurologists have extensively studied techniques that effectively re-wire our brains. They've shown that consistent behavioral changes create new pathways, known as neuroplasticity, which can positively impact our lives and solidify new habits. However, quieting our inner doubts is challenging; skepticism often undermines our efforts. Confronting these doubts is critical; we must analyze and acknowledge them with empathy, without self-criticism. Past failures should be viewed as learning experiences, not permanent setbacks. Adopting a positive, forward-looking attitude and establishing actionable plans can lead to a better life, leaving negative thoughts behind.[33]

Language plays a significant role in projecting confidence. The following suggestions can help with this challenge:

- Excessive use of filler words like "like," "yeah," "uh," and "um" can diminish perceived confidence. It's beneficial to eliminate such words from your vocabulary to enhance trust and credibility. Similarly, avoid repetitive words that don't add meaning to your communication.

- Frequent apologetic statements can undermine confidence. While mistakes happen, constant apologies are unnecessary. Trust in your resourcefulness and seek alternatives.

- Over-communicating, including over-talking or over-explaining, may signal insecurity. Aim for concise messages, prioritizing quality over quantity. Respect conversation boundaries and avoid volunteering excessive information.

- Using slang or informal language in formal settings can detract from confidence. Strive for professionalism and clarity in your speech, particularly in formal contexts. Articulate and be specific with your language to convey confidence effectively.

Some additional ways to develop a confident mindset are as follows:

- Define your purpose. Knowing why you're doing something will make you more confident and purpose-driven.

- Avoid comparing yourself to others. This enables you to avoid negative self-talk.

- Focus on solutions, not on problems. Acknowledge that when issues arise, that is a part of life and not something to avoid. Overcoming problems, when solved, increases confidence.

- Sometimes, it pays to project confidence, even when you're not. However, your competency must be visible to others and defendable. If you know you're competent, then you should be confident in your competence.

- Take action to overcome fear. The more you allow fear to control you, the stronger your negative inner voice will become.

- Take pride in your appearance and how you project yourself. When you look and feel confident, you become confident. If you fail to look and act the part, imposter syndrome can take root, further undermining confidence.

- Prepare for every situation. Whether you're making a presentation or arriving for an interview, preparedness shows.

- Body language counts and sometimes speaks louder than words. Hold your head high, adopt a positive and powerful (but not threatening) posture, and take command of your presence.

- Confidence is cultivated through consistent practice, experience, and positive actions. As you accumulate wins, your comfort and confidence naturally grow. Be patient with yourself and your progress; minor setbacks are normal. You can't prepare for every possibility, so stay committed to your path and persevere to achieve success.[34]

As a manager, consistently encouraging your workers can pay dividends in their pursuit of self-confidence. The amount of encouragement you offer often depends on the worker's personality and the difficulty of their projects and assignments. Workers don't always provide hints when they need encouragement, so remain vigilant in assessing their needs. For example, if you're seeing a reduction in volunteer rates or projects and tasks are taking longer than usual, those could indicate that your workers are struggling with their workloads and possibly with their confidence.

Likewise, if your supportive and light-hearted work culture has become humor-free and rather tense or stressful, that could indicate underlying turmoil. Be generous with your appreciation, and ensure that your workers feel appreciated. Help them over the hump when their courage ebbs. Remember that while reasonable challenges are healthy, unreasonable ones are not.[35]

We all struggle with self-confidence from time to time. Being judged throughout our careers is a given, whether by our peers, subordinates, superiors, customers, or stakeholders. But with confidence comes an ability to deal with and tolerate criticism effectively.

Accomplishment and advancement are ultimately underpinned by confidence. One rarely occurs without the other. When coupled with performance, confidence brings new and more challenging assignments and higher levels of responsibility and achievement. With confidence, you're more likely to accomplish difficult tasks and goals.

When you're confident, you're more likely to see and accept failure as a learning opportunity rather than an attack on your ability and ego. Without confidence, you'll never put yourself out there so that you're front and center to grab the brass rings as they avail themselves.[36]

Whether you believe you can do a thing or not, you are right.
—Henry Ford, American industrialist, industry magnate, and founder of Ford Motor Company.

Curiosity

Curiosity inspires learning, which fuels knowledge and capability. If you embrace it, encourage it, and feed it, curiosity will energize your career. Curiosity drives invention, innovation, and continuous improvement, and it's a shared behavior that propels the most successful teams. It also inspires travel, adventure, and other pursuits that enrich our lives. Without curiosity, we stagnate in our boredom.

Recent research has found that we are particularly curious when we face an *information gap*—some mystery or unanswered question. The more curious we feel when searching for an answer, the better we'll remember it.[37]

Curiosity warms up circuits including the hippocampus to prepare the brain to learn. —Matthias Gruber, cognitive neuroscientist, researcher, and author.

Productive curiosity requires intent and discipline. It endures when we avoid allowing naysayers or critics to drown us out with their noise or shout down our thoughts and ideas because we're bucking the norms. For those who are innately curious, the desire to learn is more important than wanting to be right or socially accepted.

Creativity is a powerful bond that unites teams in collaboration and enables them to overcome the fear of failure when considering unconventional ideas. Steve Jobs exemplified this approach with exceptional curiosity and reverence for the creative process. Like Jobs, the most creative individuals learn to shift their focus from fixating on the problem to exploring ideas and possibilities.

Steve Jobs stands out prominently when seeking examples of the most creative individuals in modern history. Jony Ive, Steve's longtime creative collaborator, described him as "...*the most profoundly inquisitive human*" he had ever met. Ive emphasized that Steve's curiosity was not constrained by his knowledge or expertise. Instead, it was ferocious, energetic, and practiced with intention and rigor. This description captures the essence of exceptional curiosity. The collaborative curiosity shared by Steve and Jony left an indelible mark on our everyday lives.[38]

> *Talking often gets in the way of listening and thinking.* — Jony Ive, British industrial and product designer, and business executive.

"Intelligent curiosity" is a skill that sets entrepreneurs and leaders apart, enabling them to become "thought leaders." It involves direct, focused, strategic, and active questioning, going beyond a casual exploration of interesting things. Intelligent curiosity explores opportunities for success—not just the obvious but also the periphery that influences it. It employs a wide-angle lens to view opportunity and solution spaces comprehensively.

Practitioners of intelligent curiosity constantly ask questions, seek knowledge from everyone they encounter, and listen actively. They excel at unpacking problems, formulating solutions, and investigating causality, impacts, and threats. This approach fosters adaptability, enabling them to pivot as the marketplace evolves.

While intelligent curiosity is a learnable skill, it requires practice and the willingness to deep-dive into subjects and questioning, especially in a world of superficial engagements and shorter attention spans.[39]

Curiosity fuels continuous learning, innovation, and personal growth throughout our careers, enabling us to adapt to change and seize new opportunities. Embracing curiosity as a guiding force encourages exploration, creativity, and a deeper understanding of our professional paths, ultimately leading to greater fulfillment and success.

Humility

I've always admired individuals who exhibit exceptional intelligence or achievement yet remain modest and humble. Despite earning significant recognition, they deflect attention away from themselves during conversations, choosing instead to focus on others. In contrast, I've never been impressed by braggarts. Their boastful demeanor strikes me as rude and annoying, often overshadowing others as they incessantly emphasize their importance, intelligence, or accomplishments.

> *I know that I know nothing.* —Socrates, ancient Greek philosopher.

Our egos can prevent us from succeeding. The best way to combat this is to adopt humility as a way of life. In today's world, finding great examples of humility is difficult. Sometimes, failure or a streak of bad luck shocks us into discovering humility to improve our lives.

In every situation, we choose to be a jerk, a braggart, or a humble soul. Our egos play a significant role in influencing this choice. Fragile egos often lead to negative behavior, especially when faced with slights or challenges. How we respond to these situations—whether a car cutting us off or poor treatment at a checkout counter—reveals our ability to react with patience and empathy, keeping frustration in check. Understanding others' perspectives and not letting ego dictate our reactions is crucial.

In business, particularly for managers, humility involves redirecting attention to your team, including subordinates, superiors, and coworkers. When discussing accomplishments, resist framing them as individual feats and instead focus on the collective "we." Avoid seeking attention when someone else is the center, and refrain from inserting yourself for personal gain. Regularly thanking your team for their contributions, publicly acknowledging their efforts, and expressing gratitude for everyday kindness fosters a humble and appreciative workplace culture.

> *Try not to be the smartest person in the room. And if you are, I suggest you invite smarter people, or find a different room.*
> —Michael Dell, American businessman, innovator, and philanthropist.

Maintaining a thankful attitude showcases humility and diminishes self-importance, which makes you more approachable and likable. It can also contribute to personal success. When you observe individuals who embody humility, emulating their behavior can curb the urge to boast or act selfishly. Without humility, even success can falter, leading to diminished status and influence, potentially branding you as another egotistical figure.[40]

In business leadership, particularly among seasoned leaders who have logged substantial achievement, there's a risk of becoming fixated on outcomes and control, viewing employees merely as tools to an end. This mindset breeds incrementalism, overemphasizing profitability, efficiency, and cost reduction initiatives, often at the expense of workforce morale and engagement. A top-down leadership approach centered on control and end goals neglects organizational culture, innovation, and employee creativity. Such an environment drains vitality from the workforce, dampens motivation, and instills fear of job insecurity among employees. Leaders who embrace humble, servant leadership actively seek ideas and contributions from their employees, fostering a sense of importance and motivation among them. Such leaders prioritize providing tangible and emotional support to their workforce, acknowledging the expertise of those below them. They empower employees by granting ownership, autonomy, and responsibility, encouraging them to excel. Rather than imposing changes, they inquire, "How can I assist you in achieving your goals?" This approach fosters a positive feedback loop where incremental employee successes spur creativity and risk-taking, leading to greater achievements. Mistakes are reframed as *innovations*, driving corporate success and fostering a culture of continual improvement.[41]

Being humble does not equate to being *meek*. Instead, it relates to being *grounded*. It's about having the confidence to admit your mistakes while recognizing other people's strengths. By acknowledging their weaknesses and imperfections, leaders also make it OK for others to be fallible. Strive to admit your faults and weaknesses to grow in character. Choosing and committing to bettering yourself daily is a goal worth striving for.

> *As the area of our knowledge grows, so too does the perimeter of our ignorance.* —Neil deGrasse Tyson, American astrophysicist, author, and science communicator.

Kindness

Plenty of brilliant individuals grace our world, accomplishing astounding feats daily. However, mere intelligence does not guarantee success. Thankfully, while you might not always be witty or clever, you can always find a way to be kind to others.

Kindness is a powerful tool. Consider the best leaders and bosses that you've had. What sets them apart from the others? Most likely, their presence was uplifting, their guidance invaluable, and their demeanor devoid of bullying or over-control. These individuals embody kindness, nurturing growth, fostering inclusivity, and prioritizing listening over speaking.[42]

In the business world, toughness often gets glorified as the key to success. Some go full-throttle with a "Take no prisoners" mindset, while others are perhaps too nice, risking being taken advantage of. But finding the right balance is crucial. A dash of kindness mixed with assertiveness can be a winning recipe for success and happiness.

Human interaction, which involves people skills and relationships with others, determines to a large degree our success or failure in life. As a manager or leader, you'll face numerous issues and challenges, including technical, business, or personnel-related. Your skills, knowledge, and experience will guide you toward solutions. However, your style and approach will shape your reputation and level of success. When leadership kindness isn't modeled and celebrated, the workplace environment may become toxic or, at best, fail to foster our full potential. Recently, there's been a growing demand for a more human leadership style, perhaps in response to societal trends toward anger, hate, and paranoia.

> *Cooperation comes from friendship, friendship comes from trust, and trust comes from kindheartedness. Once you have a genuine concern for others, there's no room for cheating, bullying or exploitation; instead, you can be honest, truthful, and transparent in your conduct.* — The Dalai Lama.

Consider a personnel issue where a worker is underperforming. Will you take a strong-handed approach, confront the individual, and demand improvement? Alternatively, a more measured approach involves showing kindness. When you offer support and coaching, you enable the individual to be part of the solution. Perhaps the person is facing challenges at home. Respectfully explore the reason for their underperformance to address the root cause rather than superficially prescribing solutions. When we show kindness, consideration, and empathy, employees often respond more positively, leading to sustained positive outcomes.

Being kind doesn't mean you're weak or unable to make tough decisions. It's about showing respect and empathy. There's a difference between being kind and being *nice*. Philosophers and psychologists have defined the difference as being dependent on *why* you do it. If it's about creating a favorable impression, it's nice, lacking benevolence. If it's to spare someone inconvenience, it's kind. Kindness involves concrete actions to help others; niceness focuses on pleasing others. Kindness is more meaningful, though it can be awkward. For instance, addressing bias in a meeting isn't nice, but it's kind. We could all benefit from more kindness. Helping others boosts happiness and resilience when needed most.[43]

If you spend your workdays seeking others' approval or worrying about whether they like you, you're squandering valuable time. What truly matters is earning their respect and fostering a good working relationship. Respect stems from the quality of your work and its impact. Don't let your desire to be perceived as nice hinder your effectiveness. For instance, don't hesitate to voice disagreement or offer dissenting opinions. Remaining silent when a situation demands your active participation isn't nice, and it contradicts your job responsibilities. When you're kind and produce excellent work, you'll naturally earn others' appreciation and respect.[44]

While kindness and decency are always appreciated, going overboard is possible. Sometimes, you must assert yourself and take charge. Consider arriving at a conference room where everyone is engaged in idle chatter. If you don't take charge and steer the conversation, time will be wasted, and productivity will suffer. Making others slightly uncomfortable isn't necessarily rude. For instance, what if someone leaves your meeting abruptly? Or drops off a conference call early? Instead of labeling these behaviors as rude, consider whether your meeting was worthwhile for them. If they felt they weren't adding value or benefiting from the meeting, it's legitimate for them to exit and focus on more impactful tasks. While staying in a meeting out of politeness may seem considerate, wasting people's time is inconsiderate. Kindness and politeness have their limits.[45]

Kindness at work fosters a supportive and positive environment where colleagues feel valued, respected, and motivated to collaborate effectively. By practicing empathy, generosity, and consideration towards others, individuals can cultivate stronger relationships, enhance team morale, and contribute to a more fulfilling and thriving workplace culture.

> *To be kind is more important than to be right. Many times what people need is not a brilliant mind that speaks, but a special heart that listens.* —Unknown.

Empathy

When you exhibit empathy, you embody care and kindness; you strive to deeply comprehend a person's circumstances, motivations, or challenges at their core. Empathy motivates you to prioritize the well-being of others, even amidst your busiest moments, to establish personal connections, especially when colleagues or friends are facing difficulties. Often, it's the simple gestures that matter—offering a kind word or a thoughtful gesture requires minimal effort. Anyone can spare a few moments from their schedule to assist another person. Demonstrating genuine care for your colleagues can significantly enhance loyalty and engagement. Moreover, it can positively impact your reputation.

> *Nobody cares how much you know, until they know how much you care.* —Theodore Roosevelt, 26th president of the United States, statesman, soldier, conservationist, naturalist, historian, and writer.

There's a growing sense of disconnection and reduced employee engagement in today's workplace. Empathy is dwindling as interactions become more remote and impersonal, with tasks shifting to computers and communication relying on texts and emails. Corporate leaders, often fixated on profits and efficiency, overlook the fundamental needs of their teams.

To address this, it's crucial to recognize the value of empathy in the workplace. Empathetic leaders humanize the workplace when genuinely caring for their teams beyond productivity. By fostering personal connections, leaders inspire loyalty and encourage peak performance. Leadership is a privilege—it involves responsibility, accountability, and the ability to harmonize diverse teams. Demonstrating empathy not only benefits employees but also drives success and impact, shaping a leader's career trajectory.[46]

Empathy and sympathy are very similar, but they are often incorrectly used interchangeably:

- Empathy involves effort. It's the active attempt to experience what someone else is feeling or thinking. In a sense, it's putting yourself into another person's shoes.

- Sympathy involves a more automatic or involuntary affinity. For example, one might automatically sympathize with someone who shares a similar background, but it would take more effort to empathize with someone who has endured a very different experience.

- Pity, on the other hand, is a very different concept. It involves sorrow prompted by others' misfortune but does not suggest shared emotional understanding.

- Compassion is beyond empathy. An example is when you acknowledge that someone is suffering and take tangible action to do what you can to help.[47]

Empathy and listening are intertwined. In a world of information overload and shrinking attention spans, the quality of our listening shapes the impact of our influence. Employees seek to be heard and respected; attentive listening communicates this respect while fostering trust. It's important to refrain from prematurely processing information before the speaker has finished talking. Take the time to fully digest their message before crafting your response.[48]

Empathy plays a critical role in customer relations. As we strive to innovate and address unmet, unarticulated needs in the market, it's important to remember that these needs ultimately belong to individuals and organizations composed of people. While it's tempting to view customers in abstract terms, we must recognize them as people with their challenges and desires. Empathy lies in understanding and sharing the feelings of others, which guides us to comprehend their needs better when contemplating innovation.[49]

Nearly every interpersonal relationship or interaction can benefit from empathy. As a leader, developing and exercising empathy will serve you well.

> *The most successful companies focus on people and relationships, and make sure that both are not just managed but led and cared for.* —Brigette Hyacinth, business executive, author, speaker, and influencer.

Positivity and Optimism

Though related, optimism and positive thinking are somewhat different. Optimism embraces the notion that things tend toward improvement rather than decline. The eternal optimist has a glass-half-full mentality and anticipates positive outcomes. Positive thinking, on the other hand, involves meeting challenges with affirmation and a can-do attitude. Actions are constructive, supportive, and collaborative.

> *We may hope, but we should not believe, in the excitement of today, that the next trip or the ones to follow are going to be particularly easy.* —Neil Armstrong, American astronaut, aeronautical engineer, and the first person to walk on the Moon.

I can fully appreciate how some people can find themselves in a situation that is so dark and bleak that they simply can't navigate to a place of optimism or recovery. For many of us, pessimism seems to creep into our thoughts each day, uninvited, as we read the daily news or witness unacceptable behavior in those we surround ourselves with. Sometimes, it almost feels that doom and gloom is pre-ordained.

Psychologists have suggested that humans are hardwired to adhere to a negative bias. When we were cave-people, preparing for the worst-case scenario kept us alive. To stay safe, we tend to react more strongly to negative stimuli and dwell on negativity more frequently. When searching for reasons to be unhappy, we find a million examples supporting our pursuit. Many politicians have focused their persistent messaging and rhetoric on fear, anger, and negativity because they understand those powerful emotions stimulate action, ultimately driving their followers to the ballot box.

A recent study found that early career setbacks can create higher degrees of success in the long run. Those who suffer setbacks or failures can become better versions of themselves, having grown and learned from their negative experiences. Failure is a core component of any successful career. Admitting failure and discussing it with others cultivates a healthier work environment by humanizing the person who failed and spurring other employees to perform better through the shared learning that failure-related discussions can provide. In a sense, success breeds success, but failure can also breed success.[50]

Be brave enough to suck at something new. —Unknown.

Another recent study highlighted that optimistic individuals are more likely to live longer, even achieving exceptional longevity by reaching age 85 or beyond.[51] In this study, the most optimistic participants had a 50-70% greater chance of living to 85 than the least optimistic. Being generous to others has also been associated with longer life spans. If embracing an optimistic lifestyle for career benefits isn't motivation enough, then perhaps the prospect of living a longer and healthier life is.

When we appreciate and express gratitude for the small joys in life, we open ourselves to discovering even more positive experiences. Enjoying life's simple pleasures, such as feeling the warmth of the sun on our skin, a gentle breeze, cozying up to a fire, sinking into a comfortable bed, or indulging in a delicious treat, can shift our mindset towards positivity, even if only temporarily. Our diet, physical activity (exercise), sufficient sleep, and minimizing exposure to negative influences are all factors that contribute to fostering positivity in our lives.

The degree to which you can conjure optimism depends on more than deliberate intent—it's also influenced by your personality, upbringing, environmental interactions, and even genetics. Some patterns of thought can become deeply ingrained and difficult to adjust.

Despite my attempts to be consistently positive, I can't claim to be continuously optimistic. For example, I tend toward cynicism about politics, which temporarily shifts with flashes of leadership or voter sanity. However, I'm hopeful new leaders will demonstrate wisdom, patriotism, ethics, and empathy, which is now lacking in government. Optimism *expects* improvement, while positive thinking *builds it* through an affirmative can-do approach. My optimism wavers, but I aspire to think positively.

Positivity and optimism carried me through immense challenges, like when my wife developed the rare, life-threatening HELLP Syndrome while pregnant. With hours until emergency delivery, uncertainty loomed over their survival. After delivery, I felt utterly helpless as I cycled between my wife's room and our 2lb-7oz baby daughter in the NICU. Thankfully, they both survived and thrived—that harrowing experience revealed my wife's strength and resilience in the face of crisis. Though positivity was hard to muster at the moment, maintaining hope and optimism ultimately buoyed us through. When severely tested, positivity and optimism provide the ballast to weather life's gravest storms.

While optimism might be a bridge too far for some in certain situations, *hope* requires only possibility. Remember to practice self-empathy toward a more positive, optimistic, or hopeful future.

Optimism is the faith that leads to achievement. Nothing can be done without hope and confidence. —Helen Keller, American author, disability rights advocate, political activist, and lecturer.

Humanity

Humanity is a virtue linked with the basic ethics of altruism. It symbolizes love and compassion towards each other. How we express our humanity reflects our character. Our shared humanity is codified in laws and norms safeguarding fundamental human rights in contemporary society. Love, kindness, and social intelligence are considered the core virtues of humanity, encompassing the understanding of interpersonal relationships, intimacy, trust, persuasion, group dynamics, and political influence.[52]

> *We think too much and feel too little. More than machinery, we need humanity. More than cleverness, we need kindness and gentleness.* —Charlie Chaplin, English comic actor, filmmaker, and composer.

Our humanity inspires us to connect and unite with one another as ordinary human beings while also celebrating our vast diversity. We all share a common DNA and universal human traits and values independent of race, sex, and gender. Yet, in today's fractured and polarized society, it's far too easy to overlook the remarkable similarities that unite us.

Recently, specific individuals have sought to undermine the progress made through our growing diversity by weaponizing the concept of "otherness." They categorize people based on race, gender, age, sexual orientation, ethnicity, nationality, religion, and political beliefs, as they view diversity as a challenge to their authority and dominance in society. This attitude is harmful and divisive and poses significant dangers to our collective well-being.[53]

Exceptional leaders embody humanity in their professional endeavors and personal lives. They exhibit qualities that elevate them beyond merely good leaders and consistently share their insights with everyone in their organization. These leaders recognize that everyone is unique and precious beyond what they contribute at work. They do *good* and do *right* despite the pressures and influences that they face every day.

Leaders who prioritize humanity create inclusive and supportive environments, empowering their teams to innovate and thrive. In turn, businesses become more resilient, adaptable, and capable of navigating complex challenges as they are built on solid relationships, mutual respect, and a shared sense of purpose. Ultimately, human-centered leadership leads to better business outcomes and a positive societal impact.

> *Our culture has accepted two huge lies. The first is that if you disagree with someone's lifestyle, you must fear or hate them. The second is that to love someone means you agree with everything they believe, say, or do. Both are nonsense, you don't have to compromise convictions to be compassionate.* —Dave Chappelle, American stand-up comedian, and actor.

CHAPTER 3

Ethical Principles and Integrity

Never let your sense of morals prevent you from doing what's right. —Isaac Asimov, Russian-born American writer, and professor.

Ethical principles guide our behavior and decision-making. They serve as the foundation for a life of integrity and trustworthiness. They are also the moral compasses that direct us personally and professionally, ensuring our actions align with our values.

Understanding and adhering to these ethical principles is crucial for building and maintaining trust, fostering healthy relationships, and positively impacting those around us. These principles are guidelines essential for living a life of purpose, honor, and authenticity.

Ethical principles and integrity are crucial in business and life because they build trust, credibility, and a strong reputation. Adhering to ethical standards fosters long-term relationships with customers, employees, and partners, creating a foundation for sustainable success. Integrity ensures that decisions are made with fairness and transparency, preventing conflicts, fraud, and other risks that can damage an organization. Ethical leadership drives a positive work culture, encourages employee engagement, and helps businesses avoid scandals or practices that could damage their reputation or lead to legal issues. Living with integrity reflects consistency between one's values and actions, earning respect and fostering meaningful connections.

However, recent events have shown us the dangerous influence of unethical leaders, politicians, and media personalities. We have seen how dishonesty, corruption, and self-serving behavior can erode the foundations of society and weaken democracy. When those in power prioritize personal gain over the common good, they create division, foster distrust, and undermine institutions meant to serve the public. This breakdown in ethics has led to increasing polarization, political gridlock, and a growing sense of disillusionment among citizens. Without integrity, leaders lose their moral authority, and the social fabric that holds communities together begins to unravel, threatening both governance and the future of democratic society.

In the business world, leaders who operate with integrity not only impact their organizations but also influence society through corporate citizenship and social responsibility. Ethical business practices, such as fair labor, environmental sustainability, and philanthropy, set an example for industries and communities alike. These leaders champion social causes, support local economies, and contribute to global well-being, demonstrating that businesses can be powerful forces for good when grounded in ethical principles. Through their influence, business leaders help shape societal norms, advance policies that benefit the public, and contribute to the betterment of society as a whole.

Ethical businesses foster trust within their communities and build a sense of responsibility that strengthens the social fabric, promoting a healthier, more equitable world. This collective influence of ethical leadership in business can counteract the adverse effects of unethical governance, acting as a stabilizing force that upholds the values of fairness, justice, and democracy.

The "Golden Rule"

Practicing the "Golden Rule"—treating others as you wish to be treated—is a timeless principle that holds profound significance in our careers and personal lives. In the workplace, it fosters respect, empathy, and collaboration, which are essential for building strong, trusting relationships with colleagues, clients, and partners. You create an environment where people feel valued, heard, and motivated to contribute their best efforts by approaching others with fairness and kindness. This enhances teamwork and productivity and strengthens your professional reputation as someone who leads with integrity.

In life, the Golden Rule serves as a compass for personal growth and emotional well-being. It encourages self-reflection, helping us understand how our actions impact those around us and inspiring us to cultivate compassion and patience. Living by this principle leads to deeper connections and a more meaningful existence as we learn to navigate challenges with grace and support others in their journeys. Ultimately, whether in our careers or personal lives, practicing the Golden Rule builds a legacy of respect and positivity, shaping our path to success and contributing to a more humane and inclusive world.

> *People will always notice the change in your attitude towards them, but they will never notice it's their behavior that made your change.* —Torgbui Agormenu III, influencer.

Effective teamwork is essential for companies and employees to succeed. We work together toward common goals, relying on each other's support and collaboration. An organization's strength and effectiveness depend on every individual's contribution. While some may possess unique skills or experience, it's important to treat everyone equally, acknowledging their valuable contributions, commitment, and dedication.

This approach reflects positive ethics and morality, instilling a sense of pride in doing what's right. It also fosters a culture of appreciation and respect among team members, driving the organization towards higher performance overall.

Respecting others and recognizing their significant contributions in the workplace aligns closely with practicing the Golden Rule. Our lead venture capital investor at Endgate, Ed Tuck, imparted his "rules" for startup behavior to our founding team when we launched the company. One of his rules resonates with the values instilled in me by my parents and merits repetition here:

> *Treat everybody the same: young, old, high or low rank. This habit is a mark of good breeding.* —Ed Tuck, venture capitalist, and serial entrepreneur.

Integrity and Trust

Integrity is an exceptional character trait. A person with integrity demonstrates sound ethical and moral values and does the right thing regardless of who's watching. In the workplace, integrity is the foundation upon which co-workers build working relationships and mutual trust. Integrity means being self-aware, accountable, responsible, and truthful and demonstrating reliably consistent actions. People who demonstrate integrity draw others to them because they are trustworthy and dependable. As employees, they can be counted upon to behave honorably.[54]

> *Real integrity is doing the right thing, knowing that nobody's going to know whether you did it or not.* —Oprah Winfrey, American talk show host, television producer, actress, author, and media proprietor.

Personal integrity breeds trust. When you're entrusted with something important and demonstrate the integrity needed to deliver on your responsibility, you can experience pride in what you've accomplished. How you treat others—a hallmark of integrity—is critical in business.

Integrity requires consistent and reliable delivery of commitments. It also requires you to treat others with kindness, respect, and empathy, as those behaviors are conducive to trust-building.

The following list describes how people with a lack of integrity might behave at work:

- They take credit for other people's work or fail to reward and recognize the efforts of others.
- They blame others for their own failures and deficiencies.
- They fail to defend their team and co-workers.
- They fail to deliver on their promises.
- They show favoritism or otherwise behave unfairly towards others.
- They attempt to make themselves look good, particularly when they put others down to do so.[55]
- They ignore the boundaries set by co-workers and fail to respect the word "no."
- They dominate entire conversations.

- They're erratic, aggressive, and unpredictable.

Integrity and trust are foundational to fostering strong relationships, enhancing collaboration, and achieving organizational success. By consistently demonstrating honesty, reliability, and ethical behavior, individuals and teams cultivate a workplace environment where mutual respect thrives, enabling sustained growth and achievement of shared goals.

> *The best way to find out if you can trust somebody is to trust them.* —Ernest Hemingway, American novelist, short-story writer, and journalist.

Respect

Respect is a cornerstone of success in our careers and personal lives, influencing how we interact with others and how they perceive us. In the workplace, respect fosters a positive and productive environment where individuals feel valued for their contributions and are more motivated to perform at their best. It cultivates trust, reduces conflicts, and promotes collaboration among colleagues, regardless of their roles or backgrounds. Demonstrating respect for others—whether through active listening, open communication, or appreciating diverse perspectives—creates a foundation for healthy professional relationships and effective teamwork, which are essential for long-term career growth.

In life, respect shapes the quality of our relationships and contributes to our overall well-being. It involves recognizing the inherent dignity and worth of others, setting boundaries and showing consideration for their needs and feelings. By practicing respect, we uplift those around us and reinforce our sense of self-worth. It guides us in navigating personal challenges, gracefully managing conflicts, and building meaningful connections. Respect is about honoring others and ourselves, laying the groundwork for a more fulfilling career and a more harmonious, balanced life.

Unfortunately, disrespect is all too common in our daily lives. Perhaps you've observed a store manager scolding a clerk for a minor error or an angry customer berating a server for something beyond their control. Some individuals perceive themselves as superior due to education, success, or social status. I've witnessed disrespect in public and at work too many times to count. The truth is, nobody deserves to be disrespected, regardless of the circumstances.

> *I don't trust anyone who's nice to me but rude to the waiter. Because they would treat me the same way if I were in that position.* —Muhammad Ali, American professional boxer, and activist.

We all deserve respect, no matter our role or situation. But respect is earned—not expected and certainly not demanded. Respect requires a degree of humility and the willingness to take responsibility for your faults and weaknesses. That, in turn, builds character. So, while nobody deserves to be disrespected, we can't expect to be respected if we misbehave.

If you find yourself being disrespected, it's important to maintain your standards of respectful behavior. You never know what challenges or circumstances others may face, and responding with disrespect only perpetuates the cycle of negativity. Instead, focus on treating others with kindness and dignity, regardless of how they treat you. By embodying respect in your actions, you contribute to a more positive and respectful environment for everyone.[56]

> *Show respect even to people who don't deserve it. Respect is a reflection of your character not theirs.* —Unknown.

Honesty

How we respond when faced with challenging or embarrassing questions speaks volumes about our honesty and integrity. Sometimes, we muster the courage to provide a complete and truthful answer, while other times, we may resort to evasion, dismissal, or redirection. However, each response reflects on our character and credibility.

I vividly recall a pivotal leadership meeting where the CEO imparted guidance on interacting with the press ahead of a significant corporate milestone. Anticipating heightened investor and media interest, he emphasized the importance of truthfulness in our responses. Yet, he also emphasized the strategic use of truth, advocating for selective disclosure that served our interests. At the time, I felt more than a little anxious as I contemplated threading a difficult needle that teetered between honesty and evasion.

Politicians have mastered the art of evading tough questions. They often refuse to provide direct and transparent answers, especially when it could reveal unpopular views or jeopardize their support. Instead, they resort to carefully crafted responses, veiled in rhetoric and half-truths, to appease their audience while safeguarding their interests. This calculated approach allows them to sidestep the potential fallout of honesty, even when it involves sacrificing clarity and authenticity.

> *Whoever is careless with the truth in small matters cannot be trusted with important matters.* —Albert Einstein.

Public-facing leaders often encounter questions they can't, shouldn't, or aren't allowed to answer, especially those leading public companies. They must balance transparency with confidentiality, providing sufficient information while safeguarding sensitive details. During quarterly earnings calls, leaders typically acknowledge questions while reframing them to align with company messaging. They often respond to inquiries about proprietary information or upcoming strategies with general statements or avoidance, protecting the company's interests. Effective communication and thoughtful responses are essential for navigating these complex situations.

Some communication techniques that corporate leaders commonly employ are as follows:

- Reframe the question. When faced with a challenging question, paraphrase it to confirm understanding, then adjust it slightly to make it more manageable for your response. This technique allows you to address the question in a way that aligns with your intentions.

- Avoid answering altogether. You might cite a legal concern or regulatory guidelines as a valid reason for not responding directly.

- Deflect. Instead of answering a question directly, offer an alternative or related information to avoid revealing too much. This takes practice.[57]

Dishonesty takes various forms, including *regular* dishonesty and *intellectual* dishonesty. Regular dishonesty involves misrepresenting easily verifiable facts, such as denying responsibility for breaking a vase when one did. This constitutes lying. *Intellectual* dishonesty is somewhat different. Someone who is close-minded or opposes other people's points of view or specific facts or information to support their agenda is demonstrating intellectual dishonesty.

In recent years, Americans have been grappling with pervasive intellectual dishonesty as lies, fake news, and disinformation inundate our daily lives, propagated by politicians and the media. This trend has normalized deceitful behavior, undermining truth and integrity. Many seem to prioritize rhetoric and lies over honesty, perpetuating a cycle of untruths that impede respectful public discourse. Without a shared foundation of facts, meaningful discussions on critical issues become nearly impossible, fueling chaos, anger, polarization, and stagnation.

One prominent example of intellectual dishonesty is evident in science denial. Science and medicine face persistent attacks from individuals and groups with ideological agendas. Climate science is dismissed as a hoax, while medical professionals at the FDA and CDC are subjected to ridicule and threats from politicians, quacks, and antivaxxers seeking to discredit life-saving treatments and medicines.

When confronted with intellectual dishonesty, we must uphold honesty and integrity. Refusing to join in, support, amplify, or emulate dishonest behavior can deter individuals from persisting in their charades. Listening to others' opinions fosters constructive dialogue and provides opportunities to counter falsehoods with truth. It's important to diplomatically question the claims of those promoting dishonesty, persisting even if they evade or dodge your inquiries. If necessary, call them out on their deception and reiterate your questions. However, when dealing with a superior who engages in dishonesty, approach the situation cautiously, as confronting them directly could have career repercussions.[58]

You'll find that many liars, grifters, and intellectual imposters refuse to accept facts and truth, given that their primary objective is to promote falsehoods, propaganda, and dogma for their gain. Recent studies have found that those who are most susceptible to false facts and conspiracy theories are more committed to their *tribes* and political ideologies than they are to facts and truth. It pays to ascertain whether those you are talking to are amenable to fact-based discussions before investing your time and energy.

Honesty at work is fundamental for building trust, fostering transparency, and maintaining ethical integrity within teams and organizations. By prioritizing truthful communication and integrity in all interactions, individuals cultivate a culture of accountability and credibility, paving the way for sustained collaboration and collective achievement

> *Honesty is a test of your competence and character. You need intelligence to know what is true, and you need strength to speak it.* —Guy Kawasaki, American marketing specialist, corporate evangelist, author, podcaster, and venture capitalist.

Truth and Lies

A fundamental lesson commonly taught by parents to their young children is: "Don't lie." This vital principle remains simple and unequivocal—period.

> *A lie can travel around the world before the truth can put on its shoes.* —Unknown.

Lies typically come to light eventually, often betraying the liar. Meanwhile, most truths tend to be discoverable. While we may at first assume that truths are naturally unambiguous, perhaps it's worth asking ourselves, "What exactly is truth?"

Some profess that there are three kinds of truths:

- Personal truth: Firm beliefs that we hold dear can't be argued away or modified.

- Political truth: Something becomes true (in our minds) because it often repeats or aligns with our biases, preferences, or ideals.

- Objective truth: Established by the methods and tools of science, validated through scientific inquiry. Once established, an objective truth can be expanded or deepened, but it cannot later become false. Objective truth is different from a hypothesis or unsettled science.

The concept of truth often varies based on interpretation and perspective. While science offers functional truths that describe what something *does*, as opposed to what something *is*, absolute truths may not exist universally. Cultural differences can shape perceptions of truth, influenced by morality, values, and interpretation. Scientific truths are grounded in evidence, while other truths may rely on belief or faith. Religion often substitutes truth with faith, allowing interpretation based on personal beliefs and convictions. Thus, truth can be subjective, shaped by individual perspectives and cultural contexts.

> *Falsehoods not only disagree with truths, but usually quarrel among themselves.* —Daniel Webster, American lawyer, and statesman.

Science seeks to produce the truth without consideration for a particular belief or moral system. We tend to consider those truths as absolute. However, given that science is ever-evolving, we find ourselves dealing with evolving truths. For some, this provides tacit permission or the rationale to resist those science-based facts on a wholesale basis. This particularly destructive manipulation prohibits the establishment of common facts and norms upon which people can agree as a foundation for discussion and discourse.

The dictionary defines truth as "...a fact or belief that is accepted as true." And in that definition, we find the critical term of acceptance. A belief or a fact must be *accepted* to be true. This is how the scientific society arrives at a consensus of what is true—through common acceptance. To accept a scientific finding, sufficient factual evidence must be presented and accepted by consensus. The danger lies in those who deliberately misstate, manipulate, or cherry-pick findings to present a contrarian conclusion and recruit others to join in the deception. Within this contrarian group-acceptance arises a new "truth" that conflicts with the settled or honest truth. From there, only broadside disagreement is possible.[59]

How might we endeavor to expose a liar? While many intelligent and savvy geniuses possess an uncanny ability to see through a lie when presented, most of us have difficulty discerning lies from truth. That said, some techniques can be employed to help expose liars in the act.

A recent study claims a 60% average success rate in detecting a lie. It involves the following process:

- Increase the cognitive load. Lying takes more mental energy than telling the truth. So, if you add more stimuli to a liar (like noise or changes in facial animations), they will struggle to maintain the cognitive energy required to continue their lie.

- Dig deeper. The more details a liar is permitted to add to their story, the greater the risk that they'll contradict themself, thus exposing the lie. Don't let them off the hook by domineering the conversation—instead, force them to talk more about the subject in question.

- Ask unanticipated questions. Practiced liars excel at preemptively developing their detailed lies. Break their momentum and train of thought by inquiring about things that do not concern your primary inquiry. Then return to questioning them on a particular element of their skeptical claim. This forces them to answer your explicit question on the spot, in a more unprepared way.

While these techniques aren't foolproof, they may prove helpful in pursuing facts. Additionally, pay attention to typical behaviors that indicate deception, such as anxiety, tension, irregular speaking cadence, etc.[60]

I recall a leadership meeting with our CEO where he explained his rationale against lying, which has stuck with me ever since. He said that when you lie, inevitably, you will forget who you lied to and what you lied about. Over one's career, repeated lying is simply impossible to manage, track, and control. Ultimately, the lies will catch up to you, with potentially catastrophic effects. I believe that his advice in this regard was wise indeed.

> *If you tell the truth, then you don't have to have a good memory.* —Judge Judy, American judge, and reality court TV show personality.

A recent poll has found that while most American adults believe in absolute truth, many adults under 30 don't. For adults younger than 30, 55% believe each person determines their own version of truth. These findings are alarming, and they speak to potentially negative consequences on mental health and the community. People who don't believe in absolute truth may be more likely to accept misinformation or succumb to conspiracy theories, which damages society.[61]

For those who reject or care little about verifiable truths, facts demand alternatives. All that matters is what they *believe*. Willful ignorance isn't a simple lack of understanding but an *obstinate* lack of understanding. It's an investment in not understanding—a refusal to hear what others say because it doesn't reinforce how they interpret the world. If a fact fails to provide them with something they value, they have no use for it and will avoid accepting it.[62]

Peter Wehner, an ex-presidential aid to Reagan and Bush, correctly states that at its core, "The repetition of lies not only causes millions of Americans to embrace them, it deforms their moral sensibility. It creates an inversion of ethics, or a transvaluation of values, in which lies become truth and unjust acts are seen as righteous." He further says, "Believing the deceptions also becomes a form of virtue signaling, a validation of one's loyalty to others in one's political tribe."[63]

And while chronic liars have learned that people tend to believe lies when repeated persistently, especially by multiple people, these liars are trafficking in more sinister pursuits—they understand that when people lose track of the truth, they also lose their ability to differentiate between right and wrong. German historian and philosopher Hannah Arendt once said, "This constant lying is not aimed at making the people believe a lie, but at ensuring that no one believes anything anymore. A people that can no longer distinguish between truth and lies cannot distinguish between right and wrong. And such a people, deprived of the power to think and judge, is, without knowing and willing it, completely subjected to the rule of lies. With such a people, you can do whatever you want."

The importance of truth cannot be overstated. If the pervasive lies Americans face daily are not countered soon, political violence may become increasingly prevalent and normalized in America's future. It is essential to confront misinformation whenever and wherever it arises. Claims made by truth-deniers must be robustly challenged, not with opinion-based arguments, but with well-reasoned, understandable, fact and data-based rebuttals. While it may take time to inoculate people against the influence of deniers, persistence will ultimately pay off in the long run. To ignore truth deniers is to empower them, putting us all at risk.[64]

> *Never worry about who will be offended if you speak the truth. Worry about who will be misled, deceived, and destroyed if you don't.* —Unknown.

Ethics

Being ethical means adhering to moral principles and values that align with societal and individual beliefs. These principles encompass honesty, fairness, equality, dignity, accountability, fidelity, and respect for others. Ethics centers on what benefits individuals and society as a whole.

Ethics is knowing the difference between what you have a right to do and what is right to do. —Potter Stewart, American lawyer, and judge.

Ethics, at its core, revolves around doing what's right in the right way. When colleagues excel, do you uplift them or belittle their success? When subordinates achieve, do you share their glory or snatch credit for yourself? When disagreement arises, do you undermine or support team efforts? In moments of dissatisfaction, do you wallow or seek solutions? Are you a builder or a detractor? A taker or a giver?

Do you spotlight coworker deficiencies in meetings to showcase expertise or address issues privately to maintain dignity? Influential leaders recognize grandstanding tactics and penalize such behavior, recognizing it as counterproductive and self-serving. Ethical conduct underscores collaboration, encouragement, and constructive problem-solving, elevating individuals and teams toward collective success.

Success, both personal and organizational, hinges on behavior, competence, and accomplishments. Attempts to gain an advantage by disparaging others, akin to tearing down competitors, often backfire. Always strive to take the high road, where exceptional conduct paves the way for lasting success, distancing you from the cutthroat practices of competitors. Upholding integrity and focusing on excellence elevates your reputation and fosters a positive work environment conducive to sustained achievement.

> *Never deviate from your sense of right and wrong. Your integrity [and ethics] must be unquestionable. It is easy to do what's right when you don't have to write a check or suffer any consequences. It's harder when you have to give something up. Always do what you say you will, and never mislead anyone for your own advantage.* —Stephen Schwarzman, American businessman, and investor.

Moral Compass

Your moral compass serves as an internal guide, helping you distinguish between right, wrong, and neutral actions based on ethical principles. It's shaped by your beliefs and values, such as kindness, justice, and fairness, often instilled through influential role models, family values, religious teachings, and other sources of inspiration.

> *'Agree to disagree' is reserved for things like 'I don't like coffee.' Not racism, homophobia, and sexism. Not human rights. Not basic common decency. We do not have a difference of opinion. We have a difference in morality.* —Unknown.

Moral virtues overlap across cultures, even though the relative ranking of each virtue may vary with each culture's history and environment. For example, vindictiveness, lying, and cheating are generally discouraged, while cooperation, modesty, courage, and empathy are praised. These universal norms are rooted in the similarity of our basic human needs and shared learning and problem-solving mechanisms and processes. Many attitudes and behaviors can shift when inappropriately applied to a given situation. For example, 1% of humans appear incapable of feeling shame, remorse, or genuine affection and are apt to lie and injure others without compunction. Some psychopaths seem to lack any semblance of a conscience. Their acts of good and evil are driven by altruism, which is ultimately selfishness in disguise.

Our moral compass, often influenced by our capacity for sympathy, guides our actions and perceptions of justice. However, justice can sometimes blur into vengeance, which fosters cruelty. Generosity and philanthropy vary depending on circumstances; individuals may pass by beggars but offer support during crises or to acquaintances. Morality, thus, reflects a complex interplay of upbringing, cultural context, and individual disposition.[65]

Warren Buffet describes making wise decisions and living a good and moral life by maintaining an inner and an outer *scorecard*. The inner scorecard defines your identity and conduct based on your values and beliefs. Conversely, the outer scorecard is an external measure of success defined by those around you. It can be influenced by societal judgment and personal greed. Buffett emphasizes the importance of instilling the principle of the inner scorecard in children so that they are driven to live a life on the high road, make sound decisions, and not rely on the judgments of others to steer their course through life. He also explains how important it is to surround yourself with people who are better than you so that they'll draw you upward towards fulfillment.[66]

Historically, profit has often been the primary driver of business strategies, with social responsibility taking a backseat or being overlooked altogether. However, a shift has occurred among many successful business leaders, who now prioritize corporate social responsibility alongside profitability. Human rights, sustainability, environmental impact, and business ethics are now fundamental corporate concerns shaped by leaders' ethics and moral compasses.

Misalignment between corporate values and those of employees can lead to significant blowback, prompting a reevaluation and refocusing of corporate strategy.

Millennials and Gen Z employees exert considerable influence in reshaping corporate priorities by emphasizing the importance of resetting the corporate moral compass. In the past, industry titans pursued strategies driven by excessive greed, especially in sectors like petroleum or tobacco. This greed-fueled deception for the sake of profit harms humans and our planet.

Conscious Capitalism is an emerging concept that places ethical and moral values at the heart of strategic business decision-making, aiming to uplift profits and the human condition in the long term. However, its adoption faces challenges, especially when influencers impede companies from striving to do what's right. Corporate misdeeds abound, with some leaders prioritizing what they *can* do rather than what they *should* do. Conversely, great leaders prioritize ethical conduct over exploiting loopholes.

Every leadership decision carries consequences. Too often, leaders test the limits of what they know is wrong, attempting to skirt accountability. Instead, it's crucial to assess the potential impact of your actions. Will they yield positive or negative outcomes? Who stands to suffer? Ultimately, unethical behaviors tend to catch up with perpetrators. Conversely, prioritizing the well-being of employees, customers, and society typically yields favorable outcomes without repercussions.[67]

A strong moral compass at work guides individuals to make principled decisions, uphold ethical standards, and prioritize integrity in their professional conduct. By consistently aligning actions with core values and ethical principles, individuals build trust and credibility and contribute to a positive workplace culture that promotes fairness, respect, and collective success.

Too many are still asking the question 'How much can we get away with?' when they should be asking 'What are the consequences?' —Tim Cook, American business executive.

CHAPTER 4

Inner Strength and Personal Growth

Champions don't become champions in the ring, they are merely recognized there. —Old Saying.

Developing inner strength and fostering personal growth are essential for navigating the complexities of life and advancing our careers. Inner strength enables us to face challenges with confidence and resilience, turning obstacles into opportunities for learning and improvement. Personal growth involves continually expanding our skills, knowledge, and emotional intelligence, allowing us to adapt to new situations and achieve our full potential.

Courage, persistence, and the ability to overcome fear are critical for taking risks and embracing failure as a stepping stone to success. Forgiveness and being present enhance our relationships and personal well-being while learning to handle life's inherent unfairness builds our capacity for resilience and perseverance.

Focusing on these attributes lays a solid foundation for personal and professional success. Strength and personal growth enrich our lives and empower us to contribute meaningfully to our communities and workplaces. Cultivating these qualities can lead to a more fulfilling, balanced, and successful life.

> *Mastering others is a strength. Mastering yourself is true power.* —Lao Tzu, Chinese philosopher, and poet.

Courage and Bravery

Courage is a *foundational* virtue because people need courage to display other virtues. Personal courage is essential in business, particularly when encouraging innovative, growth-oriented behaviors that promote continuous learning.

> *Courage is the most important of all the virtues, because without courage you can't practice any other virtue consistently.* —Maya Angelou, American memoirist, poet, and civil rights activist.

Courage is often underutilized and modeled infrequently in the workplace despite its significance. Studies indicate that exercising courage correlates with better outcomes in organizational performance, team cohesion, and individual well-being and learning. Standing up and speaking out are crucial for personal, team, and organizational growth. In private life, courage remains vital, especially in combating widespread lying, misinformation, and disinformation.[68]

Steve Jobs described how he reached out to Bill Hewlett (cofounder of Hewlett Packard) as a high school student. At the time, Steve was working to build a frequency counter and asked Bill if he could have some spare parts for his project. Bill not only provided parts, but he also offered Steve a summer job at HP. Steve's takeaway was the importance of having the courage to ask for what you need.

Reaching out to an industry titan like Bill Hewlett was a remarkable show of courage for a high schooler to exhibit.

Steve emphasized that he was seldom turned down for what he wanted throughout his career, which motivated him to reciprocate favors as well long term. While people invest in professional networks and education, the most successful individuals risk failure and embarrassment but muster the courage to take action. If met with initial rejection, persist until you achieve a "yes."[69]

> *Courage doesn't always roar. Sometimes courage is the little voice at the end of the day that says I'll try again tomorrow.*
> —Mary Anne Radmacher, Consultant Author, Artist, and professional speaker.

Many leaders, by default, tend to align themselves with the team consensus when faced with a decision point. Everyone, including leaders, wants to avoid looking foolish. Many are naturally risk-averse and worry that failing to conform could harm their careers. However, while it may be tempting to align with the team or superiors to avoid potential risks or conflicts, meaningful progress often emerges from challenging the status quo. Fostering an environment where diverse perspectives are valued and encouraged is essential.

In my experience, the more energetic, controversial, and sometimes contentious a discussion becomes, the better the chance that nuggets of genius will be mined. Those wild and unpopular ideas often contain groundbreaking ideas that can change an entire paradigm, which can lead to great success. I've found that the more often I've supported the occasional stretch or controversial idea to solve a problem, the more we've experienced exceptional outcomes. With practice, it became far easier to resist consensus thinking—our repeated successes provided me the confidence to routinely consider some of the more non-conventional approaches and solutions because we seemingly always found a way to make them work to our advantage.

This takes courage, trust, conviction, practice, and faith in the team's ability. It also demands that your power of persuasion be exercised effectively to convince superiors to support and underwrite the riskier pursuits when seeking approval to proceed.

Bravery and courage go together. Nelson Mandela, for example, *pretended* to be brave while imprisoned, which is a form of bravery in itself. Mandela was a social revolutionary who was considered a courageous leader, even when he was genuinely terrified. Throughout his most stressful situations, Mandela remained calm, refusing to show his fear.

Courage and bravery are choices; anyone can be courageous by learning to cope daily with their anxieties and fears.

> *With courage you will dare to take risks, have the strength to be compassionate, and the wisdom to be humble. Courage is the foundation of integrity.* —Mark Twain, American author, humorist, entrepreneur, publisher, and lecturer.

Conquering Fear

Conquering fear is essential for personal and professional growth. Fear often holds us back from pursuing opportunities, stepping outside our comfort zones, or taking the risks necessary to advance in our careers and enrich our lives. Whether it's the fear of failure, rejection, or uncertainty, allowing these feelings to dominate our decisions can limit our potential. Overcoming fear empowers us to take on new challenges, make bold career moves, and embrace opportunities that lead to growth and success. By confronting our fears head-on, we build resilience, strengthen our problem-solving skills, and develop the confidence to navigate the inevitable setbacks and uncertainties in life and work.

In our personal lives, conquering fear allows us to fully engage with the world around us and pursue our passions without hesitation. It helps us to cultivate deeper relationships, explore new experiences, and achieve personal fulfillment. When we learn to manage and channel fear productively, it can become a catalyst for creativity and innovation. Ultimately, conquering fear is not about eliminating it but learning to act despite it, turning obstacles into stepping stones toward a more courageous, fulfilling life and career.

Many struggle to initiate new tasks, stay motivated, form successful habits, or overcome their fears or phobias. The first step is often the most difficult, as objects at rest tend to remain at rest, as Newton's first law of motion explains. Humans naturally avoid pain, discomfort, uncertainty, or fear, which can lead to hesitation or procrastination.

Fear, driven by the threat of pain, harm, or danger, combined with inertia (avoidance), leads to procrastination or hesitation. When we put things off for reasons other than laziness or lack of availability, we're often fearful of something related to the task we're avoiding, such as fear of criticism or failure. Understanding this dynamic allows us to confront our fears and move beyond our comfort zone toward growth, accomplishment, and success.

When the sting of inaction outweighs the pain of action, it's crucial to recognize and address this behavior, unpacking the underlying fears that drive it. Passive acceptance of inertia perpetuates inaction.

Contemplating how a task fits into the bigger picture, such as long-term goals or overarching missions, can motivate action. Breaking tasks into smaller pieces fosters incremental progress and a sense of accomplishment. Overcoming the fear associated with the first step is critical to tackling more significant projects.

Motivation can be sustained through planning, positive reinforcement, and positive habits and rituals. If you encounter difficulties, practice self-empathy, take breaks when needed, and return to the task with a fresh perspective. Don't overthink it; dive in and get started.[70]

Fear kills more dreams than failure ever will. —Unknown.

Persistence

Persistence is a powerful behavior. It is generally defined as "... the act of refusing to give up or let go despite difficulty or opposition." It can often be the difference between successful and failed outcomes.

Research indicates that mental toughness, grit, and persistence are essential factors for success, even more so than intelligence. Regardless, there are no shortcuts or silver bullets for success. Without persistence, achievement, accomplishment, and fulfillment can seem unattainable.[71]

> *Nothing in the world can take the place of Persistence. Talent will not; nothing is more common than unsuccessful men with talent. Genius will not; unrewarded genius is almost a proverb. Education will not; the world is full of educated derelicts. Persistence and determination alone are omnipotent. The slogan 'Press On' has solved and always will solve the problems of the human race.* —Calvin Coolidge, American attorney, politician, and 30th president of the United States.

We can develop persistence by adopting and following a few essential steps:

- Goals: Set reasonable goals so that you know what you want. In one study, researchers found that people who set clear, concise goals succeeded in achieving them 95% of the time when they refused to quit and bounced back from difficulties along the way.

- Preparation: Prepare for obstacles and setbacks. Pursuits worth undertaking often involve challenges and adversity. Effective plans entail assessing risks and anticipating the unexpected. Mental preparation for potential outcomes helps avoid or mitigate surprise and disappointment, which could otherwise derail progress. Planning and preparation foster the psychological readiness needed to persist and ultimately succeed.

- Flexibility: Remember the mantra: "Nothing ever goes according to plan." Every plan is subject to adjustment, optimization, and readjustment. When something goes wrong, it's helpful to remain calm, evaluate what went wrong and why, and then revise and adjust your strategy as necessary for success. This process is iterative, so don't expect perfection on the first try.

Some have suggested that persistence is the key to success in startups. As an entrepreneur, you'll face unparalleled challenges. People may judge, be rude, or even bully you. Upholding your mission, energy, and confidence despite adversity is crucial. Leading by example and inspiring others becomes critical. Managing the demands of a startup while safeguarding your well-being is essential.[72]

From an early age, I embraced the notion that hard work, perseverance, and a refusal to give up were essential ingredients for achievement. During my college years, I encountered courses that seemed excruciatingly difficult. I often spent days grappling with a single homework problem, hoping for even partial credit from the professor. Despite the difficulties, I reminded myself that each course would eventually conclude, offering a fresh start with new challenges. Persistence became my guiding force, propelling me forward through every obstacle. While the outcomes of my efforts weren't always exceptional, they were usually sufficient.

I applied the same persistent attitude to my professional work, where seemingly impossible tasks or over-constrained program requirements could often feel insurmountable. Adopting an optimistic attitude based on the notion that every undertaking is finite in its duration and then grinding toward the finish line was a consistently successful strategy.

Stick to your plan, adjust as necessary, and keep at it as you marshal towards eventual success. Ignore the noise. It can be an emotional rollercoaster, so don't forget to celebrate the highs.

> *A lot of life is about how you react to setbacks. I was turned down by every record company in existence, including the one I'm signed to now. I kept going until I finally turned those noes into a yes.* —John Legend, American singer, songwriter, pianist, and record producer.

Perseverance and Resilience

While persistence is the firm continuation of a course of action despite difficulty or opposition, perseverance is steadfastness or steady persistence in doing something despite difficulties in achieving success. The difference is a nuance but a critical one.

There's an important distinction between persisting on a negative path and persevering towards a meaningful goal. While persistence on a negative path prolongs suffering and disappointment, perseverance is a positive trait that involves working towards significant objectives despite obstacles. Unlike stubbornness or obstinance, perseverance requires mindfulness and awareness, often associated with long-term goals that span a lifetime.[73]

> *Perseverance is the work that you do after you're already exhausted from doing the work you just did.* —Unknown.

Success in one's career, particularly entrepreneurship, demands persistence *and* perseverance. While intelligence, creativity, and ambition are essential, persistence and perseverance drive a business idea to fruition despite challenges. Grit allows entrepreneurs to navigate obstacles, learn from failures, and continue forward. Those who embody these traits persist and persevere when others might quit.[74]

While we persevere toward our important goals, resilience is the strength and speed of our response to adversity. Resilience allows us to bend in the face of a challenge and bounce back. It keeps us moving forward despite whatever life throws in our path. In life and business, we can expect surprises, detours, and occasional disasters—hopefully, we can avoid ruination. We all encounter hardship, but how do we react, adapt, and overcome it? Is this a skill, and can it be learned and strengthened?

When confronted with surprises, hardship, or even tragedy, our responses vary based on individual experiences and coping mechanisms. We may seek solutions through research, advice from others, or introspection. However, there are no foolproof answers or perfect resolutions to every challenge. Life's outcomes are not always fair or favorable, and we cannot always control or influence them entirely.[75]

Studies indicate that alongside perseverance, adopting a strategic mindset is crucial for achieving goals. This mindset involves refining processes, routines, and habits to overcome setbacks and improve the likelihood of success. Rather than abandoning tasks when faced with obstacles, individuals with a strategic mindset assess what worked and what didn't, adjusting and optimizing their approach accordingly. They continuously seek improvement by asking questions like "How can I help myself?" and "Is there a better way?" This willingness to adapt and find better methods is as important as determination, persistence, and resilience.[76]

Some people naturally have more resilience than others—they tend to bounce back from challenges with less effort. Fortunately, studies show that we can create a greater capacity for resilience. Managers can build team resilience by staying ahead of events, doing what they say they'll do, and trusting their leaders. Senior leaders are expected to look around the corner and rally people around uncertainty. While nothing is certain and nobody has a crystal ball, employees look to their leaders for a demonstrated commitment to plans and customers in the near term and to convert plans to action.

Team leaders build resilience by effectively and proactively communicating important information and instructions. This involves regular check-ins, one-on-ones, etc. They ask their team what they can do to help. Team leaders also encourage risk-taking.

People experience psychological safety when they are free to try new things, especially during difficult times. This builds resiliency within teams. As an individual contributor, enjoying the freedom to make choices when figuring out how to get work done under pressure also fuels resiliency.

The key to resilience is providing workers adequate *recovery* time after sprints. When people overwork for extended periods without being provided time to recover, the risk of burnout becomes almost inevitable. Rest and recovery are not equivalent—stopping does not equal recovering. And the longer and harder you work, the more recovery you'll need to reestablish a state of balance. Our brains need to rest as much as our bodies do.[77]

Perseverance and resilience are foundational traits that enable individuals to overcome challenges, setbacks, and career obstacles. By cultivating these qualities, individuals enhance their capacity to navigate adversity and strengthen their determination to achieve long-term goals and personal fulfillment in their professional journeys.

> *I'm convinced that about half of what separates the successful entrepreneurs from the non-successful ones is pure perseverance...Unless you have a lot of passion about this, you're not going to survive. You're going to give it up. So, you've got to have an idea, or a problem or a wrong that you want to right that you're passionate about; otherwise, you're not going to have the perseverance to stick it through.* — Steve Jobs, American entrepreneur, industrial designer, business magnate, media proprietor, investor, and co-founder and CEO of Apple.

Failure and Risk-Taking

Fear of failure is a universal experience, with the fear of looking bad in front of others being particularly prevalent. Studies suggest that some people dread public speaking more than they fear death, while CEOs acknowledge that fear of failure keeps them awake at night more than any other concern. This fear, known as atychiphobia, can lead to debilitating anxiety and depression, prompting individuals to avoid failure at all costs. Perfectionism often accompanies fear of failure, perpetuating the belief that success is about avoiding mistakes rather than achieving excellence.[78]

> *No matter how many mistakes you make, or how slow you progress, you are still way ahead of everyone who isn't trying.* —Tony Robbins, American author, coach, speaker, and philanthropist.

Innovation involves disrupting norms by exercising creativity, experimentation, grit, and perseverance. It necessitates fostering a culture that embraces risk-taking and acknowledges failure as part of the journey. Failure should be valued and seen as feedback essential for growth. It signifies progress and the courage to venture into uncharted territory, attempting what has not been done before.

Elon Musk, for example, epitomizes bold risk-taking while grappling with substantial fear. He confronts this fear by applying fatalism, methodically assessing worst-case scenarios and the probability of success. This approach mitigates uncertainty and allows for confident decision-making or, at the very least, a reduction in fear of the unknown. Confronting failure imaginatively can diminish its paralyzing grip, enabling progress with clarity and resolve.

Richard Branson, on the other hand, avoids contemplating the worst-case scenario and instead focuses on the learning potential of any risky pursuit. Focusing on what a potentially negative experience is teaching us shifts the attention from the short-term discomfort of failure to the long-term potential gain of lessons learned, which helps to boost courage.[79]

> *Try and fail, but don't fail to try.* —John Quincy Adams, 6th president of the United States, statesman, diplomat, lawyer, and diarist.

I like to reflect on Steve Jobs' career when I contemplate embracing failure: Despite facing setbacks, including being fired from the company he founded, Jobs persevered and continued to pursue his vision. His ventures with NeXT and Pixar faced significant challenges and setbacks, but Jobs remained resilient and focused on his goals.

The failure of NeXT and Pixar's initial struggles could have discouraged many individuals, but Jobs remained undeterred. His ability to learn from these experiences and adapt his approach ultimately led to groundbreaking successes. Toy Story's success marked a turning point for Pixar, leading to a string of hit films and financial success.

Jobs' eventual return to Apple and the acquisition of NeXT reshaped the company and set the stage for its resurgence. His leadership and innovative vision propelled Apple to unprecedented heights, solidifying its place as a global technology leader.

Steve Jobs' journey is a testament to the transformative power of perseverance, resilience, and embracing failure as a catalyst for growth and success. His willingness to confront adversity head-on and learn from his mistakes continues to inspire entrepreneurs and leaders worldwide.

By analyzing Jobs' process for overcoming the effects of failure, we can adopt similar behaviors to reverse setbacks and enable success:

- Take big risks. Nothing truly great comes from being conservative in your pursuits.

- Remain confident. Don't let yourself become dismayed if things don't work out. If you left nothing on the field, you can rest easy knowing that you did everything possible to succeed.

- Keep going after a setback. First, take a break, clear your mind, and perhaps consider an alternative approach.

- Setbacks and failures provide valuable learning and feedback. These can make you stronger, wiser, and more capable of avoiding future failures.

- You can't predict the future, so do what you can and maintain confidence—in your ideas, yourself, and your team.

- Embrace ambiguity and the unknown. Those comfortable navigating that realm and creating an exciting new future (i.e., putting a dent in the universe) may experience exponential success.[80]

- Remove yourself from the echo chambers of naysayers—they could all be wrong. Sometimes, being the underdog can be an advantage—they won't see you coming.

- Allow yourself to fail so that you can experience what that feels like. This can be a cure in and of itself. Failure can truly set you free.

My wife Elaine and I recently binge-watched the TV series *Ted Lasso*. Ted is an ex-football coach who finds himself coaching soccer in England—a sport he knows little about. Ted's advice to "Be a goldfish" after a painful loss encourages his team to adopt a short-term memory similar to that of a happy goldfish. By doing so, the team maintains a positive outlook and resilience by swiftly moving past setbacks and focusing on future victories. It's a simple yet profound lesson in embracing optimism and living in the moment, beautifully portrayed in the series. Ted's wisdom resonates far beyond the soccer field, offering valuable insights for navigating life's challenges with a hopeful mindset. Bravo Ted!

> *You miss 100 percent of the shots you don't take.* —Wayne Gretzky, Canadian-born hockey player, and NHL Hall of Famer.

Presence

Presence is vital in our careers and personal lives, as it reflects our ability to be fully engaged in the moment and connect meaningfully with others. In a professional setting, being present means more than just showing up physically—it involves actively listening, contributing thoughtfully, and maintaining awareness of the dynamics around you. When you demonstrate presence, you build trust and credibility, showing your colleagues, clients, or team members that you value their time and input. This attentiveness often leads to better collaboration, clearer communication, and stronger professional relationships. Presence also fosters greater decision-making abilities, as being fully focused allows you to process information more accurately and respond more effectively.

In life, presence is equally important. It encourages us to live more intentionally and appreciate the moments that make up our daily experiences. Whether in personal relationships, family interactions, or moments of self-reflection, practicing presence allows us to form deeper connections and enhance our overall sense of fulfillment. We can lead more enriched, balanced lives by putting distractions aside and focusing on what truly matters. Presence also helps reduce stress, as it encourages mindfulness and helps prevent us from getting lost in worries about the future or regrets about the past. Ultimately, presence is the foundation of meaningful engagement in both work and life.

At work it's frustrating to lead or participate in a meeting only to discover that some attendees aren't fully engaged. You've likely witnessed it yourself—individuals who open their laptops or reach for their phones, seemingly preoccupied with their other tasks while the meeting unfolds around them. When posed a question, they scramble to catch up, admitting they didn't hear, inadvertently embarrassing themselves by letting their minds drift elsewhere. By succumbing to distractions, they deprive the group of their potential contribution and convey that their tasks outweigh the importance of the meeting and its participants.

To be present, strive to bring your whole self—your attention, energy, and enthusiasm—into the moment, igniting the meeting with your presence. This is the opportune time for collaboration and mutual support as you work together to address the issues at hand. Your thoughts, ideas, and insights are invaluable; otherwise, you wouldn't have been invited.

Rest assured, the world won't stop spinning if you momentarily set aside other tasks during the meeting. Your work can patiently await your return, whether for a few minutes or an hour. Disable notifications, close your email and ignore distractions. Listen attentively to others without mentally preparing responses or anticipating the next topic. Allow their words to resonate fully, embracing their perspective before formulating your thoughts. Only then should you contribute. Doing so will enhance your effectiveness, organize your thoughts more coherently, and garner greater appreciation for your input.[81]

> *Be fully in the moment, open yourself to the powerful energies dancing around you.* —Ernest Hemingway.

Forgiveness

Kindness and forgiveness are intertwined. It's challenging to genuinely extend kindness to someone who has wronged you without first forgiving their transgression. Yet, forgiveness remains one of life's toughest aspirations—easier said than done for many.

> *Those who cannot forgive others break the bridge over which they themselves must pass.* —Confucius, Chinese philosopher, teacher, and political theorist.

In business, holding a grudge or bottling up unhealthy anger resulting from being wronged by others acts like an anchor on your career. It's hard to conceal anger. People see it in your expressions and in how you carry yourself. When you carry a grudge or outwardly condemn or undermine others, your opportunity to move forward, excel, or advance diminishes.

When I've felt aggrieved, I've found it crucial to consciously commit to moving forward. Staying in the moment and dwelling on the issue only invites brooding and stewing. Committing to engage in a new task can help break this cycle. Sometimes, taking a brief break, such as going for a walk for fresh air and a change of scenery, can be beneficial in resetting your emotions. These intentional actions help disrupt negative thought patterns and transition to more productive endeavors. You may also choose to avoid toxic individuals who provoke anger, or discontinue business dealings with those who have wronged you. It's important to note that forgiveness doesn't necessarily entail forgetting. Every experience is an opportunity for learning and growth.

If you've done or said something that hurt someone else, start by forgiving yourself. Understand that none of us are perfect, and it's human to make mistakes. It's not productive to dwell on self-judgment for your shortcomings. Shift your focus to the present, and strive to be your best self as you progress from your mistakes.

Consider these essential next steps:

- Acknowledge that you've made a mistake, and own it.

- Apologize as soon as possible—delayed apologies are far less genuine, effective, or impactful. When you apologize, don't overthink it. Gather the courage to say the words: "I'm sorry."

- Go beyond simply apologizing. Invite them to lunch or take them for a walk to discuss it further, clear the air, or improve your relationship.

You might also review what led you to make a mistake in the first place. Do you harbor a bias that requires some critical introspection and adjustment? Is there something about the other person that bothers you and warrants attention?[82]

Forgiveness at work promotes healing and growth and restores trust in professional relationships. By embracing forgiveness, individuals and teams can overcome conflicts, foster empathy, and create a more resilient and cohesive work environment conducive to personal and collective success.

The weak can never forgive. Forgiveness is the attribute of the strong. —Mahatma Gandhi, Indian lawyer, anti-colonial nationalist, and political ethicist.

Dealing with Unfairness

Unfairness is an inevitable aspect of life, spanning personal and professional domains. For example, it's common to witness individuals less intelligent, skilled, or competent than oneself receiving promotions and higher pay. Some fortunate individuals secure executive positions and substantial stock options in startups just before an IPO, leapfrogging those who have devoted years to building the company. Recognition and notoriety are sometimes bestowed upon those who did not perform the work. Additionally, *good-ole-boy* networks perpetuate unfairness by overlooking capable leaders for promotions, leaving many feeling frustrated and powerless to effect change. Unfairness in business seems endless, which contributes to a sense of frustration and helplessness among those affected.

We can complain because rose bushes have thorns... or rejoice because thorn bushes have roses. —Abraham Lincoln, 16th president of the United States, statesman, and lawyer.

Consider the pervasive issue of pay inequality in the workforce today. Over the past 40 years, CEOs have seen a staggering increase in their earnings, with a 940% rise compared to a mere 12% increase for the average worker. In 2018, the average CEO pay for the largest 350 companies in the U.S. reached $17.2 million, signifying a stark contrast with the average worker's earnings. Chief executives now make approximately $278 for every $1 an average worker makes, an increase of $258 compared to 1965 pay rates. This disparity spans not only CEOs but also the entire executive suite. Interestingly, CEOs' increased earnings are often attributed to their ability to set their own pay rather than their contribution to corporate performance or productivity. In some cases, CEOs within poor-performing companies have received excessive compensation packages, personally benefiting from rising share prices within their industry or sector without driving better corporate outcomes.[83]

While you may not control every aspect of your environment, you alone, are responsible for how you react to challenges. A common adage suggests two ways to build the tallest building—constructing the tallest structure or tearing down the taller buildings of others. Chronic complaining can strain relationships and tarnish your professional image, especially when directed at colleagues or superiors.

Instead of fixating on personal grievances, strive to shift your focus outward. Resist the corrosive emotions of envy and jealousy, and celebrate the successes of others. Recognize that success is not a zero-sum game; others' achievements do not diminish your potential for success. Embracing this mindset fosters a healthier perspective and cultivates positive interactions in both personal and professional spheres.

Rather than dwelling on personal setbacks, redirect your energy towards assisting those who are less fortunate. This shift can transform negative emotions into a rewarding and enriching endeavor, fostering a sense of fulfillment. If you consistently feel undervalued, exploited, or hindered from realizing your full potential, consider seeking work elsewhere. A change in leadership or a fresh new environment may provide the opportunity for your talents to flourish.

Living well amidst career challenges and unfairness involves cultivating resilience, prioritizing personal well-being, and maintaining a positive outlook. By focusing on self-care, meaningful connections, and pursuing passions beyond work, individuals can navigate adversity with greater resilience and find fulfillment beyond the constraints of professional setbacks.

Living well is the best revenge. —George Herbert, English poet, orator, and priest.

CHAPTER 5

Emotional and Psychological Management

Control your emotions, or they will control you. —Unknown.

Emotional and psychological management is crucial for maintaining a healthy, balanced, and successful life. Effective management of our emotions and psychological well-being directly impacts our ability to handle stress, build strong relationships, and make sound decisions. Navigating the complexities of imposter syndrome, managing ego and arrogance, and maintaining emotional equilibrium are all essential aspects of this process. The practice of pausing before reacting is a critical emotional regulation that helps individuals manage their immediate emotional responses and prevent impulsive reactions.

By mastering emotional and psychological management, we become more resilient and adaptive, better equipped to face challenges and seize opportunities. This inner stability enhances our well-being and boosts our professional performance, allowing us to lead with empathy, clarity, and confidence. Understanding and implementing these skills can profoundly influence our career trajectory and overall quality of life, enabling us to thrive in our personal and professional domains.

Managing Your Emotions

We're all human—we experience good and bad emotions, whether at work or away. Problems at work arise when those emotions become counterproductive or even destructive.

Emotions can be categorized into two main types: *integral* and *incidental*. Integral emotions are directly tied to the choice we are facing, whereas incidental emotions are unrelated to the decision at hand. Envy and regret are examples of integral emotions, while sadness and anger are examples of incidental emotions.

Envy arises when we perceive that others possess something we desire, often accompanied by feelings of shame when we acknowledge this emotion. Addressing envy productively involves taking action to make a change and focusing on achieving our desired outcome. With personal success, it becomes easier to mitigate envy and appreciate one's accomplishments, recognizing that they are sufficient and well-earned.

Regret is one of the most challenging emotions to avoid. When faced with a decision or an action, try picking the option that will minimize regret. If you're afraid of change, remember that change may bring a better outcome (less regret) than maintaining the status quo.

Sadness and gratitude represent opposite emotional states. While sadness often arises from loss or disappointment, gratitude emanates from appreciation and acknowledgment of positive experiences or acts of kindness. If you tend to adopt a "glass half empty" attitude towards life, cultivating gratitude can be transformative. Expressing gratitude through simple acts, such as writing and delivering a letter of appreciation to someone who has shown kindness, can profoundly elevate happiness and well-being.

Gratitude turns what we have into enough. —Unknown.

Like many, I've struggled with my emotions at work from time to time, having experienced varying degrees of conflict, regret, and criticism. Admittedly, I haven't always responded to those emotions positively or effectively, especially during my early years as an engineer. I sometimes allowed myself to be easily provoked, reacting angrily or hastily launching fiery emails. However, I developed a more measured approach as I matured and learned from those experiences. I learned the value of restraint, holding back on immediate responses, and taking time to cool down before addressing issues. Often, upon revisiting unsent email responses the next day, I opted to discard them entirely. I also discovered that open communication through phone calls or face-to-face discussions was far more effective in resolving conflicts and clearing the air.

Encountering bullying bosses or toxic co-workers has been one of the toughest challenges in my career—working with such individuals was, at times, deeply unsettling. Usually, the most effective solution involved seeking new opportunities elsewhere. Transitioning to different roles allowed me to work alongside individuals I admired in a healthier and more fulfilling work environment. Fortunately, most bosses genuinely care about their teams and strive to foster positive and respectful workplaces.

Every manager should know that yelling at employees is unacceptable, regardless of the circumstances. Such behavior is not only demeaning to the individual being yelled at but also creates a culture of fear and discomfort for everyone in the workplace. Moreover, it undermines the manager's authority and damages their reputation, ultimately driving away talented employees.

Managers occasionally resort to yelling because they lack effective strategies for achieving their objectives without resorting to anger. Some may feel desperate or frustrated, while others may yell out of convenience or be unwilling to explore more constructive approaches to motivation and leadership.

Managers should never forget that they have various tools to motivate their teams and achieve results. Anger should be a tool of last resort if ever used. And when an employee displays anger, the manager should address the behavior promptly and respectfully. Understanding the root cause of the employee's frustration is essential. The manager should remind the employee of the importance of respectful behavior toward colleagues, collaborate with them to identify solutions, and communicate the consequences of repeating the behavior. This approach fosters a constructive and respectful work environment while addressing issues effectively.

If you find yourself in a situation where you have yelled at someone, regardless of your position, it's important to apologize immediately. Don't let anger or frustration dictate your actions. Admit that your behavior was wrong, and acknowledge that nobody deserves to be yelled at, especially in a professional setting. Ensure that your apology comes across as genuine and sincere. Next, address the root cause of the issue calmly and professionally. Explore what triggered your outburst, and collaborate with the other person to find a resolution and prevent similar incidents from occurring in the future. Taking responsibility and resolving conflicts constructively can help maintain a positive work environment and foster healthier relationships among team members.[84]

Reflecting on the struggles many face worldwide can provide a valuable perspective on our challenges and circumstances. It reminds us to appreciate what we often take for granted and keeps us grounded in reality. By redirecting our emotional energy towards more constructive endeavors, we can focus on productive pursuits that benefit ourselves and those in need. Ideally, these reflections inspire us to take action and extend a helping hand to those who are less fortunate, creating a mutually beneficial outcome for everyone involved.

> *Being happy doesn't mean you have it all. It simply means you're thankful for all you have.* —Unknown.

Pause First

When you find yourself angered at work, how do you react? Perhaps you've been called out by a co-worker or superior, wrongly challenged by a peer, or targeted by a bully. What do you do? Likewise, when asked a difficult question, do you immediately blurt out the first thought that comes to your mind? Are you motivated to answer quickly because you associate that with superior intellect?

> *Before you react, take a pause. Give yourself time to decide if it's worth responding to. Sometimes silence is the best response.* —Unknown.

When someone wrongs you, and you immediately respond by lashing out, you miss a significant opportunity to establish cause and perspective. Most people don't act out without reason; they often start from a place of innocence, and something triggers their adverse action or response. Taking a pause allows you to investigate and comprehend the source of the issue before reacting. This moment of reflection enables a more empathetic response, valued by leaders and co-workers alike.[85]

Similarly, when faced with a difficult question, many respond hastily, offering an incomplete thought or opinion. Intellectuals may swiftly compose a reply, while thoughtful individuals take a moment to consider the question and possible responses before providing a quality answer. They refuse to be rushed, preferring to take their time to respond thoughtfully. Wise individuals refrain from constantly sharing opinions to impress others and only contribute when they can positively impact the conversation. They avoid unnecessary attention to feed their ego.[86]

Elon Musk and the late Steve Jobs exemplify the "Rule of awkward silence" when confronted with challenging questions. They take a pause to deeply contemplate their responses, even if it lasts 15 seconds or more. This moment of reflection often yields remarkable answers, as it allows our brains to suppress the urge to react quickly and emotionally under pressure.

When we receive a written request, our instinct is to reply promptly. However, delaying our response enables us to craft a more thoughtful reply. If the delay frustrates the requester, that's part of the awkward silence; it's important not to yield. With practice, this technique becomes more comfortable, and others come to expect it. The pause empowers us to manage our emotions and deliver optimal responses. Initially awkward, with practice, the pause becomes natural as we replace emotion with considered thought.[87]

The pause—that impressive silence, that eloquent silence, that geometrically progressive silence which often achieves a desired effect where no combination of words, howsoever felicitous, could accomplish it. —Mark Twain.

Imposter Syndrome

Almost everyone experiences imposter syndrome from time to time. This form of self-doubt can make workers feel inadequate, regardless of their accomplishments or abilities.

> *Imposter Syndrome is just fear's vegan cousin.* —Unknown.

Some individuals who grapple with imposter syndrome often undermine their achievements by attributing their success to luck rather than merit. They dwell on their mistakes while dismissing accomplishments as mere chance. Despite evidence of competence, they harbor doubts about their intelligence and qualifications, fearing exposure as frauds. These beliefs hinder their ability to internalize success and can lead to self-sabotage. Imposter syndrome manifests in behaviors such as withdrawal in meetings, reluctance to share ideas, or procrastination to evade scrutiny. Some may resort to job-hopping in a bid to evade discovery.

Rapid change is a hallmark of today's workplace. In recent years, we've transitioned from empirical developments to wide-scale computer-based design—we're experiencing the pervasive utilization of computers and mobile devices and the hastened integration of AI and machine learning. With such rapid change, it's easy to fall behind while others evolve, leading to a sense of incompetence. At the same time, we set the bar for our success and competence so high that we're practically assured of failure. And then we experience shame as a consequence.

> *There are still days I wake up feeling like a fraud, not sure I should be where I am.* —Sheryl Sandberg, American business executive, author, philanthropist, and women's rights advocate.

To combat these unhelpful feelings, observing and recognizing them when they arise is essential. We must allow ourselves to acknowledge our victories and successes, attributing them to *our* efforts rather than dismissing them as fraudulent. Success rarely follows a linear trajectory, and recognizing the non-linearity of our achievements doesn't diminish their legitimacy. Reflecting on past failures, we can acknowledge that we did our best in each situation, eliminating the need for shame. If we learn or grow from each failure, we should take pride in our self-improvement journey.[88]

Surrounding yourself with friends or mentors who offer helpful perspectives can quiet your restless mind. Sharing your fears with them may reveal that others experience similar feelings, which can provide valuable reassurance. Setting reasonable expectations for yourself is also important; constantly striving for the unachievable reinforces the destructive narrative of inadequacy. Permit yourself to acknowledge personal wins and achievements without comparing yourself to others.[89]

It's important to understand that new hires are especially vulnerable to imposter syndrome. I first learned of this term during my initial orientation week at Facebook. Alongside approximately a hundred other recruits, I participated in a series of engaging talks led by various company leaders. These sessions illuminated Facebook's mission and unveiled the intricate network of roles within the organization, showing how each contributed to the collective mission.

During one such session, a speaker addressed the common phenomenon of feeling unprepared or unqualified for our new roles in a fast-paced, results-driven enterprise like Facebook. They acknowledged the inner voice that sometimes doubts our worthiness and qualifications, suggesting we may have somehow faked or cheated our way into the company. However, the speaker's message was refreshingly empowering. They encouraged us to recognize that nobody is ever a perfect job fit from the start, and that's perfectly normal.

Despite Facebook's rigorous interviewing process, there's always room for growth and learning in any new role. The company values employees willing to embark on a journey of exploration, learning, and contribution. Facebook encourages individuals to be authentic, follow their passions, and evolve into impactful team members. Whether someone perfectly aligns with their initial role is less critical than their willingness and ability to grow and contribute positively. Ultimately, attitude, behavior, and character matter more than specific skills.

It's important to remember that none of us are imposters, and we're not alone in experiencing such thoughts. When feelings of inadequacy arise, it's essential to redirect our thoughts and summon the courage to dispel the notion of being unqualified frauds. Regardless of the mission or task, we all have something valuable to offer. We are unique, skilled, and inherently valuable in our own right.

The best companies understand this reality and actively work to bolster the confidence of their recruits. They remind them that everyone has room to learn, grow, and contribute without the need to measure up immediately. Even highly successful individuals like Albert Einstein and former Starbucks CEO Howard Schultz have openly admitted to sometimes feeling like impostors. It's a natural phenomenon and should not be misconstrued as a lack of competence or belonging.

> *The exaggerated esteem in which my lifework is held makes me very ill at ease. I feel compelled to think of myself as an involuntary swindler.* —Albert Einstein.

Ego and Arrogance

The higher a person rises within the organization, the more power they gain and the higher the risk of developing an inflated ego. Likewise, suppose a worker has experienced remarkable success. In that case, they might convince themselves that each of their accomplishments was theirs alone rather than the byproduct of exceptional team achievements.

> *The trouble with the world is that the stupid are cocksure and the intelligent are full of doubt.* —Bertrand Russell, British philosopher, logician, and mathematician.

The influence of increased responsibility and authority varies among individuals. While some rise to the occasion with maturity and humility, others succumb to self-interest, often putting others down. Many high-performing individuals strike a balance between self-confidence and humility. They learn along the way while they build, grow, and nurture their teams. Conversely, some individuals become arrogant, prioritizing their interests over collective success. They dominate discussions, emphasizing their intelligence at the expense of others. In hiring, some managers avoid recruiting exceptionally talented individuals, fearing that new hires might steal their limelight or dim their glow by comparison.

As ego expands, there's a heightened risk of becoming insulated from the organization and its people, which inhibits their ability to receive honest and factual data or feedback from their subordinates and coworkers. Subordinates may tell leaders what they *want* to hear, fueling further ego inflation. This pattern, known as the "Hubris syndrome," characterizes a disorder associated with prolonged power and success. The ego can prompt self-manipulation, fostering corruption and compromising personal values.

To avoid this pitfall, committing to keeping your ego in check is necessary. Cultivate humility and gratitude as strategies for fostering selflessness. Regularly acknowledge and reward those who have contributed to your success, reinforcing the reality that success is a collective effort. Resist insulating yourself by engaging with individuals who challenge rather than cater to your ego. Hire and surround yourself with intelligent, independent thinkers who aren't afraid to question you when necessary. This practice helps maintain humility and prevents unchecked self-importance.

Continuously evaluate your behavior for signs of rudeness, selfishness, and a tendency to interrupt others. Reflect on how you handle setbacks and criticism—are you open to accepting feedback from others? An inflated ego hinders our ability to learn from mistakes. Watch out for confirmation bias, which can lead to a distorted perspective and a reluctance to consider alternative viewpoints. Avoid creating a leadership bubble where you only accept feedback that aligns with your views and preferences.[90]

Research indicates that people are often drawn to over-confident and arrogant leaders, highlighting the importance of promoting humility in leadership. Further, individuals struggle to assess competence within their leaders accurately. Consequently, they rely on more visible traits like confidence. Psychologists suggest that overconfidence and arrogance in leaders stem from self-deception. Even lacking critical leadership skills, convincing oneself of competence can increase popularity and marketability. Others may falsely perceive confidence as a sign of skill.

> *In all that surrounds him the egotist sees only the frame of his own portrait (Petit-Senn). Good leaders are self-aware but not self-absorbed. They understand the importance of both confidence and compassion.* —Martin E. Dempsey, American general, statesman, and teacher.

While arrogance and false credentials might not have impeded career success 100 years ago, they're far more dangerous in today's complex world. *Fake it 'till you make it* is hardly a winning leadership strategy these days, when knowledge, expertise, critical thought, curiosity, and creativity are essential prerequisites for most ventures.

To make matters worse, our societal norms often prioritize style over substance, perpetuating biases where men are rated higher on leadership traits than women, regardless of qualifications. While demonstrated self-awareness, including the ability to admit uncertainty with phrases like "I don't know," signals strength and competence in leadership, many visible leaders fall short in modeling this exceptional behavior for others to emulate.

Arrogant leaders often harbor insecurities rather than competence despite outward appearance. Recognizing arrogance in a worker provides an opportunity to investigate further, which can reveal underlying insecurities or weaknesses that can be addressed for the benefit of both the worker and the company. However, directly confronting arrogant individuals poses risks depending on their position and response to such confrontation. Nevertheless, leaving arrogance unresolved risks weakening teams and undermining positive work cultures.[91]

It's important to remember that ego and arrogance can hinder collaboration, stifle personal growth, and damage professional relationships. Embracing humility, empathy, and a willingness to learn fosters a healthier work environment, promotes sustainable success, and encourages genuine connections with colleagues and stakeholders.

> *You have to be ruthlessly open-minded and constantly willing to reexamine your assumptions. You have to take the ego out of ideas.* —Marc Andreessen, American entrepreneur, and tech investor.

CHAPTER 6

Influences and External Factors

Your beauty and status are to be remembered for some time, but your good behavior and sincerity will rule over the hearts forever. —Ritu Ghatourey, Indian author.

The influences and external factors in our lives profoundly shape our behaviors, decisions, and overall trajectory. From upbringing and societal norms to the impact of luck and office politics, these external elements can support or hinder our personal and professional development.

Social and behavioral psychologists have extensively studied the intricate interplay between attitude, behavior, and reaction. Understanding how these forces affect us allows for greater self-awareness and enhanced strategic decision-making. [92]

Our perceptions of fairness, the influence of wealth on behavior, and the dynamics of image and reputation are all critical components in navigating our careers. Recognizing and effectively managing these external influences enables us to maintain our integrity and align our actions with our core values, even in complex and challenging environments. By gaining insight into these factors, we empower ourselves to create a more intentional and fulfilling path in our personal lives and careers.

Upbringing and Norms

Social factors such as learning, conditioning, and observation can shape attitudes. The relationship between attitude and behavior is complex and only sometimes consistent. Sometimes, a positive attitude can stimulate poor behavior. Other times, we change our attitude to match our behavior or to combat conflicting attitudes that complicate our behavior. At times, we all act in ways we later regret, influenced by our environment, external pressures, and innate impulses. Nevertheless, we generally strive to uphold positive behavior consistent with our values, ethics, morals, and upbringing.

We tend to judge others by their behavior, and ourselves by our intentions. —Unknown.

When I grew up in the 1960s, strict discipline was the norm. Parents and even teachers routinely administered spankings for misbehavior. We were expected to display proper manners and honesty at all times. My parents consistently taught values like empathy, humility, and respect for others. Bad behavior carried strict consequences, regardless of age.

Times have changed, and so have parenting norms. But teaching our children what's right and wrong and instilling in them an expectation of how they should behave, especially regarding how they treat others and conduct themselves, is perhaps the most important and influential role a parent can play.

Our behavior, aided by self-awareness and emotional intelligence, can often have more influence on our career success than knowledge, skill, or intellect. Sometimes, the simple act of holding the door open for a boss or co-worker is enough to differentiate yourself from the many other workers who won't expend the same effort or who perhaps don't know any better.

As our workforce becomes increasingly diverse, we experience a range of behaviors at work. Expecting individuals from different countries, raised with distinct value systems, to behave exactly as I was taught is an unreasonable expectation. Some people, often those in positions of power or with high levels of education, may pay less attention to their behavior, appearing arrogant or entitled. The most extreme cases may even resort to bullying, displaying little or no emotional intelligence. Others may not have been taught common courtesy or manners by their parents. It's important to recognize that different cultures embrace different norms.

As leaders and colleagues, it's our responsibility to consistently model positive behavior in how we treat one another. We should also establish clear and consistent expectations for behavior to foster a positive, safe, and supportive corporate culture. Neglecting this responsibility allows our culture to evolve without guardrails, potentially leading to undesirable outcomes.

> *Your desired behavior must become just as much a habit as your undesired behavior was before.* —Mike Hawkins, author, executive coach, speaker, and thought leader.

Luck

Is there such a thing as *luck* in life or business? Perhaps, but I believe that luck is essentially a construct of our minds, a simplified explanation or excuse for the events that unfold around us. It's easier to attribute outcomes to luck than to take responsibility for our actions and the influences of our environment. While others may influence us, we still possess agency over our lives. Our personal and professional journeys are shaped by a continuum of cause and effect, where our actions can wield significant influence.

In many ways, we have the power to shape our own lives and attract the opportunities we desire, increasing our chances of encountering *good luck* when it presents itself. During periods of difficulty or perceived lousy luck, we either remain trapped in a cycle of rumination and victimhood or take proactive steps to break free from the pattern.[93]

Breaking the cycle of chronic unhappiness or prolonged streaks of bad luck requires adopting a mindset of appreciation and gratitude, often referred to as seeing the *glass half full*. By focusing on the positives, or at least acknowledging what isn't going wrong, we can find solace in the notion that situations could be far worse than they are. I've discovered that expressing appreciation and gratitude for others often leads to reciprocal responses, creating a ripple effect of positivity that can significantly impact attitudes and outcomes.

It's also observed that individuals who appear to have good luck tend to maintain a positive attitude and outlook. In my experience, those who radiate positivity often attract more favorable circumstances, reinforcing the belief that attitude plays a pivotal role in shaping our experiences.

Embrace the notion that change often starts with small, incremental steps, just like physical training; forming new habits and taking risks become easier with practice over time. If minor changes don't yield the desired outcomes, challenge yourself to take more significant risks that push you beyond your comfort zone.

Look for the good. Even bad ideas may have nuggets of positive potential. We can all be good and nice, even when experiencing a tough patch. If all you see is bad, that's probably exactly what you'll get—it becomes a self-fulfilling prophecy. Allow yourself to see the good before your optimism *muscle* atrophies.

At certain points in my career, I've encountered what could be interpreted as bouts of bad luck. For instance, I've faced the sting of being laid off twice, a victim of circumstance. During the "dot-com bust" in the early 2000s, Endwave, the company I co-founded, felt the repercussions as telecom orders retracted post-IPO. To weather the storm, our CEO streamlined operations, cutting ancillary activities, including my antenna business unit. Despite our team's exceptional efforts and achievements, we found ourselves unemployed in a market plagued by hiring freezes. Years later, multiple cycles of layoffs swept through Space Systems Loral, eventually claiming my position along with other personnel within my department despite a decade of dedication and extraordinary accomplishment.

Thankfully, my wife, Elaine, provided her reliable perspective at every turn. She reminded me that each setback presented an opportunity to pivot toward something even better, and in every instance, she proved correct.

Diligent effort paves the way for success, and exceptional effort leads to extraordinary success. Success generates the favorable circumstances we often attribute to good luck.

Luck in career success often intertwines with preparation, persistence, and seizing opportunities. While chance plays a role, proactive effort, continuous learning, and cultivating a support network enhance the likelihood of capitalizing on fortunate circumstances and achieving long-term career goals.

We cannot direct the wind, but we can adjust the sails. — Unknown.

Behavioral Effects of Wealth

Money and success tend to change people, often for the worse. This phenomenon has been well studied and documented. People tend to yearn for more and more, even when they've been remarkably successful. Cold-hearted behavior demonstrated by the wealthiest among us has been coined the "Rich Asshole Syndrome" (RAS). When people make more money, they use it to insulate themselves from risk, noise, and inconvenience—resulting in isolation. And research confirms that the rich are less generous than the poor. They are four times more likely to cut in front of other drivers, cheat at tasks and games, lie during negotiations, and excuse unethical behavior at work.

> *Rich people are poor people with money.* —George Orwell, English novelist, essayist, journalist, and critic.

One study found that affluent individuals were more likely to engage in shoplifting behaviors and demonstrated a reduced ability to recognize emotions in others' facial expressions. Furthermore, brain imaging studies indicated that wealthy individuals exhibited lower levels of brain activity when exposed to images depicting the suffering of others, such as children with cancer. This suggests wealth may lead to a psychological adaptation characterized by diminished empathy and compassion towards others.

Other studies have echoed similar findings, proposing that wealth triggers chemical reactions in the brain that contribute to increased feelings of entitlement, reduced empathy, and heightened focus on self-interest among affluent individuals. Fortunately, research has also found that generosity and charitable behaviors can be learned through small psychological interventions—nudges in specific directions that can lead to sustained behavioral change.

Experts recommend that we regularly monitor our behavior, attitude, and values as we achieve higher levels of success and wealth. Remember to focus on empathy, humility, and respecting others. Give back as a way to maintain balance and perspective. Keep your ego in check, remain humble, and continue to raise others through continuous recognition of their achievement. You'll be helping yourself as a by-product of helping others, which may lead to a more fulfilling life.[94]

Acquiring great wealth can change *some* things, but it doesn't have to change who you are, how you act, how you treat others, and what you value most. Appreciate what you've earned, and don't take it for granted. Refrain from turning inward and contracting your circle of friends or familial relations. Instead, focus on sharing your generosity with those who can benefit most. You may find that your benevolent charity or philanthropy can provide more personal satisfaction and happiness than your unfettered wealth accumulation ever will.

> *Too many people spend money they haven't earned, to buy things they don't want, to impress people they don't like.* — Unknown.

Image and Reputation

Building and maintaining a positive image and reputation is essential for long-term career success. While it may take years to establish these, missteps can erase them instantly.

> *Character is like a tree, and reputation like a shadow. The shadow is what we think of it; the tree is the real thing.* — Abraham Lincoln.

Trust your instinct; if something feels wrong, it probably is. If you find yourself in a situation that could harm your image or reputation, remove yourself promptly. Don't make excuses or doubt your intuition; trust it and move forward.

Consistently defend your reputation. If someone posts something negative about you, address the issue immediately and work to resolve the issue or complaint. Consider having the post removed. Some individuals thrive on spreading negativity; in such cases, it may be best to ignore them and disengage rather than fuel their behavior. Choose your actions and responses wisely.

It's important to exceed expectations and avoid taking shortcuts. This principle relates to doing what's *right*. Rise above the fray and establish a reputation built on excellence and accomplishment. You'll earn even greater admiration and respect when you surpass people's expectations. Your work's quality, detail, and thoroughness directly contribute to your reputation. If you gain a reputation for taking shortcuts or providing shoddy or incomplete work, your prospects for advancement and plum assignments may become jeopardized.

Your image is enhanced when you positively accept and respond to criticism and failure. Criticism and setbacks are inevitable; nobody is immune to them. How you handle failure shapes your reputation and growth.

Strive to be truthful, transparent, and consistent. Your relationship with facts and truth significantly influences your reputation. People will respect you when you behave consistently and hold yourself to the highest level of integrity.[95]

> *The way to gain a good reputation is to endeavor to be what you desire to appear.* —Socrates.

CHAPTER 7

Professional Conduct and Behaviors

Talent is never enough. There's no substitute for it, but there's also no guarantee of success with it. To turn talent into influence, a person must prepare it with hard work, surround it with the right relationships, strengthen it by taking responsibility, and protect it with character. —John C. Maxwell, American author, speaker, and pastor.

Professional conduct and work-related behaviors are pivotal in shaping our career success and workplace relationships. Our professional identity and reputation define how we conduct ourselves, from showing initiative and maintaining a "can-do" attitude to respecting boundaries and the chain of command. Navigating office politics tactfully and avoiding unprofessional behaviors, such as excessive swearing at work, are crucial for maintaining a respectful and collaborative environment. These behaviors reflect our values and influence how we are perceived and treated by colleagues and superiors.

Certain behaviors and attitudes are inspirational and transformative in life and business. When applied effectively, consistently, and judiciously, these enablers can change your life and career. While behavioral changes may seem daunting or even impossible, they can be learned, practiced, and reinforced until they become second nature. Adhering to high standards of professional conduct fosters a positive and productive work environment. It enhances collaboration, builds trust, and opens doors to opportunities for growth and advancement. By embodying these behaviors, we can navigate the complexities of the workplace with integrity and effectiveness, contributing to both our personal fulfillment and professional achievement.

Initiative

Initiative is a cornerstone of success in both careers and life, as it embodies the drive to take proactive steps toward achieving goals without being prompted or instructed. In the workplace, demonstrating initiative sets individuals apart, showing they are willing to go beyond the minimum requirements, tackle challenges head-on, and think creatively to solve problems. Those who take initiative often find more opportunities for career advancement, as they exhibit leadership potential and a commitment to personal and professional growth. Employers value individuals who can identify needs, propose solutions, and execute them, even in uncertain or ambiguous situations. Initiative is also essential for navigating career transitions, as it pushes individuals to seek new opportunities, pursue further education, or make strategic moves to stay ahead in an ever-changing market.

In life, initiative plays a similarly transformative role. It encourages personal growth by inspiring people to pursue their passions, take risks, and embrace challenges that foster development. Whether learning a new skill, nurturing relationships, or contributing to the community, initiative empowers us to shape our experiences rather than waiting for opportunities to come to us. Taking the first step in any endeavor sets a course for achievement and self-fulfillment. Furthermore, initiative cultivates resilience, as it often requires stepping out of comfort zones and facing potential failures—key experiences that lead to long-term success and personal satisfaction. Ultimately, initiative transforms intentions into actions and dreams into realities, making it an indispensable quality in every facet of life.

Many ambitious, self-directed leaders begin to lead long before being promoted to leadership positions. They assume responsibility, step up to the plate, fill an existing leadership void, and take the initiative to get things done. I learned this lesson through personal experience.

> *Without initiative, leaders are simply workers in leadership positions.* —Bo Bennett, Psychologist, administrator, author, and educator.

Early in my career, I assumed I needed a promotion to "manager" before taking charge of a languishing project. When I approached my boss for a promotion, he told me that people lead efforts and earn promotions through their demonstrated leadership, not vice versa. That message resonated with me, and with implicit approval, I took charge of the project without waiting for formal authority.

You don't need a formal leadership role to be a leader—persuasion and inspiration, not job titles, secure support. Leadership is about building connections that enable collective action; the more effective you are, the more people will want to follow you.

There's a lot to be said for taking initiative. Progress comes through action, and action happens when we take that crucial first step. Taking imperfect action rather than overthinking and remaining stalled builds trust and confidence in our resourcefulness. This goes to trusting your *gut* or intuition. Pairing intuition with analytical thinking helps you make better and faster decisions and creates greater confidence. Sometimes, the difference between greatness and mediocrity is simply learning to get out of our own way.[96]

Even one person with clarity of conscience and a willingness to speak up can make a real difference. When leaders bring their voice and vision, others may follow, leading to extraordinary outcomes. Hone your skills at challenging the status quo for the greater good. Gather the courage to make your voice heard and avoid succumbing to groupthink. Believe in the "Power of one," which requires courage, initiative, and persistence to drive change.[97]

You'll never plough a field by turning it over in your mind.
—Irish Proverb.

Boundaries

Setting personal or professional boundaries is inexorably linked to other behavioral traits such as confidence, courage, integrity, pride, and respect. It relates to knowing when to say "no" to preserve your integrity, mental health, and even your personal safety. Learning how to set protective boundaries is a skill that everyone should learn, even from an early age.

Boundaries are a part of self-care. They are healthy, normal, and necessary. —Doreen Virtue, American author, and motivational speaker.

Setting boundaries and saying "no" can be challenging, especially for individuals who face discrimination or marginalization in their professional or personal lives. Women and minorities often experience pressure to over-perform as a means to counteract systemic biases and discrimination. This dynamic extends to academia, where additional expectations and barriers may exist for women and minorities, including the need to be likable and grateful for acceptance and engaging in service activities not required of their male counterparts. Recognizing and asserting one's boundaries becomes crucial for maintaining well-being and navigating power imbalances.

> *One of the things dad instilled in me... is that you had to be twice as good to be given half a chance* —Tiger Woods, American professional golfer, golf course architect, entrepreneur, and philanthropist.

Athletes often face immense pressure to display toughness, strength, and even perfection and are expected always to compete regardless of their physical or mental well-being. When athletes like Simone Biles decide to prioritize their mental health and withdraw from events, they may face criticism and contempt from fans and media. However, Biles' decision to withdraw from the Olympics, especially in solidarity with athletes facing racial abuse, was widely supported by many who saw it as a courageous stance against societal pressures and expectations. Despite facing backlash, Biles' choice sparked essential conversations about mental health in sports and highlighted the need for athletes to prioritize their well-being over external pressures.[98]

It's normal to feel hesitant about pushing back on your boss, fearing it may harm your career prospects. However, it's essential to recognize and uphold reasonable personal boundaries in the workplace. While earning the trust and respect of your colleagues is important, it shouldn't come at the expense of your integrity. There are situations when we must consider pushing back against unreasonable expectations, such as being on call 24/7 for extended periods. I faced this challenge in my career when working for overly demanding bosses. Fortunately, I usually achieved a reasonable balance by establishing boundaries and committing to personal priorities.

Employees should not feel obligated to provide their boss with constant accessibility. It's unreasonable to expect immediate responses to emails at all hours or to be tethered to a phone 24/7, especially during vacations. While some occasions warrant extraordinary availability, that shouldn't become the norm. Such expectations are not sustainable and create stress for employees while eroding work culture. That said, pushing against corporate norms or opposing your boss's demand for continuous, around-the-clock availability could land you in hot water—bosses don't always do what's *right* when pushing for increased output. For example, when "Shark Tank" personality and investor Kevin O'Leary was asked whether he ever encounters employees who silence their phones outside of work, he responded: "*The next moment is—I just fire them.*"[99]

As leaders, it's essential to recognize that demanding perfection from employees is unreasonable. While doing your best, learning from mistakes, and striving for improvement are reasonable, sacrificing your health or shouldering unreasonable stress is unacceptable. Your health should always come first, and it's important to prioritize self-care. Remember, you are of little use to others when your health becomes compromised.

Bosses who expect constant agreement without valuing diverse opinions can create a toxic work environment. The best leaders understand the value of different perspectives and ideas. Employees should not feel pressured to agree with their boss at all times, as healthy disagreement can lead to better outcomes and innovation.

Likewise, employees should not feel obligated to *like* their boss simply because of their position of authority. Respect should be mutual, and likability must be earned through actions and behavior, not imposed due to hierarchy. Employees should focus on performing their best while maintaining their integrity and individuality.

In the past, bosses demanded and expected worker loyalty. This is no longer the case. You don't owe your boss anything when you choose whether to continue working for them or stay at the same company. It's a fair and open market for all workers, and remembering that is both important and empowering.[100]

Setting boundaries in our jobs is essential for maintaining work-life balance, preserving mental and physical well-being, and fostering productive relationships. By establishing clear limits around time, tasks, and personal needs, individuals can cultivate a healthier and more sustainable approach to work while achieving greater overall satisfaction and success.

> *The only people who get upset when you set boundaries are the ones who benefited from you having none.* —Unknown.

"Can-Do" Attitude

When evaluating a person's performance or considering a new hire, possessing a "can-do" attitude consistently ranks at the top of my behavioral metrics. I've observed that the most effective and valued employees contribute in every possible way to support an effort. I seek out individuals who go above and beyond the minimum requirements, exceeding expectations and aiding others in their pursuit of success, even if it means taking on tasks that might reasonably be considered subordinate.

For instance, as co-founder and director of Endgate, I endeavored to embrace every task with humility; whether making coffee for others, unclogging toilets, or trapping rats that frequented our office hallway, no job was beneath me. Once, as VP at Safeview, I sat behind the wheel of a large box truck, transporting our prototype body scanner across snowy mountains from Colorado to California to ensure our entire team could focus on last-minute design tweaks before a critical demonstration. It's critically important to take pride in one's work and willingly take on any task necessary to support the team and benefit the company.

I've never felt prouder than when I witnessed my children embodying the same attitude. Growing up, they were exposed to various opportunities to contribute to the community, from volunteering at soup kitchens to participating in park clean-ups and tree-planting events. One notable instance was when my son Kyler joined his high school basketball team during his junior year. Despite possessing impressive skills, he found himself on a team of seasoned players who had been competing together since freshman year. Consequently, he saw little competitive playtime, much to our disappointment as parents. Nevertheless, he attended every practice and game, becoming his team's most dedicated and vocal supporter from the bench. He encouraged his teammates and maintained a positive attitude, regardless of his own playing time. Despite our frustration with his lack of opportunities on the court, we couldn't have been prouder of his unwavering passion and positivity. That's what truly matters.

> *I'll do whatever it takes to win games. Whether it's sitting on a bench waving a towel, handing a cup of water to a teammate, or hitting the game winning shot.* —Kobe Bryant, American NBA All-Star.

Adopting a can-do attitude is straightforward. It doesn't require special training or knowledge; it involves taking initiative and maintaining positivity. Everyone can strive to do a little more than what's expected, surpassing the efforts of others. This might mean arriving at work a bit early, staying a few minutes late, making an extra phone call, or sending another email before the day ends. It could also involve conducting additional research beyond the minimum requirement or assisting customers with their belongings. Helping with tasks like unloading shipments demonstrates proactive engagement. Instead of waiting to be asked, offer assistance, or simply take the initiative to act. Rather than merely instructing employees, lead by example and work alongside them. Over time, these seemingly minor contributions and a positive attitude can make a real impact.[101]

Individuals who consistently exhibit a can-do attitude often find themselves highly sought after, securing the best jobs and commanding top pay. By setting aside ego and prioritizing success, they support the endeavors of their colleagues and contribute to their success. Embracing this mindset has the potential to catalyze positive transformations in various aspects of life.

Office Politics

Gossip, often synonymous with office politics, has historically served as a means of bonding and group cohesion. But despite its familiar presence, gossip is inherently destructive. It allows individuals to reinforce biases and undermine transparent relationships and cultures that value direct feedback. Gossip can also serve as ammunition in interpersonal conflicts.[102]

Over the years, I've encountered workplaces where certain employees seemed to dedicate most of their time to spreading rumors and discord, engaging in what I refer to as "stirring the shit." The most energetic among them make it their mission to involve others in their drama and intrigue, turning gossip into their daily focus. These gossipers can poison the work culture, creating a toxic environment.

> *Rumors are carried by haters, spread by fools, and accepted by idiots.* —Unknown.

If someone on your team consistently creates drama or stirs division, as their boss, it's crucial to take swift, corrective action. Gossipers breed negativity and can significantly harm team dynamics, leading to increased turnover and damage to the company culture. Even if these toxic employees are high performers, the overall benefit of removing them from the team often outweighs the value they may bring.

The following steps can utilized effectively to deal with the corrosive effects of office politics:

- Stop gossip as soon as it's identified by setting a consistent example of refusal to engage.

- Encourage others to follow the example of taking the "high road" and abstaining from gossip.

- Understand personal tendencies towards gossip and seek less destructive ways to achieve important goals.

- Redirect attention to impactful and productive activities.

- Foster a healthy environment of timely and respectful feedback where issues and complaints can be addressed directly.

- Encourage individuals to communicate concerns directly rather than through gossip channels.

- Prioritize open and honest discussions to rectify situations or issues promptly.

A healthy environment of bidirectional feedback is an effective method of neutralizing the tendency for gossip. If you can succeed in this pursuit, your relationships and organization will be provided the opportunity to flourish and thrive.[103]

> *Great minds discuss ideas; average minds discuss events; small minds discuss people.* —Eleanor Roosevelt.

Swearing at Work

Mild profanity has become increasingly common in everyday speech, even in professional settings. It's not uncommon to hear an occasional F-bomb or other choice curse words slip out, especially in moments of frustration or when things go wrong. However, swearing at work can have unintended consequences that may backfire on you unexpectedly.

That said, research suggests mild swearing can have positive effects, even in the workplace. Occasional curse words can ignite urgency, increase persuasiveness, ease tension, or alleviate stress in certain situations. Moreover, swearing may help foster camaraderie among colleagues and contribute to a sense of fitting in. Recent studies have also shown that swearing can temporarily increase our pain threshold, with the F-word being particularly effective in this regard.[104] However, it's essential to remember that swearing without purpose is simply cursing.

Leaders may find mild profanity acceptable in companies that prioritize authenticity among employees in specific contexts. Nonetheless, there are well-accepted boundaries regarding profanity. George Carlin's "Seven Words You Can Never Say On Television" monologue from 1972 highlighted taboo words, many of which remain inappropriate for public discourse today. While societal acceptance of profanity has evolved, racial or homophobic slurs remain highly offensive and unacceptable, especially in the workplace, where such language can lead to severe consequences. It's prudent to exercise restraint and avoid using potentially offensive language, erring on the side of caution when unsure of appropriateness.[105]

While mild or occasional swearing has become normalized in Western society, it also carries the risk of portraying you as someone prone to anger, a hothead, or lacking control over your emotions. In the worst-case scenario, it could adversely affect your assignments and professional reputation. For instance, if your swearing becomes problematic, you might miss out on exceptional job opportunities, perhaps involving customer interaction, as leaders may question your suitability to represent the company. Swearing at work also risks annoying or offending co-workers. In extreme cases, a co-worker might perceive your language as abusive or threatening and report it accordingly. This risk is exacerbated as our workforces become increasingly diverse, with individuals who may struggle to interpret the nuances of English profanity, including its context and intent.

How companies monitor and police profanity can vary widely. At one company I worked for, even mild swear words could lead to dismissal, while at another, swearing was commonplace and considered a part of being authentic. It's important to understand your company's policies and norms regarding profanity and avoid saying anything that could jeopardize your reputation or employment.

The following guidelines may help you to avoid any negative consequences of mild swearing at work:

- Refrain from using profanity in written communications, as it could be used against you later.

- Be self-aware and mindful of your surroundings and audience. Use profanity sparingly and appropriately to express emotions, but avoid it if there's a chance it could upset or offend anyone nearby.

- If you accidentally swear during a presentation, acknowledge it briefly and move on without making a big deal about it.

- Occasional and reactive swearing may be more accepted, but apologize if necessary.

- Never use swearing as a weapon in anger, especially when providing negative feedback or reprimanding an employee, as it could escalate the situation quickly.

In my experience, when management or HR personnel are overly strict in monitoring or policing workplace speech, such oversight can become an unnecessary annoyance. Employees should generally be trusted to behave appropriately and avoid offending others. Encouraging authenticity, even if it means occasional swearing, can contribute to a healthier work culture.

When applied judicially and sparingly, swearing at work can provide some degree of positive benefit in certain situations. However, swearing can impact perceptions of professionalism, team cohesion, and organizational culture, potentially leading to misunderstandings and strained relationships. By fostering accepted communication norms and respectful dialogue, workplaces can promote a more inclusive and productive environment conducive to mutual respect and collaboration.

Vulgarity is like a fine wine: it should only be uncorked on a special occasion, and then only shared with the right group of people. —James Rozoff, American author.

Chain of Command

Disregarding the chain of command is almost guaranteed to upset or frustrate managers. While your company may promote an open-door policy for addressing issues, it's important to respect the established hierarchy and engage with managers appropriately before escalating.

Skipping over managers is generally considered disrespectful. Managers are expected to handle problems within their scope of responsibility, and bypassing them signals a lack of confidence in their abilities or intent. This can lead to resentment and reflects poorly on you and the manager you bypassed. It may also annoy the higher-level manager you reached out to directly.

Generally, every manager should have the opportunity to lead or be involved in resolving issues, especially those within their area of responsibility. The circumvented manager is usually best equipped to address the problem directly since they likely possess valuable insight and knowledge. It's generally in everyone's best interest to involve them in finding a solution.

That said, escalating beyond your immediate boss may be justified in certain situations. But first, if your boss is exhibiting signs of being unaware or out of touch with what's happening, someone should bring it to their attention. Leaders are human and may have personal or professional challenges that affect their ability to focus, or they might be temporarily distracted. It's important to approach the situation with empathy and understanding, considering that your boss may be dealing with other priorities or personal issues.[106]

The following suggestions are worth considering as you navigate what may prove to be difficult conversations with your boss:

- Rely on facts and data to support your points. Prepare your arguments with critical and relevant information and present them clearly and deliberately. This will make it difficult for your boss to ignore the evidence presented to them.

- Avoid confrontation; present the data and allow your boss to make an informed decision.

- Rather than making bold statements, consider asking pointed questions that challenge your boss to assess the situation and its implications. This approach stimulates critical thinking and may lead them to reconsider their stance.

- Highlight the consequences of inaction or the risks of maintaining the status quo. Presenting potential worst-case scenarios can prompt your boss to take decisive action or make positive changes.

- Ensure your boss understands the positive and negative outcomes, and express your willingness to support their decision.

While truthfulness and transparency may not always yield immediate results, they are often the most effective approach to addressing conflicts or issues with your boss.

If you find it impossible to resolve an issue with your boss directly, escalation might be the only remaining path to resolution, assuming you're not willing to grin and bear it. When this happens, the best leaders will avoid retribution for your escalating an issue or complaint.

> ...no one likes someone going over his head. But if in an employee's opinion, such a step ultimately becomes necessary, it must be understood that he has every right to do so. Any effort to prevent such going 'up the line' through intimidation, or any other means, is absolutely contrary to company policy. Any such action will be considered as a serious breach of management responsibility, and will be dealt with appropriately. —William R. (Bill) Hewlett, American engineer, entrepreneur, business executive, and philanthropist.

These days, the landscape of leadership and communication is evolving rapidly, with an increasing emphasis on efficiency and agility. Traditional hierarchies and communication channels are being reevaluated for faster, more direct methods. Elon Musk's approach underscores the importance of prioritizing efficiency over rigid chains of command. He advocates for communication to follow the shortest path necessary to achieve objectives rather than adhering strictly to hierarchical structures.

For companies experiencing communication inefficiencies and bottlenecks, adopting a more direct approach may be beneficial. However, it's essential to understand and adhere to the guidance and norms established by leadership and the company culture. Transitioning to more direct communication paths should align with the organization's approved processes and accepted practices.[107]

CHAPTER 8

Skill Building

The capacity to learn is a gift; the ability to learn is a skill; the willingness to learn is a choice. —Brian Herbert, American author.

Skill development is the cornerstone of a successful and fulfilling career. Building and refining skills such as effective questioning, writing, and listening are essential for clear communication and strong relationships. Diversifying your skill set and enhancing your abilities in public speaking, storytelling, and presentations can set you apart and make you a more versatile and dynamic professional. Charisma and the ability to captivate an audience are invaluable traits that can significantly impact your career trajectory.

Climbing the corporate ladder requires a strategic approach to professional growth. By continually investing in your development, you improve your immediate job performance and position yourself for future opportunities. Mastery in these areas fosters confidence and competence, enabling you to navigate the complexities of the corporate world with poise and effectiveness. You can achieve long-term career success and personal satisfaction through focused and intentional professional development.

Career Diversification

If you're new to the workforce, I wish you great happiness and fulfillment as you navigate your career path. I would point you to something Guy Kawasaki once said as essential guidance for young or new employees:

> *Don't sweat your first few jobs as long as you're learning, and don't leave in less than a year. You have to stay some place at least a year.* —Guy Kawasaki.

As you add years of experience to your résumé, you may find a variety of reasons to adjust the vector of your career. For example, you might have started working at a job or in an industry that has since dried up or transitioned to something else. When this happens, you don't want to be caught flat-footed, or you might find yourself unemployed and unemployable. Business is constantly changing, so every worker must prepare for the worst and be positioned for the best.

In the current economy, taking your work for granted can be risky. Layoffs happen, jobs become automated, and skills become obsolete. The U.S. Census Bureau reports that Americans will average seven careers over their lifetimes. Many of us find that we can't make ends meet on a single income, which motivates us to secure multiple jobs. That often requires that we learn new skills.

Specializing can also provide job opportunities when you select a skill that the market won't soon move past. Most jobs enable role and salary advancement opportunities to those who gain expertise through work experience, coursework, or training, so specializing can be a path toward marketability and job security.

Ultimately, though, to prepare for uncertainty and position yourself for long-term success, sometimes the best thing you can do is diversify. Part-time freelancing and consulting have become easy and popular paths towards diversification. Some experts predict that there will be more freelancers than employees in the not-too-distant future.[108]

Some people take up a side hobby, often leading them to a new career. There are countless ways to expand your work horizons, but relying solely on chance and letting yourself drift aimlessly is typically not the most effective approach. Instead, consider the following tangible actions:

- Make a plan.

- Research job postings in the areas that interest you to understand the skills they require.

- Reach out to people already doing those jobs and request advice on transitioning into those roles.

- Learn new skills. Read books, magazines, and journals. Take some courses.

- Once you've established a plan forward, execute it!

Commitment and persistence often lead to success in career transitions.

Like many careers, mine took numerous unexpected twists and turns. It's often only in hindsight that you can make sense of these changes. Building a broad skill set enhances your marketability and widens the range of accessible roles. With technology advancing rapidly, keeping pace, evolving, and adapting are more crucial than ever.

Career diversification empowers individuals to cultivate resilience and adaptability, enhancing professional fulfillment and financial stability. Embracing diverse opportunities mitigates risks and fosters personal growth, enabling individuals to navigate dynamic job markets and achieve sustainable career longevity.

> *Never get complacent. Nothing is forever. Whether it is an individual or a business, your competition will defeat you if you are not constantly seeking ways to reinvent and improve yourself. Organizations, especially, are more fragile than you think.* —Stephen Schwarzman.

Climbing the Ladder

There are many paths to career advancement, but progression hinges on skill development. Some individuals may prioritize a superior professional title over higher pay, equating it with success. However, a prestigious title doesn't always guarantee swifter career growth or advancement. While titles hold significance, they shouldn't be the primary driving force behind your career aspirations.

> *It's better to be at the bottom of the ladder you want to climb than on the top of the one you don't.* —Unknown.

Building a solid skill foundation opens doors for career growth. Conversely, lacking essential capabilities can lead to early plateaus or stalling out. As you ascend the corporate ladder, performance expectations rise from managers, stakeholders, and customers. Executive teams face intense scrutiny from boards and the public, making the "Fake it 'til you make it" strategy ineffective. Skill building is vital for job security; staying current in your industry with high-demand skills ensures ongoing career success.

Consider the following strategy as you pursue career advancement:

- Set Clear Goals. Define where you aim to be professionally in five years, aiming for roles two or three levels above your current position.

- Research and Identify Skills. Explore the requirements for success in higher roles through research and reviewing job postings on platforms like LinkedIn.

- Network. Connect with professionals in those positions to gain insights into the critical skills needed.

- Commit to Skill Development. Acquiring new skills demands time, commitment, and sometimes financial investment. Understand that skill acquisition is a gradual process that cannot be rushed or achieved overnight.

- Prioritize Learning. Dedicate time and effort to long-term skill building despite busy work and personal schedules. This requires dedication and persistence. Find ways to integrate learning into daily routines through morning, evening, or weekend classes.

- Start Early. Begin building new skills early in your career journey to mitigate the increasing costs associated with advanced learning as you progress.

Not everyone aspires to climb the corporate ladder—many individuals find fulfillment and success in their current roles, and that's commendable. There should be no pressure to pursue management positions if they don't align with your interests or preferences. However, it's worth considering that some of the most effective managers didn't initially aspire to such roles. These individuals excel in management because of their dedication to achieving results and exceptional skills in getting the job done efficiently and effectively.

> *You know who the best managers are? They're the great individual contributors who never, ever want to be a manager, but decide they want to be a manager, because no one else is going to be able to do as good a job as them.* —Steve Jobs.

Climbing the corporate ladder requires a blend of strategic networking, continuous skill development, and a proactive approach to seizing opportunities. By navigating challenges with resilience and cultivating leadership qualities, individuals can advance their careers and achieve long-term professional success in competitive environments.

Strategy and Execution

Demonstrating an ability to think strategically can be critical to your career advancement. It shows your superiors that you can think for yourself and make decisions that affect the organization beyond your current role and responsibility. It also shows that you can integrate and synthesize broad and disparate viewpoints, desires, and demands (i.e., those of your stakeholders and customers) and resolve plans and actions that fuel organizational progress and success.

Being exposed to various strategic roles accelerates the development of strategic thinking. This is why many leadership development programs include job rotations, cross-functional projects, and close exposure to executive leadership. Immersing oneself in how organizations operate and function provides the ability and experience to think strategically and holistically.

Strategic thinking encompasses formulating and articulating plans or solutions, effectively communicating them to stakeholders and superiors, and garnering support for their implementation. It necessitates the courage to challenge existing norms, persuade others to endorse your ideas, and execute them proficiently to achieve favorable results.

Individuals grappling with strategic thought often exhibit tunnel vision, focusing solely on their personal or local concerns rather than adopting a broader perspective that acknowledges how ideas and actions impact various functions and external entities. What benefits one department may detrimentally affect others. Strategic clarity is fostered through dialogue, involvement, and collaborative brainstorming.[109]

Successfully launching your strategic idea hinges on garnering support and endorsement from others. Crafting an effective strategy is just the beginning; execution is equally vital for sustained success. Any misstep in execution could undermine your reputation and credibility as a strategic thinker. Embracing the philosophy of "under-promising and over-performing" can be beneficial. It's important to secure buy-in and commitment from stakeholders who will aid in your success, maintain transparent communication, and adopt a "no-excuses" approach to leadership. Securing the support of a proficient program manager can be invaluable for expansive, complex, innovative projects.

Becoming a successful leader necessitates proficiency in strategic thinking. It involves delivering present business results while anticipating future opportunities, issues, risks, and concerns. These skills are attainable and can be cultivated by individuals with determination and dedication.

> *Strategy without tactics is the slowest route to victory. Tactics without strategy is the noise before defeat.* —Sun Tzu, Chinese military strategist, philosopher, and writer.

Communication Skills

Consider the various ways we communicate today: We engage in small talk, answer questions, provide feedback, give or receive direction, brainstorm, and utilize multiple mediums such as phone calls, texts, and emails. Social expectations and norms guide our communication in both professional and personal spheres. Clear and appropriate communication is vital for success, whether conversing with a recruiter, friend, spouse, co-worker, or superior. When executed skillfully, the possibilities are endless; however, poor communication can lead to significant consequences.

> *The art of communication is the language of leadership.* — James Humes, American author, and presidential speechwriter.

Recent research that analyzed 400 companies with 100,000 employees or more revealed that inadequate communication resulted in average annual losses of approximately $62 million per company. It's reasonable to infer that smaller companies suffer even greater losses proportionally due to poor communication. A separate 2018 study surveyed 403 executives, with nearly half reporting project delays or failures from communication deficiencies within their organizations, particularly impacting midlevel managers. Conversely, companies led by executives proficient in communication who prioritize effective communication within their organizations yield significantly higher returns for shareholders. Despite compelling evidence, poor communicators are often excused from accountability.

At the extremes, ineffectual communication can be exhibited as screaming or silence. Both are equally damaging. People who constantly interrupt others are both disrespectful and disruptive. People who communicate their disparaging feelings through facial expressions are just as corrosive as those who use their words. Despite their training, people who insist on shutting down ideas and comments from others during brainstorming sessions are troublesome. And those who weaponize sarcasm to attack others while attempting to maintain a degree of plausible deniability are especially problematic.[110]

> *The single biggest problem in communication is the illusion that it has taken place.* —George Bernard Shaw, Irish playwright, critic, and political activist.

Our communication skills are fundamentally tied to our success and happiness at work. If you speak poorly, you will lose your audience and perhaps undermine your confidence or authority. You might also diminish your prospects for promotion or advancement. When you communicate effectively, you'll stand above the crowd, gain trust from those you engage, and more likely earn a reputation for excellence. This applies to written as well as spoken communications.

Generally, when you verbally communicate at work, it's important to structure your communication as follows:

- Be concise and relevant. This will enable your audience to better process and remember what you say.

- Start with the "what". Define your crucial point, idea, or argument. Present it clearly, devoid of jargon.

- Next, present the relevance or the reason that you're speaking. What is your point (so what)?

- Finally, bring your message to a close with the "now what?". This summarizes your point and presents a conclusion or proposal for action or next steps.[111]

Mastering the art of balancing masculine and feminine communication styles is central to effective communication, often referred to as the "Goldilocks Dilemma." Individuals, especially women, face heightened scrutiny regarding their speech and presentation. Women are frequently judged more harshly, with their style labeled as either too aggressive, competitive, demanding, or caring and soft, seldom hitting the mark. In contrast, men typically enjoy more leeway to express aggression, disgust, or anger, whereas such displays are rarely deemed acceptable from women.

This disparity underscores the uneven communication landscape that persists today. Until this unfortunate imbalance is rectified, it's important to be aware of your communication approach in every scenario. Pay close attention to nonverbal cues, including appearance, demeanor, posture, language, body language, voice, and diction, as they significantly impact your perceived confidence, approachability, professionalism, and authority. Practice makes perfect.[112]

As workplaces become more diverse, communicating with individuals with limited English proficiency or hearing impairments presents challenges. Speaking slowly and clearly and occasionally asking for confirmation of understanding can help ensure effective communication. Assuming your message was understood without confirmation may lead to later difficulties and frustrations.

Effective communication skills at work are pivotal for fostering clarity, collaboration, and productivity among team members. They serve as the cornerstone for building solid relationships, resolving conflicts constructively, and achieving collective success within organizations.

Half the world is composed of people who have something to say and can't, and the other half who have nothing to say and keep on saying it. —Robert Frost, American poet.

Deep Listening

Many people focus solely on the speaker's perspective when discussing effective communication. However, how the listener receives and understands the information is equally important. Effective communication involves ensuring the listener comprehends and processes the information with relevance and perspective. For instance, it's beneficial for speakers to follow up after answering a question to ensure that their response fully addresses the question and is clearly understood by the listener.

> *Know how to listen and you will profit even from those who talk badly.* —Plutarch, Greek philosopher, historian, biographer, essayist, and priest.

In sales and marketing, it's important to practice active and attentive listening, also known as "Deep listening." Your main goal in every interaction is to gain insights into each customer's business, challenges, needs, and plans. This means engaging in genuine, unhurried discussions that enable spontaneous exploration and sometimes unexpected tangents, which often prove invaluable. It is perfectly acceptable to conclude a meeting without covering every item on your agenda, understanding that relationship-building is an ongoing process that unfolds over multiple conversations. Rushing or cutting corners in this process is often counterproductive.

The following listening process can enhance effective communication:

- Let others speak first and validate their ideas before offering your opinion.

- After actively listening to your customer or audience, summarize what you've heard to ensure complete understanding.

- Document the conversation for future reference and share your notes transparently with all involved parties. This lays the groundwork for future discussions and serves as a historical reference.

- Empathizing with others allows you to understand their objectives, challenges, passions, and possibilities. Through empathy, you can assess whether your solution truly addresses their problems and resonates with their end users, making your offering more compelling. The deeper your understanding of your customer, the more valuable you become as a provider.[113]

Deep listening at work involves hearing words and understanding their meaning and context, which fosters trust and empathy among colleagues. By cultivating this skill, individuals can forge stronger relationships, enhance collaboration, and contribute more effectively to team success and organizational goals.

> *ALOE (Ask, Listen, Observe, Empathize).* —Spencer Huang, technologist, and growth leader.

The Art of Questioning

If curiosity is communication's secret weapon, asking questions is its tool. Asking questions helps you to build trust and connect with your audience. It also enables you to become a more authentic communicator. The value of the information you receive is highly influenced by the questions you ask.

> *Without a good question, a good answer has no place to go.*
> —Clayton Christensen, professor, and business consultant.

When you ask questions, you signal that you value the other person and their opinions. It's an investment of time and attention to understanding their perspective. Asking questions deepens mutual understanding and fosters a meaningful connection. Importantly, questioning can spark ideas and encourage creativity. However, when questioning is misused, it can become interrogative or intimidating.

Influential mentors and coaches become skilled in the art of questioning. They know which answers to ask and when to break an unproductive train of thought or to take a discussion to a higher level where discovery is possible. They use questioning to motivate the other person to self-assess or contemplate answers to their own questions.

Asking the right questions takes as much skill as giving the right answers. —Robert Half, author, and talent industry expert.

As a leader and mentor, I often avoided giving immediate answers to difficult questions from my subordinates or mentees. Instead, I preferred asking probing questions, sometimes circularly, to help them uncover information that could guide their own answers, strategies, or conclusions. This approach prevented me from being seen as the sole source of answers and encouraged independent critical thinking. Moreover, I viewed problems as opportunities for learning, allowing others to develop and refine their problem-solving skills.

The art of questioning hinges on trust. Without it, questions can be perceived as threats, regardless of the intent behind them. I have a friend who possesses an insatiable curiosity about various subjects. During our conversations, his questions start innocently but gradually delve deeper. At times, it feels like an interrogation. However, knowing him well, I understand his intent isn't to expose my knowledge gaps but to satisfy his curiosity.

Questioning should always lead to a positive outcome for both parties involved. It should never devolve into a power struggle or a means to expose weaknesses. Be mindful of the other person's reactions and signals during questioning. Adjusting or redirecting the conversation can be helpful if discomfort arises or the interaction becomes unproductive. If someone appears hesitant or uncomfortable, respecting their boundaries and moving on to a different topic is wise. Deep and relentless questioning solely for extracting information can be perceived as disinterest in the individual, prompting them to disengage.

Mastering the art of questioning at work empowers individuals to foster deeper understanding, drive innovative solutions, and cultivate a collaborative and learning-oriented environment. Effective questioning enhances communication, encourages critical thinking, and promotes creative problem-solving within teams and across organizational boundaries.

> *Questioning is the ability to organize our thinking around what we don't know.* —Unknown.

Writing Skills

Effective writing is a critical enabler for almost everyone, especially anyone aspiring to advance their career. Writing effectively requires deep thinking. It forces us to contemplate what we seek to explain and describe. Only when we've mastered our thoughts can we put them to paper.

Great writing makes you persuasive and believable. It enables you to convey knowledge, gain trust, and even seem smarter to others. Bad writing, on the other hand, can give the appearance of being uneducated and incompetent. Our writing prowess can significantly influence outcomes, underscoring its importance in professional spheres.

> *Good writing is clear thinking made visible.* —Bill Wheeler, author, and illustrator.

Creative writing courses in high school and college can equip us with indispensable skills that shape us into influential writers—which can prove pivotal throughout our careers. Writing proficiency is a compounded skill that improves with practice and diverse application.

For example, while writing was initially limited to documenting my designs as a junior engineer, my writing responsibilities expanded with each promotion. I began to craft detailed design reviews, and test reports and eventually wrote technical proposals and business plans. I authored sections of our company's prospectus for our IPO, published technical papers, drafted patent and product line strategies and developed MarCom product brochures. Over time, my audience diversified from engineering peers to executives, investors, customers, and business partners. Writing emerged as a cornerstone of my success, complementing my engineering and leadership abilities.

To write effectively, it's important to identify good writing by reading extensively. Focus on materials relevant to your writing context, such as business documents for business writing. Technical papers demand a distinct style compared to internal memos or personal letters. When you write, revise your document carefully and thoroughly and seek feedback from colleagues to enhance its quality. Allocate ample time for this process, recognizing that collaboration and revisions demand patience.

Writers today can benefit substantially from the many powerful AI writing tools like ChatGPT, QuilBot AI, Claude, Grammarly, and others. These tools utilize deep learning algorithms to analyze text and generate human-like responses, simplifying the writing process. Whether you seek grammar corrections or content suggestions, AI writers are exceptional enablers, providing corrected and often improved content. Comparing the tool's output to your original writing helps improve your writing skills over time.

Another advantage of AI tools is their ability to generate new content, saving time when developing a first draft. For instance, you can ask them to outline a business report or prepare the lead-in for a pitch to investors. They can also help articulate gratitude for an award. AI provides various possibilities within seconds, making editing rough content quicker than developing initial verbiage.[114]

AI writing tools can also help you write emails, reports, social media posts, customer presentations, data sheets, sales pitches, product brochures, performance reviews, or almost anything else. You can ask them to list the pros and cons of something you're indecisive about. Or perhaps you're looking for ideas for team activities or things to do while on vacation. They can translate text and documents and can also understand and write code.[115]

However, it's important to exercise caution, as with most computer tools, the output is only as good as the input ("Garbage-in, garbage-out"). Sometimes, AI tools make mistakes and misunderstand requests, and their effectiveness is limited by the data they were provided during their learning phase. Further, if you fail to detail your objectives and set boundaries and constraints adequately, the tool may yield a less desirable result. Despite these drawbacks, the benefits of using AI writers in terms of cost and time savings are well worth the effort.

Mastering writing skills enhances career success by enabling workers to communicate effectively, think critically, and establish credibility across various industries and roles. It is a foundational tool for advancing one's career through clear articulation of ideas and persuasive communication with stakeholders and peers alike.

> *The skill of writing is to create a context in which other people can think.* —Edwin Schlossberg, American designer, author, and artist.

Conversation and Public Speaking

Conversation is an act of information gathering and selling. It's how we learn about things that inform our thoughts, opinions, points of view, and stories. It's also how you tell your stories and sell yourself and your ideas. Conversation is an all-powerful tool that you can use to further yourself and your business. Public speaking is the formalized and structured embodiment of conversation.

Conversation also informs others about yourself. You can learn a lot about someone by how they engage in conversation. Some people command or demand attention, droning on and on, weaving from one idea or subject to another, leaving you exhausted when they finally come up for air. This can be described as "competition disguised as conversation," where the speaker strokes their own ego or attempts to demonstrate their brilliance by jumping from idea to idea non-stop. Some are witty and spellbinding, with endless stories of adventure or intrigue. Others are awe-inspiring in a way that makes us envious. But sadly, many are simply tiresome bores.[116]

Striking up a conversation can feel rather daunting, cognitively demanding, tiring, and even stressful, especially for introverts like myself. We never know where the conversation is going, and when speaking to strangers, we need to pay closer attention than when talking to someone familiar.

However, psychologists have found that making small talk with strangers can boost our mental performance and even help us approach public speaking more comfortably and confidently. Additionally, talking to strangers can be fun, enhance our well-being, make us smarter, and expand our social and professional networks.

Initiating a conversation involves making the other person feel safe and quickly conveying that you don't have an agenda—you're just being friendly and curious. Many people hate small talk, but that's because they don't think about what small talk is for. Small talk isn't a conversation. It's simply the opener for a better conversation. It's the way to get comfortable with one another and explore things that you eventually want to talk about. When someone asks, "What do you do?" they're essentially asking, "What should we talk about?"

For example, in improv, a comedian will start a sketch with something familiar to everyone in the audience—something relevant, timely, or present in the room—to bind the room together. Only then can they take the audience on a ride. When someone comments to a stranger about the weather, the weather isn't the point—it's a vehicle to help us overcome our natural reserve so we can talk to each other. Once you've established a safe and common ground, you can move incrementally towards something of mutual interest.

Conversely, when you go into a store and ask, "How are you doing?" and the clerk says, "Fine; how are you?", that's more of a script to make interactions more efficient. The intent is not to expand the interaction into a conversation but to facilitate whatever you hope to accomplish, like finding an item in the store.[117]

Effective conversations begin with the notion that asking questions initiates engagement.

The following process can further enhance most conversations:

- Ask questions and offer the other person time to develop their point of view while you listen intently.

- Don't focus on who is right or wrong.

- Refrain from dominating the conversation or overwhelming others with stories or opinions.

- Relax and curb your domineering tendencies. This requires give-and-take, which improves with practice.

- When you complete a thought, incorporate transitions or off-ramps and invite the other person to interject. This makes them part of the conversation instead of just an audience. That, in turn, makes them feel appreciated and heard.
- Continue to ask questions, demonstrating you're paying attention and caring about what they're saying. This deepens your bond with the other person.[118]

Public speaking is an essential skill for most professions—it can be crucial to your success regardless of your career path. If you're a salesperson, you want people to follow your advice, and buy what you're selling. If you're a manager, you want them to follow you in business. The higher you advance in your career, the more likely and more regularly you'll find yourself speaking in public.

Unfortunately, many people fail to grasp the fundamentals of public speaking, which can result in flat speeches that fail to meet the desired objective.

The following suggestions can improve your speech-giving ability:

- Giving a speech to an audience is your gift to them. Each speech should provide an epiphany or at least a call to action.
- Usually, the objective of a speech is to educate, communicate, inspire, or stimulate action. If you don't deeply understand the purpose of your speech, you'll just be wasting everyone's time.
- If you're proposing comprehensive change, breaking your proposal into discrete, bite-sized, actionable morsels may become necessary to facilitate comprehension without overwhelming your audience.
- If you're offering a solution your audience seeks, ensure you're hitting the mark. Don't solve a problem they're not struggling with or answer a question that isn't being asked.

- Sometimes, it makes sense to make a presentation interactive, where you can field questions in real-time to increase your effectiveness.[119]

- Most people seek engaging stories that transport them from their current concerns. They crave narratives that evoke emotions and offer respite from mundane facts. A well-told tale captivates with clarity and passion, supported by relevant data and insights, leading to a satisfying conclusion.

- Crafting a compelling narrative requires careful consideration of themes, plots, and critical points. Injecting humor and integrating relevant data adds depth and credibility without inducing boredom.

- Starting with a captivating story and ending with a logical conclusion ensures audience engagement and positive responses.[120]

- Psychologists have determined that we tend to remember best what we hear first and last rather than what is said in the middle. Therefore, you should have a powerful, relevant, relatable intro and a strong finish. It's important to craft compelling openings and closings that resonate with the audience and reinforce key messages.

- Rather than memorizing speeches verbatim, focusing on mastering content and allowing flexibility in delivery promotes a relaxed and confident demeanor onstage.[121]

Public speaking discomfort is common. Some people are moderately uncomfortable, while others are rather petrified. Rarely have I encountered someone who is entirely comfortable with public speaking and relishes the opportunity.

> *According to most studies, people's number one fear is public speaking. Number two is death. This means to the average person, if you go to a funeral, you're better off in the casket than doing the eulogy.* —Jerry Seinfield, comedian, actor, writer, and producer.

Thankfully, your speaking effectiveness and confidence will usually increase over time due to preparation and repetition (practice). The more you experience public speaking, the easier it gets. The more deeply prepared you are, the better the delivery.

Even if you're nervous, you can project confidence by applying some basic tactics. Various studies have found that body language and the expressions we use during a speech can convey impressions about us and evoke positive (or negative) emotions in the audience. For example, positive signals involve smiling, maintaining eye contact, and persuasive, open gesturing. Negative signals include fidgeting, stiff hand movements, and averted eyes. The right kinds of nonverbal gestures correlate with confidence and success. When you gesture, control your hands within a small space (imagine a small box). Keeping them generally still, combined with positive facial expressions, conveys a relaxed, confident posture. A wide, confident stance conveys control.[122]

Neuroscientist Andrew Huberman highlights physical actions that help manage nervousness and enhance performance. Taking a step forward toward the source of anxiety triggers the release of dopamine, promoting confidence and enjoyment in subsequent actions. Additionally, techniques like Eye Movement Desensitization and Reprocessing (EMDR) Therapy and double inhaling serve to alleviate fear and anxiety, facilitating a calm and composed state before presentations.[123]

It's OK to embrace your natural nervousness regarding public speaking. Own it, and see if you can channel your nervous energy into the excitement that stems from the opportunity to impart something impactful and meaningful to your audience. Your audience will detect your passion, which may translate well into their perception of a better speech. It's important not to dwell on stumbling over words—if you make a mistake, move forward without looking back. After giving your best effort, let go of worries about how you've been perceived or judged. Embrace your performance, whether it's good or bad. Learn from any missteps to improve for next time, and celebrate your successes when they come.[124]

I've discovered the value of studying great presentations, such as TED Talks, and analyzing what makes them effective. The opening sets the tone—whether a provocative statement or a relatable story, it draws the audience in. Influential speakers use metaphors and analogies to make their message resonate, and they pause after important points to let them sink in. Inflections, tone modulation, and self-deprecating humor keep the delivery engaging. Making eye contact with the audience and moving around the stage adds a personal touch. Like comedians, they circle back to tie all points together and leave the audience with a memorable takeaway.

Observing skilled communicators in social settings is also enlightening. What sets them apart? Take advantage of everyday opportunities to learn and adapt your style organically. With practice and observation, you'll notice positive results and a boost in self-confidence sooner than you think.

> *There are always three speeches, for every one you actually gave. The one you practiced, the one you gave, and the one you wish you gave.* —Dale Carnegie, American author, and lecturer.

PowerPoint Presentations

The primary goal of a slide presentation is to inform or persuade—to convey critical information or influence a decision. Unfortunately, presentations can also miss the mark, leaving the audience over- or underwhelmed, confused, and exhausted. Slide decks filled with bullet points tend to be dull and lackluster. Audiences struggle to connect with bullet points alone, so focusing on crafting a compelling story and conveying a clear overarching message is essential. Instead of relying solely on bullet points, speak to your slides by adding context and insight that give meaning to the facts and figures. Slides should serve to illustrate and support your points, not overshadow them.[125]

Slide presentations are another example of public speaking. Success can be improved by following these additional suggestions:

- Avoid wasting time with slide decks that serve no purpose beyond background information, self-promotion, or ego-boosting. Ensure your presentation is focused on achieving your defined objective.

- Provide only the information your audience needs to accomplish the presentation's objective. Cut down on unnecessary details and streamline your message to facilitate decision-making.

- Determine the most effective way to convey information. Minimize visual clutter by avoiding outlines and excessive text on slides. Use visuals sparingly, and opt for precise, efficient communication methods.

- Keep slides concise, with a maximum of 12-15 words per slide. Clearly label all data and graphs and highlight critical takeaways for emphasis. Use language familiar to your audience and avoid unnecessary technical jargon or acronyms.

- Be prepared to address follow-up questions and drill-downs efficiently. Have supplementary details ready as a reference, and promise to follow up on unanswered questions promptly.

- Foster audience engagement by encouraging interactive questions throughout the presentation. Embrace interruptions as opportunities for dialogue and clarification.

- Steer the discussion toward a decision. Summarize key points and lead the group to a conclusion based on the information presented. Accept the outcome, even if it differs from your expectations, and articulate a follow-up plan if necessary.

- Remember to compliment others and acknowledge those who contributed to your effort or presentation. Use "we" instead of "I," recognizing that most achievements involve collaboration.

- Maintain humility while exuding confidence; deflate your ego before addressing the audience.

- Document the meeting outcome. Codify decisions and follow-up plans and ensure all stakeholders, including non-attendees, are informed. Provide a list of attendees to keep everyone informed and aligned.

Remember that your presentation isn't for *your* benefit, and your audience may not be as familiar with your content as you are. Craft your narrative at a level that resonates with your audience and is easily digestible. Avoid using your presentation as a platform to indulge in self-importance, showcase brilliance, or boast.

When delivering a presentation, adjusting your speaking pace can be a valuable tool for engaging your audience and managing the duration of your speech. For content you anticipate will resonate with the audience or is crucial to your argument, slowing down allows them to digest the information and form their opinions in real time.

Conversely, for less critical or potentially controversial points, speaking slightly faster limits the time available for opposition to formulate. However, it's important to avoid rushing the audience for agreement or decisions, as some individuals may need more time to process complex information. If a decision is obvious or the audience is quick to comprehend, refrain from unnecessary delays or repetition.

Companies should recognize the substantial benefits of employees improving their presentation skills. Encouraging and funding training initiatives aimed at enhancing presentation abilities is worthwhile. Leadership should prioritize creating a safe environment conducive to practicing this skill. It's important to remember that even managers and executives were once nervous presenters themselves. They should lead by example, ensuring that all presenters receive consistent celebration, recognition, and encouragement.

It usually takes me more than three weeks to prepare a good impromptu speech. —Mark Twain.

Slide Deck Alternative

PowerPoint and other modern publishing tools have empowered virtually anyone to create visually stunning presentations with vibrant colors and animations. However, the utility of these tools doesn't necessarily suggest their usage in every situation. Moreover, even if we decide to use them, is it sensible to monopolize an audience's time for an hour or more, bombarding them with slide after slide until we inevitably arrive at the logical endpoint?

There's been extensive discourse on enhancing PowerPoint presentations, and the preceding discussion has further contributed to that dialogue. Yet, we can push the boundaries further and challenge ourselves to achieve even greater excellence. How can we significantly elevate the standard presentation or transcend it altogether?

As a matter of principle, Steve Jobs and several other renowned CEOs have vocally opposed PowerPoint slideshows. Perhaps Jobs preferred Apple's product, Keynote, but given his well-documented opposition, it went beyond that. He suggested that meetings have become forums for sharing long, monotonous bullet-slide decks rather than engaging others interactively. Slide decks put the presenter in command and relegate everyone else to be passive observers. This inhibits the creative process by reducing the opportunity to hash things out as a group exercise. Presenters who aren't prepared read their slides as a crutch or a reminder of what they want to say. Bullet points become simply disjointed text.

Building a 20-page slide deck with a smattering of facts and comments is straightforward. However, slide decks enable the presenter to gloss over ideas, dilute any sense of relative importance, and ignore the interconnectedness of ideas. Some advocate for limiting slide decks to situations involving large audiences rather than as a general tool for running routine meetings.[126]

In the extreme, we may consider eliminating presentations completely. Jeff Bezos, CEO of Amazon, has paved the way for this thinking. Bezos previously banned PowerPoint from meetings at Amazon. Instead, he requires every meeting attendee to silently read a hardcopy document at the beginning of every meeting, which contains the critical information needed to discuss an issue. He calls these documents "Briefing Documents". This strategy achieves several key objectives:

- Using briefing documents instead of slide presentations saves considerable time. Participants can read at their own pace, condensing an hour-long presentation into just 5-10 minutes of silent reading during meetings without interruptions for discussion.

- Briefing documents facilitate faster information transfer compared to presentations. All relevant information is shared upfront, ensuring everyone starts the conversation on the same page. Consequently, discussions are shorter and more focused.

- By providing a comprehensive document, individuals seeking information can read it and opt out of the meeting entirely. Skipping a slide presentation may result in significant gaps in understanding for those who choose not to attend.

Given the considerable time executives spend in meetings, Bezos' approach can substantially improve efficiency and productivity while enhancing time management within the organization, particularly at the senior levels of leadership.[127]

> *The magic to a great meeting is all of the work that's done beforehand.* —Bill Russell, NBA legend, and civil rights activist.

Executive Presentations

Presenting to executives differs somewhat from delivering to customers or peers. Executive audiences often pose more challenging, strategic, thought-provoking, or unexpected questions that may catch presenters off guard. In such instances, it's crucial not to panic. Underestimating an executive's knowledge or intelligence can have serious consequences, so avoid evading difficult questions with vague answers—it's likely to backfire. Furthermore, don't attempt to overpower their queries with complex jargon or technical terms. Instead, communicate using language familiar to your audience—words they understand and resonate with.[128]

> *It doesn't matter what you thought you said. It's what the audience believes you meant.* —George Torok, executive speech coach.

Consider following these steps when addressing questions from executives:

- Always be thoroughly prepared for any discussion or question.

- Take the time to formulate your answer thoughtfully and deliver it confidently.

- If the question seems complex, consider seeking clarification or offering multiple response options for the executive to choose from.

- Avoid the urge to rush through your answer to avoid further scrutiny. Instead, engage in a measured, deliberate response that invites further discussion and input from the executive audience.

- Resist the temptation to ramble or prolong your response with unnecessary details or buildup, as it may lead to disinterest or loss of confidence.

- Present your key points upfront and provide additional information only when requested.

- Honesty is essential—if you don't have an answer, admit it.

- Commit to follow up with the necessary information when it becomes available.

- Move on to the next topic when appropriate and practice regularly to refine your skills.

Executives value integrity and transparency over attempts to manipulate or evade questions.

Remember that they were once in your position—great leaders will empathize with your situation and challenges. Stay composed and confident, knowing that difficult situations will eventually resolve.

Presenting to executives shouldn't create fear and apprehension. Instead, when your presentation is crafted with clarity and conciseness, emphasizing strategic alignment and showcasing your expertise, you'll be afforded a unique opportunity to build your reputation and enhance your confidence.

> *People will forget what you said, people will forget what you did, but people will never forget how you made them feel.* — Mark Twain.

Story Telling and Charisma

Consider, for a moment, when you encounter an individual who effortlessly captures the attention of a room. They exude a sense of natural leadership, presence, or professional maturity. Some might call it gravitas. These individuals possess charm and likability, drawing others to them. In their presence, you feel valued and important. They demonstrate a genuine interest in your thoughts and contributions. These charismatic leaders usually possess a remarkable ability to inspire loyalty and diffuse tension with their light-hearted humor and engaging personalities, even during challenging times. Their unwavering leadership inspires the entire team to enthusiastically tackle any challenge they present.

The ancient Greeks described charisma as a "Gift of grace." It is a learned behavior and a skill that can be developed. In the most basic sense, charisma consists of three components:

- Presence: When you're present, you're fully aware, residing in the moment.

- Power: Accumulating power involves removing self-doubt and convincing yourself that your skills and passions are valuable and interesting to others.

- Warmth: Projecting warmth to others is hard to fake. It involves radiating a positive vibe and signaling kindness and acceptance.

Charismatic individuals often embody these traits, ranging from confidence and success to warmth and generosity. While some exude all these qualities, others may excel in specific areas. Experience and success in one's career can bolster confidence, making it easier to convey power. For instance, figures like Steve Jobs and Elon Musk are recognized for their presence and authority, though they may lack warmth, unlike Sheryl Sandberg, who embodies all three attributes.

Charismatic individuals employ metaphorical language, anecdotes, and comparisons to communicate effectively in social settings. They utilize facial expressions, dynamic body language, and vocal variations to emphasize critical points while posing questions to maintain engagement. What sets them apart is their ability to make others feel valued and special, fostering personal connections that transcend distractions and make individuals feel uniquely appreciated in their presence.[129]

In business, leaders who exude charisma can instill confidence, securing cooperation and commitment from strangers. A CEO's charisma can directly affect a company's share price and buoy the CEO, even when performance is flat or ambiguous. Charismatic leaders possess an almost magical air. They present as charming and even lucky. Most people typically appreciate a handshake or a hug from someone charismatic over someone who is merely hardworking or successful.[130]

Consider the following if you seek to enhance your personal charisma:

- Maintaining consistent eye contact throughout a conversation signals genuine interest and engagement.

- A warm greeting accompanied by a firm handshake and positive body language conveys sincerity and attentiveness.

- Asking relevant questions demonstrates respect for the other person's knowledge and interests, fostering meaningful dialogue.

- Smiling can create a welcoming atmosphere and elevate the mood of the interaction, eliciting positive responses.

- Strategic use of compliments can enhance rapport but should be sincere and moderate to avoid insincerity.

- Humor is an effective icebreaker, initiating conversations on a light and engaging note.[131]

Public speaking is an excellent way of generating confidence and honing skills that improve your presence and power. According to research, participants who shared slightly embarrassing stories generated 28% more ideas in a creativity test than those who shared a prideful story. This suggests that when you share something that exposes you to embarrassing feelings, it reminds your audience that you're human, you're vulnerable, and you're fallible. This frees us up to explore ideas more openly.[132]

What's most important is your story, more so than how well you tell it. Leaders tell stories that carry meaning and impact—that are relatable to the audience. If you tell a story that is unhelpful or irrelevant, you will waste everyone's time.

Here is an abbreviated list of stories that every business leader should be able to tell:

- Founding Story: Why was the company formed? This story pulls the team together with a sense of shared purpose, and instills passion.

- Vision or Mission Story: Where is the company headed, and what is the motive for going there? For example, why is your mission meaningful, worthwhile, and impactful? What are you planning to solve, and why is that a compelling pursuit?

- Investor Story: Who are your investors, and why did you select them from all others? What are their values? What do they expect from you? What do you expect from them? How will they provide value that will help you succeed?

- Recruiting Story: Why should people want to work at your company? Why is your team so incredible?

- Strategy Story: How will you execute to achieve the end goal? This is a forecast of the journey.

- Corporate Values Story: How does the organization behave? What's important, and how will you be tested?

- Customer Story: Who are your customers, what are their challenges, what do they want, and how will you meet their needs? What constitutes a customer that is a good match, and why do you need to be careful not to align with the wrong customers?

- Advantage or Marketing Story: What is your advantage, and why is it compelling? How will you beat the competition, and how will you sustainably maintain your advantage? How are you doing things differently and better for your customers?[133]

Ultimately, charisma and public speaking are powerful combinations in business. Charisma captivates and engages an audience, while strong public speaking skills effectively convey ideas with clarity and impact. Together, they reinforce one another, enabling leaders to inspire, influence, and motivate with presence and persuasion.

Charisma without character is postponed calamity. —Peter Ajisafe, author, and preacher.

Meetings

Effective meetings are invaluable. When transacted effectively, they bring teams together to strategize, address challenging issues, generate new ideas, tackle tough questions, and reach important decisions. These discussions foster real-time, interactive, and dynamic exchanges that are nearly impossible to replicate outside a meeting setting.

However, meetings can consume significant time, especially as you ascend the organizational ladder. While some are indispensable and fruitful, many are not. There are distinctions between good and bad meetings, between those that are useful and those that are a waste of time. Effective meetings don't spontaneously occur—they demand appropriate attendance, active participation, meticulous planning, adept leadership, and skillful execution.

> *You have a meeting to make a decision, not to decide on the question.* —Bill Gates, American business magnate, investor, philanthropist, and writer.

At many companies, the implicit assumption is that meeting attendance is mandatory once invited. However, employees should proactively safeguard their time, ensuring every work hour is devoted to high-priority and meaningful endeavors. A mere invitation to a meeting shouldn't automatically imply attendance. Moreover, if the purpose and goals of the meeting are unclear or vague, attendees should request clarification from the host to determine the need for their attendance.

> *No agenda, no attenda.* —Unknown.

During my time at Facebook, management strongly supported employees in declining meetings when justified and appropriate. Workers were encouraged and empowered to identify and eliminate time-wasting activities, including low-value meetings. Embracing this philosophy, I refined my meeting preparation and planning, ensuring that only essential contributors were invited. Stakeholders with interest but not critical involvement were designated as "optional" attendees and included in post-meeting briefs, signaling their presence wasn't essential. This approach facilitated more efficient use of everyone's time and resources.

In contrast, at many companies, declining a meeting invitation, regardless of the reason, may be perceived as defiance, especially if the host is a superior. How you can manage your meeting attendance depends on your company's culture, norms, and management expectations. Exceptional managers empower their employees to assess their own attendance needs, provided they can justify their decisions and exhibit sound judgment. Of course, some meetings are deemed mandatory.

In my experience, effective meetings boil down to a few simple and common-sense guidelines:

- Clearly define the meeting objective and critical attendees before sending invitations, including a descriptive meeting title for easy assessment.

- Clarify any required decisions and important ground rules at the outset.

- Start and end meetings punctually to emphasize the importance of everyone's time, allowing slight leniency for back-to-back meetings.

- Avoid scheduling excessively long meetings. Aim to finish within the allotted time (preferably earlier) without unnecessary extensions.

- Provide pre-meeting materials for review to ensure all attendees come prepared, rescheduling if necessary if participants arrive unprepared. If one or more attendees arrive late, don't waste everyone else's time by bringing them up to speed. Doing so sets a poor example for the future, disrespecting those who arrived on time and fully prepared.

- Keep the meeting agenda concise, focusing ideally on one or two topics. Maintain control over the meeting agenda and timetable to prevent hijacking. If a detour is warranted, proceed deliberately, not casually or randomly.

- Encourage active participation from all attendees, valuing everyone's ideas and comments.

- Avoid putting anyone on the spot or using tactics that may embarrass attendees.

- Foster open interaction and brainstorming while staying flexible in exploring tangents. Over-controlling can stifle interaction and creative collaboration.

- Address unresolved discussions by assigning them to a "parking lot" for future consideration. Refrain from allowing a protracted collateral discussion to derail your ability to meet other essential meeting objectives.

- Conclude meetings with a recap of decisions, next steps, and assigned actions, ensuring accountability. Document and distribute meeting notes to attendees and stakeholders to keep everyone consistently informed.

- Maintain a positive, optimistic atmosphere to encourage future attendance and engagement. Make your meetings fun, and inject some light-hearted humor as appropriate to lighten the mood, especially when the team is experiencing heightened pressure or stress.

When you make an effort to ensure meetings are purpose-driven, inclusive, and result-oriented, you'll likely maximize your team's productivity and engagement.

> *When the outcome of the meeting is to have another meeting, it has been a lousy meeting.* —Herbert Hoover, American President, politician, and humanitarian.

CHAPTER 9

Unlocking Soft Skills

There is a big difference between being human, and human being. —Unknown.

Describing a valuable and impactful employee involves considering a range of attributes beyond just hard skills. While experience, knowledge, skill, and work ethic are essential, soft skills substantially influence a candidate's long-term contribution to an organization. Soft skills such as adaptability, conflict resolution, teamwork, and humility are key indicators of how well a candidate will integrate into the organizational culture and navigate challenges. Evaluating how candidates respond to change, handle conflict, and collaborate within diverse teams provides insights into their potential to drive the company forward. Prioritizing soft skills alongside hard skills ensures a more comprehensive assessment of job candidates and their ability to thrive within the organization.

By some estimates, as little as 2% of a person's success is attributed to IQ. Most of us are not blessed with the brains of Einstein—we all struggle with self-confidence or imposter syndrome occasionally. When searching for a new job, how often have we avoided applying for a particular position because we're afraid that we might not possess precisely what the job description requires? Recent research has shown that in almost every case, personality outweighs intelligence regarding one's future success at any level. Character traits, such as conscientiousness, openness, and curiosity, are far more predictive of life outcomes than grades, test results, or IQ scores.[134]

> *People skills, EQ, 'soft' skills, HUMAN skills—these are our anchors. They ground us, and remind us that we are real. Without these we fly away.* —Claude Silver, inspirational speaker, and influencer.

IQ and Intelligence

Intelligence is a term used to describe a person's mind regarding their capability to think, solve problems, reason, study, and understand complex concepts. It's the rich stew of personality, knowledge, creativity, performance, and wisdom. IQ, on the other hand, stands for intelligence quotient. It describes the calculated value of a person's mind. The factors that influence a person's IQ are mortality and morbidity, parental IQ, social status of parents, and others. While IQ is determined primarily by mathematical knowledge and literacy, intelligence spans a broad spectrum of knowledge and ability.[135]

While there are several recognized forms of intelligence, two are worth mentioning here:

- *Crystallized intelligence* is accumulated knowledge. It includes facts and figures and is otherwise known as *book smarts*. Improving crystallized intelligence requires delving deeper into a particular topic.

- *Fluid intelligence* is the ability to learn and retain new information and use it to solve a problem, learn a new skill, or recall memories and modify them with new knowledge. This is otherwise termed as *street smarts*. Improving fluid intelligence requires deep-diving, then moving to something new, rinse and repeat. The only way to increase and sustain fluid intelligence is through experience, learning, and trying new things continuously.[136]

In general, people who possess high levels of intelligence tend to demonstrate the following behaviors:

- They have an insatiable appetite for information, knowledge, and learning. Their need goes beyond mere curiosity.

- They can quickly understand and grasp complex arguments with little explanation and can identify interesting implications and consequences of arguments.

- They display a strong capacity for learning, keen perception, and robust problem-solving abilities.

- Their depth and breadth of knowledge are broad, and they can identify, perceive, and appreciate the talents and accomplishments of others.[137]

- They often exhibit active listening rather than chronic speaking. Intelligence is highly correlated with the capacity for introspection.

- They usually refrain from small talk or conversation about superficial topics deemed low-value. Instead, they guide the conversation to more interesting, conceptual, or big-picture topics.

- They tend to exhibit humility. They are capable of understanding that subjective opinion is separate from objective truth. Therefore, they can admit when they don't know something or don't have an answer, and their opinions are always a work in progress.

- They exhibit an unrelenting pursuit of truth. This requires the ability to perform abstract thought, which complements a focus on data and facts, to arrive at the truth.[138]

Our intellectual capacity may be fixed, but how we employ our knowledge and talents makes a difference. Learning to avoid pitfalls and solve complex problems can make you seem more intelligent and even sentient. This takes time, repetition, and practice. While solving brain teasers can provide you bragging rights, the ability to solve problems and improve the world creatively is a demonstrated genius worth pursuing.[139]

Years of research have revealed a surprising trend: Individuals with average IQs often outperform those with the highest IQs—a staggering 70% of the time.[140] This finding challenges the notion of the *lone genius*—the idea that those with exceptional intellect achieve success independently. In reality, many outstanding achievements are the result of collaboration. Take Michelangelo, for instance, who collaborated with a team while painting the Sistine Chapel ceiling. Similarly, Einstein's groundbreaking ideas were cultivated through years of analyzing patents at the Swiss patent office, where he built upon the work of others. Additionally, he may have drawn inspiration from his first wife's profound understanding of physics and mathematics.[141]

While people might be impressed by what you know, they're unlikely to be *inspired* by it. Ultimately, it's not *what* you know that matters—*who* you are and how you treat and relate to others that counts most. Lots of people possess elevated IQs and go on to squander their lives on meaningless or destructive pursuits. On the flip side, I've worked with people who aren't exceptionally intelligent but are far more productive, impactful, influential, and successful than those blessed with mind-numbing intelligence.

Intelligence and IQ can influence work performance by shaping problem-solving abilities, decision-making skills, and overall cognitive capacity. But while IQ is often a valuable factor, emotional intelligence and adaptability also play critical roles in navigating complexities, fostering innovation, and achieving sustained success in diverse professional environments.

Knowledge is the accumulation of information. Intelligence is the potential to understand. Wisdom is the ability to discern. —Unknown.

EI and EQ

Emotional Intelligence (EI) is a form of intelligence that involves the ability to monitor one's own emotions and feelings, as well as those of others, and use that information to guide one's thinking and action.

Emotional quotient (EQ) plays a vital role in expressing emotions, fostering relationships, handling challenges, and making sound decisions. Alongside IQ and personality, EQ significantly influences job performance, leadership effectiveness, overall well-being, and life success. EQ, IQ, and personality traits shape our identities, govern our tendencies, and define how we interact with the world around us.[142]

EI and EQ have been used interchangeably for decades to describe emotional intelligence. EQ can be further broken down into domains:

- Self-management: Involves controlling your feelings, adapting, and developing and maintaining a positive outlook.

- Self-awareness: Involves recognizing your own feelings.

- Social awareness: Involves recognizing the feelings of others and demonstrating empathy.

- Relationship management or social skills: Involves developing and maintaining relationships, managing conflict and teamwork, and coaching, influencing, and mentoring.

Several competencies that enable exceptional performance are nested within each of these domains. They include empathy, positive outlook, self-control, achievement, influence, conflict management, teamwork, and inspirational leadership.

Unlike hard skills, which are specific technical abilities, EQ encompasses a range of soft skills, behaviors, cognitive abilities, and personal traits. While hard skills pertain to the "what" and "how" of a role, soft skills address the "why" and are applicable across various roles. Leaders need a balance of EQ competencies to excel, as EQ enables effective coaching and sets high performers apart. It involves understanding and managing your emotions and influencing others, essential for successful leadership, especially during crises.[143]

EQ is what helps leaders coach others effectively and navigate challenges with grace. Great leaders excel at leading their teams during difficult times, inspiring others to produce their best work while remaining composed under pressure. Understanding and managing emotions, both one's own and those of others is crucial for effective leadership. Leaders who lack EQ may struggle to motivate their teams and navigate complex interpersonal dynamics, which can ultimately undermine a company's success.[144]

EQ can profoundly impact career advancement. Exceptionally talented individuals can sabotage themselves by behaving in destructive ways when their actions lack the tact, self-awareness, and guardrails that EQ provides.

If you are deficient in EQ, you may experience the following:

- You have a limited emotional vocabulary.

- You make assumptions quickly and defend them vehemently.

- You're easily offended and hold grudges.

- You get stressed easily
- You have difficulty asserting yourself.
- You don't let go of mistakes.
- You often feel misunderstood.
- You don't know your triggers.
- You blame others for how they make you feel.[145]

Soft skills can be learned and honed through practice. As you train your brain by repeatedly practicing new EQ behaviors, they become new habits. These habits become reinforced while old and destructive behaviors diminish. EQ is fostered by practicing empathy, active listening, and taking a genuine interest in considering diverse perspectives. Modulating your behavior based on what you're observing within yourself and from others is the key to EQ. Perception is essential—requesting and processing feedback from others demonstrates your commitment to developing this vital skill.

> *Developing emotional intelligence is what really makes a great leader. When you can adjust your approach for every context, only then can you truly conquer every challenge.* — Matt Bereman, business executive, and strategist.

Emotional Discipline

People are recognized for their accomplishments and how they deal with challenges, failures, and despair. Those who have demonstrated remarkable achievement, leadership, or caring for others when faced with the most challenging circumstances are the most impressive and memorable.

While our feelings are strong forces that sometimes overcome our better judgment, we always possess the power to choose how we feel. This is at the root of emotional discipline. It is not a one-size-fits-all process but something we can develop and customize to our needs. This, in turn, enables us to more effectively and successfully deal with current and future challenges.

> *I don't want to be at the mercy of my emotions. I want to use them, to enjoy them, and to dominate them.* —Oscar Wilde, Irish poet, and playwright.

Abraham Lincoln's legacy is often associated with his remarkable emotional discipline, particularly during the tumultuous era of the Civil War. However, what is less widely recognized are the numerous setbacks and personal tragedies he endured, which profoundly shaped his resilience and leadership.

Despite facing multiple defeats in critical elections and enduring the loss of loved ones, including his mother and young son, Lincoln persevered through bouts of severe depression that, at times, threatened his very life. His ability to navigate through despair and cultivate self-awareness became hallmarks of his character, enabling him to guide the nation through its most trying times. Lincoln's willingness to seize opportunities and continuously educate himself, from mastering fundamental skills like reading and writing to pursuing legal studies, exemplifies his unwavering determination and adaptability in the face of adversity.

Throughout his tumultuous experiences, Lincoln cultivated a profound capacity for empathy, particularly as he grappled with the complexities of slavery during his presidency. Faced with a deeply divided nation and the threat of secession, Lincoln navigated through unprecedented challenges with remarkable composure and resilience. Despite facing vehement opposition and enduring the horrors of war, he refrained from succumbing to anger and instead approached each crisis with thoughtful deliberation. As a leader, Lincoln bore the weight of intense scrutiny and hatred. Yet, he persevered, ultimately guiding the nation through its darkest hours and fostering unity in the aftermath of despair.[146]

Anyone can lead, shine, or excel when the going is easy. However, demonstrating greatness when the going is tough separates the average from the exceptional.

> *Only when you combine sound intellect with emotional discipline do you get rational behavior.* —Warren Buffett, American investor, entrepreneur, and businessman.

EQ and Optimism

Optimism is another vital trait of EQ. In my experience, optimism and job satisfaction go hand in hand. I've found that the best and most inspirational bosses are consistently optimistic—they possess the wisdom of experience and know that if they model optimism, their workers will follow suit. Optimists believe no challenge is insurmountable and every storm can be weathered with calm and confidence. When we embrace an optimistic outlook, things become easier, and worries fade away, enabling us to tackle our work without the hindrance of doubt.

Studies reveal the profound impact of optimism on overall well-being, from enhanced resilience to improved physical health. Specifically, optimists tend to experience better pain management, enhanced immune and cardiovascular function, and overall greater physical well-being compared to pessimists. Optimists view failures as temporary detours. They exhibit a willingness to change, which leads to personal and organizational development. This mindset not only bolsters individual growth but also contributes to the success and adaptability of their companies.[147]

> *A pessimist sees the difficulty in every opportunity; an optimist sees the opportunity in every difficulty.* —Winston Churchill, British Prime Minister, statesman, orator, and author.

Adapting to change and uncertainty requires confidence and composure in the face of the unknown. While none of us can predict or control the future, we can regulate our responses to uncertainty and manage emotions like fear and anxiety. Meditation, unplugging, and reflective walks can quiet the mind and promote self-compassion and empathy. By treating ourselves and others with patience and kindness while accepting the presence of fear and uncertainty, we build resilience and the capacity to navigate challenges and periods of high stress.

I've learned that every project or pursuit has a natural endpoint in business, which becomes more palpable as we approach it. Despite our challenges, we always find a solution or compromise that allows us to complete the effort and transition to the next phase. Even failure provides a path to learning opportunities. Understanding that nothing lasts forever can be empowering and comforting during tough times.

Young and inexperienced workers often grapple with daily challenges or feel overwhelmed by seemingly insurmountable tasks or situations because they lack the experience to resolve them. This can lead to feelings of fear and uncertainty, which can be paralyzing. Seasoned leaders, however, bring confidence, comfort, and perspective to such situations, reassuring their team that every challenge can be overcome. By fostering encouragement and support rather than criticism when things don't go as planned, exceptional leaders motivate their team members to persevere, learn, and grow. Optimism fosters a sense of calming confidence that helps navigate through uncertainties.

> *Optimism is a happiness magnet. If you stay positive, good things and good people will be drawn to you.* —Mary Lou Retton, American retired gymnast.

EQ and Leadership

Among the most critical behavioral traits that distinguish a leader is emotional intelligence. Exceptional leaders constantly monitor their emotions and how they impact their thinking and judgment. They're effective at self-regulating or modulating their behavior and emotional response to avoid acting out or saying something they regret later. They also demonstrate social awareness, which is the ability to read others. They are supremely observant and notice subtle signals that others might overlook. Some might refer to this ability as *reading the room*.

When you reflect on the qualities of a leader within your company or organization, it's unlikely that you'll be disappointed by their knowledge or intellect. Instead, it's more likely that you'll wish your boss cared more or showed more interest in you, your pursuits, or your challenges. Or perhaps you'd like to see them display more trust, compassion, or empathy. These deficiencies are all *soft skills*.[148]

Studies have confirmed that practicing effective EQ can enable leaders to excel and drive higher corporate performance. In one study of the impact of EQ on performance, executives with high EQ generated 10% more productivity, experienced an 87% reduction in turnover, and added substantial economic value to their companies. Emotionally intelligent leaders demonstrate empathy, which can transform a cutthroat culture into one of openness, collaboration, and continuous learning.

Leadership behavior influences every aspect of an organization. Employees at all levels tend to emulate a leader's good or bad behavior. When leaders demonstrate strong and consistent EQ, they can improve activities throughout their sphere of influence. For example, within product design, understanding the end user's needs, desires, tendencies, and mode of engagement is foundational to defining requirements. By embracing empathetic EQ, it becomes more straightforward to ask questions, to reflect on and contemplate possibilities, and to challenge assumptions. As a designer, simplicity and ease of use are hallmarks of a great design. Applying EQ to the design process can enable a deeper exploration into use cases, ease of use (actual and perceived), and user enjoyment.[149]

> *CEOs are hired for their intellect and business expertise— and fired for a lack of emotional intelligence.* —Daniel Goleman, author, psychologist, and science journalist.

CHAPTER 10

Cognition and Bias

To know the true reality of yourself, you must be aware not only of your conscious thoughts, but also of your unconscious prejudices, bias and habits. —Unknown.

Cognition encompasses the fundamental process of thinking. Every decision we make results from a complex mental action or process, which we experience as high-order thinkers. This involves tapping into various brain functions, including intuition, knowledge, emotions, experience, judgment, and more. Our cognitive abilities enable us to solve intricate problems and reach conclusive decisions, a capability that distinguishes humans from other animals.

"Fast thinking" is relatively intuitive and almost automatic, whereas "slow thinking" takes time and energy to analyze data and inputs before reaching a conclusion. These processes are not, by any stretch, perfect or fool-proof, and several human traits can come into play that can compromise their effectiveness.

Bias is a fundamental aspect of human cognition, which shapes our perceptions and judgments, often without our awareness. While we may claim to be objective in our opinions and observations, our minds mislead us by applying our biased impressions of reality. In so doing, we delude ourselves as we find ways to justify, rationalize, and reinforce our opinions, arguments, and actions. Extensive research on Cognitive Behavioral Therapy, Naive Realism, the Benjamin Franklin Effect, Impression Management Theory, and Self-Perception Theory delves into this phenomenon, offering valuable insights for those interested in understanding the intricacies of human behavior.

Bias and misperceptions impact business and personnel in various ways, often leading to suboptimal outcomes. Recognizing these influences is critical to increasing awareness and avoiding biased decisions and interactions. This awareness is crucial for promoting objectivity and improving decision-making processes.[150]

Cognitive Bias

Our biases can often cloud our judgment, leading to consequences that range from minor to disastrous. Confirmation bias stands out as particularly dangerous among the various forms of bias. It involves favoring information that confirms our beliefs while discounting conflicting evidence, thus reinforcing pre-existing expectations. Confirmation bias underlies many societal issues today and can significantly impact decision-making and behavior.

> *Confirmation bias is the most effective way to go on living a lie.* —Criss Jami, American poet, essayist, musician, singer, designer, lyricist, and existentialist philosopher.

I've seen many examples of confirmation bias in the business world by workers at every level. Those who fall victim to this treacherous form of cognitive bias tend to seek out, highlight, or over-emphasize information reinforcing their position or opinion. Competing information or data is then de-prioritized, overlooked, or disregarded intentionally or subconsciously. This occurs when we are deliberately biased for a particular decision or outcome and half-heartedly (perhaps disingenuously) prepare a supporting defense based on incomplete, cherry-picked, or erroneous data. It can also result when our investigation, research, or analysis is scattered, lazy, or overly rushed.

As managers, we create confirmation bias when we overly focus on upsides rather than risks or potential paths to failure. When we do, we tend to rely on preferential data to support a predetermined decision or approach rather than make a fact-based, sound decision.

The Shuttle Challenger disaster is an unfortunate example of confirmation bias in action. Engineers and leaders, disregarding concerns about the booster rocket's O-ring seals and cold temperatures, proceeded with the launch, leading to catastrophic failure and the loss of all astronauts on board. Similarly, the Iraq war stands as a significant consequence of confirmation bias—or ulterior motives—at the highest levels of leadership. Despite doubts and alternative viewpoints, the invasion was falsely justified and approved, resulting in immense human sacrifice and financial costs over the years.

One way to overcome confirmation bias is to act as your own devil's advocate: perform a comprehensive search for evidence that could overturn the theory you are testing. Another is to encourage or demand a wholly balanced approach, to question the pluses and minuses of a theory and its evidence.[151]

Confirmation Bias is only one of several forms of cognitive bias. Briefly, here are some other biases to be aware of. Note that this is not an exhaustive list:

- Authority bias: Involves being influenced by authority figures. This behavior is at the root of authoritarianism and fascism.

- Blind Spot bias: Involves being unaware of our own bias—we see it in others more than ourselves.

- Dunning-Kruger effect: The less we know, the more confident we are—the inability to recognize our own incompetence.

- Implicit bias: Involves applying mental shortcuts to make sense of the flood of information we take in every moment of every day. We accept daily information at face value without investigating for accuracy or truthfulness.

- Negativity bias: Our brains prioritize negative things and events over positive ones, which leads people to prefer to focus on and consume negative news instinctively.

- Optimism bias: We sometimes become over-optimistic about good outcomes.

- Pessimism bias: We overestimate the likelihood of bad outcomes.[152]

- Sunken-cost Fallacy: The tendency to continue investing in a lost cause because we're unwilling to abandon what we've already spent substantial money on—spending good money after bad.

- Survivorship bias: The tendency to overestimate the likelihood of success in risky ventures.[153]

Optimistic bias is common in business. Many entrepreneurs and CEOs ignore the potential for bad things to happen to their companies. They overlook the importance of having a comprehensive risk management plan and take unreasonable risks that endanger their company's survival. Although unexpected "black swan" events can impact any business, addressing more probable risks like competition or market changes is essential when preparing for the future.

> *Some people have the attitude that if they agree with something, they don't need proof. If they don't agree with something, then no proof is sufficient.* —Unknown.

In leading teams and projects, I've learned that promoting a thorough risk and opportunities analysis demands careful consideration of the pros and cons of a design, service, or product. We delve into tough questions like: What are the potential pitfalls of our plan? How might our strategy or roadmap encounter obstacles? Could our assumptions be incorrect? On the flip side, what positive outcomes are possible? Are there opportunities we can seize to achieve results beyond our expectations? And how can we foster these opportunities to increase their likelihood of occurrence?

Initially, most people often resist the idea of risk/opportunity analysis and planning, seeing it as mere busy work that detracts from their everyday work. However, with practice, open-minded people come to appreciate the value of challenging assumptions and biases, which clarifies discussions and improves decision-making. Identifying risks highlights weaknesses in designs or processes that could jeopardize outcomes, prompting proactive measures to mitigate those risks if necessary. Over time, I've witnessed my teams embrace robust risk management processes for their consistently positive impact on business outcomes.

Bias affects many aspects of our lives, especially in American politics. People are becoming more divided and polarized in their thinking and ideologies, and bias plays a substantial role. People tend to stand by others who share their beliefs and listen only to news that agrees with them. This creates echo chambers where people repeatedly hear the same ideas, further reinforcing their beliefs. To break free from this cycle, it's essential to connect with diverse groups of people and seek information from various sources that are balanced, trusted, truthful, and fact-based.

> *The difference between someone guided by principle and someone driven by bias: A person who is guided by principle will stand up to his allies and side with his 'opponents' if truth and morality dictate it. A person who is driven by bias will go to war against reality to defend the identity of the herd.* —Unknown.

Cognitive Dissonance

Human stubbornness is a fascinating aspect of our psychology. We often find it challenging to admit our mistakes or reconsider our beliefs, even when faced with overwhelming evidence that refutes our tenuous convictions. This phenomenon, known as cognitive dissonance, motivates us to maintain our positions and dismiss conflicting evidence, even if it means ignoring potential risks to ourselves or others.[154]

> *There are two ways to be fooled. One is to believe what isn't true. The other is to refuse to accept what is true.* —Soren Kierkegaard, Danish theologian, existentialist philosopher, poet, social critic, and religious author.

The ongoing resistance to evidence-based measures like mask-wearing in the face of the COVID-19 pandemic highlights the destructive impact of cognitive dissonance. Despite overwhelming scientific evidence supporting the efficacy of NIOSH-approved masks in combatting viral spread by reducing viral load, many individuals continue to view mask mandates as nothing more than an infringement on their personal freedoms. This ideological stance, fueled by opinion rather than facts, contributed to the perpetuation of the pandemic and undermined public health efforts.

This refusal to acknowledge the effectiveness of mask-wearing, combined with vaccine hesitancy, reflects a more profound reluctance to admit mistakes or reconsider beliefs, even in the face of mounting evidence. As a result, the pandemic response became mired in political polarization and tribalism, with individuals prioritizing loyalty to ideological camps over public health imperatives. This entrenched mindset impeded rational discourse and hampered efforts to combat the spread of the virus, which led to further harm and unnecessary loss of life.

> *Those who can make you believe absurdities can make you commit atrocities.* —Voltaire, French Enlightenment writer, historian, and philosopher.

I've witnessed many examples where dissonance played out in the workplace. At one company I worked for, we invested significant time and resources into developing a core technology fueled by venture funding. Despite numerous warning signs indicating its potential limitations, we persisted in our pursuit, pouring millions into designs, intellectual property, and specialized processes. However, as time passed, it became increasingly clear that our technology wouldn't deliver the required performance or competitive edge. Eventually, we had to confront the harsh reality we'd been avoiding.

Stubbornness is a common affliction. If we admit a mistake or acknowledge our underlying assumptions are faulty, we might be ridiculed, punished, disrespected, or even fired. This fear motivates us to allow our dissonance to play out boldly, damaging ourselves, our co-workers, and our companies.

Organizations must foster a culture of openness, adaptability, and accountability to combat dissonance effectively. When we constantly monitor our progress and success in the context of what we expect, make the most informed and data-driven decisions we can, and, most importantly, adjust and modify them when evidence, facts, and science dictate, we can avoid the harmful effects of dissonance. It takes courage, confidence, and self-reflection to remain flexible and admit we're wrong.

Effective leaders maintain vigilance in overseeing their projects, continuously evaluating whether to continue or cancel ongoing pursuits based on their progress relative to the initial plan. They should embrace the philosophy that the "sunk cost" invested in a project should not be a rationale for its continuation. Don't spend good money after bad simply because continuing a long-term losing pursuit is easier (or less embarrassing) than canceling it.

Humans have an amazing capacity for believing what they choose and excluding that which is painful. —Star Trek character, Spock.

CHAPTER 11

Decisions and Problem-Solving

> *The key to good decision-making is not knowledge. It is understanding. We are swimming in the former. We are desperately lacking in the latter.* —Malcolm Gladwell, English-born Canadian journalist, author, and public speaker.

Whether you're an entry-level employee or a C-level executive, improving problem-solving skills benefits individuals and businesses alike. Indecisiveness among managers can lead to mental paralysis, draining organizational energy and fostering resentment. The lingering uncertainty resulting from indecision undermines focus and self-motivation across the board.

Decision-making is a skill that improves with practice and repetition. While some overly self-confident individuals may make snap decisions, others exhibit great patience, believing that the best decisions stem from thorough data collection and analysis. There's a debate about the optimal timing for decisions. Delaying them may lead to lost opportunities—time that cannot be recovered—while quick decisions allow for adjustments downstream, maximizing the benefits of decisive action.

Warren Buffett exemplifies steadfastness in decision-making and strategy. While he adjusts his stock portfolio in response to changes and acknowledges mistakes, he rigorously adheres to a long-term "buy and hold" approach. Likewise, he maintains routine throughout most aspects of his life. On the other hand, Elon Musk represents a more adaptable leadership style. He swiftly adjusts his strategies and reshapes his companies and industries based on new information. Musk seizes opportunities quickly and is known for his bold risk-taking, often forging ahead without seeking approval or permission from others.[155]

I've observed a broad spectrum of decision-making approaches and techniques and have seen where each strategy can be effective or destructive, depending on how and when it's applied. The key to success is knowing when decisiveness and quick action are prudent and justified, and when it becomes advantageous to postpone a decision and focus on gathering additional data to inform it further.

I tend to prioritize gathering facts, data, and expert insights for significant decisions to understand the options and situation fully. Once I feel confident in my grasp of the risks and implications, I proceed with a well-informed decision I can defend. However, I tend to act more swiftly for less critical decisions, knowing adjustments can be made as circumstances evolve. Either way, I prioritize transparency, ensuring stakeholders understand the rationale and potential risks of the chosen course of action.

In today's digital age, we rely heavily on the internet and smartphones to quickly access vast information. However, while Siri and Google can provide all sorts of data and information, they generally can't help with complex decision-making. And while our tendency to trust our *gut* or instincts might be an adequate approach to decision-making in some situations, it can be wholly deficient in others.

Effective decision-making often requires a circular feedback loop, where we gather information, contemplate a path forward, and then circle back to review anything we overlooked or disregarded the first time. Significant and consequential decisions usually consist of smaller decisions. At a certain point, we cannot possibly keep everything organized and resident in our brains, which suggests the importance of notebooks or spreadsheets to keep important information safe, available, and organized.

Emotions and personal biases frequently influence our decision-making process. There's often more than one viable solution to a problem; as the saying goes, "There's more than one way to skin a cat." This highlights the importance of considering diverse perspectives and approaches when tackling challenges.

Decisiveness is crucial, yet allowing time for processing information before making decisions is equally essential. Sometimes, taking a "cheetah pause" is beneficial, inspired by the cheetah's ability to swiftly decelerate and change direction while hunting. During this pause, we reflect on our emotions, collected information, and the potential impacts of our decisions on ourselves, our goals, and our business endeavors. It's a moment to reconsider overlooked details, missing information, and the potential effects of our decision on others.[156]

Jeff Bezos claims that the most successful leaders change their minds often. They escape the trap of getting too caught in the weeds, overly focusing on details that support only one point of view. Instead, exceptional leaders accept the possibility of being wrong, fostering an environment where feedback is valued and adjustments are seen as natural steps in the decision-making process. This approach promotes continuous learning and innovation, empowering individuals to challenge assumptions without fear of repercussion.

Steve Jobs is another highly effective leader who changed his mind quickly and often. Sometimes, he would flip 180 degrees from his position the day before. This is something that takes courage to say, "I was wrong." These leaders don't wait for negative feedback—they're quick to own up, admit a mistake, and adjust their decisions to benefit the company. It usually pays to be flexible and adjust plans when necessary rather than to be fixed, unwavering and determined to be right.[157]

> *Make decisions when you are ready, not under pressure. Others will always push you to make a decision for their own purposes, internal politics, or some other external need. But you can almost always say, 'I think I need a little more time to think about this. I'll get back to you.' This tactic is very effective at defusing even the most difficult and uncomfortable situations.* —Stephen Schwarzman.

Difficult Decisions

I've often said, "*Everyone gets their turn over the pully*." This means that while you may not always experience chronic overtime, there will be times when you face critical deadlines requiring extra time and effort. Similarly, you'll occasionally face tough decisions that substantially affect the organization and multiple careers. The more significant the decision, the greater the tendency to delay or procrastinate. However, those who confront difficult decisions with resolve and deliberate action often emerge as leaders, surpassing their peers.

In any moment of decision, the best thing you can do is the right thing, the next best thing is the wrong thing, and the worst thing you can do is nothing. —Theodore Roosevelt.

While much has been written regarding effective decision-making processes, the most difficult decisions occur when those processes become inadequate. Judgment comes into play, which involves a fusion of thinking, intuition, feelings, experience, imagination, creativity, and character. When this happens, it pays to ask a few essential questions to make a sound judgment:

- Consequences: Given the variety of possible actions, what are the tangible implications of each? Ask "What can we do?" and "What should we do?"

- Obligations: What are your duties and core obligations? When you recognize your biases and blind spots, assess your obligations, and consider the impact of your decision on others, you can arrive at the penultimate duty you must uphold, informing your decision.

- Practicality: Nothing is ideal in the world or life. Leaders excel when they operate pragmatically, acknowledging realities and constraints when struggling with painful choices. Which decision will most likely work, providing a resilient, persistent, desirable result? How will outside forces influence the outcome? How can you influence the outcome positively through persistence, commitment, creativity, and prudent risk-taking?

- Values: Great leaders are bound by their values and those of the organization. When faced with a difficult decision, assessing how the various options reflect what matters most to your team, company, culture, customers, and local community is essential. Which of your choices best reflects, represents, and expresses those belief systems?

- Acceptance: Once you make your choice, you must live with the consequences. What matters most, and what matters less? Reflect on your decision. How does it make you feel? Can you live with it and yourself? Solicit the opinions of those you trust most on your path to acceptance.[158]

During the late 90s at Endwave, my team and I developed an impressive product line of innovative millimeter wave antennas for the booming cellular backhaul market. Energized by orders from market leaders, our backlog grew steadily. However, in 2000, the "Dotcom Bust" hit us hard. Orders were rescinded, delayed, or canceled overnight, and many companies went bankrupt.

Fortunately, we were the last hi-tech Silicon Valley company to go public before the crash, which provided a sizeable cash infusion to weather the storm. With little visibility as to the timing of an eventual market recovery, our CEO decided to divest our antenna business to shed costs. Tasked with finding a buyer, we accepted the first offer, which included our designs, inventory, backlog, and IP. However, the acquiring company wasn't interested in our antenna team, so I had to lay everyone off, including myself. It was excruciating to let go of an exceptionally talented team amid a challenging business climate.

Reflecting on that time, I appreciate the process behind our CEO's difficult decision to divest our antenna business. First, our leadership team didn't shy away from tough decisions. We assessed the impact of the drop in customer demand, consulted experts, and explored steps to maintain solvency and emerge stronger. Once the divesting strategy was decided, we broke it into actionable steps. We formulated a messaging plan to present the decision positively to the company and investors.

I was tasked with finding a buyer and relocating our office, labs, and test facility to a remote site to make it a more attractive offering for a potential buyer. Simultaneously, I crafted a business plan for potential investment but found no backers due to the industry crash. After accepting a purchase offer, we provided a comprehensive severance package to the team and sponsored a celebration to honor the departing employees and their contributions.

Taking the required time and effort to contemplate, analyze, plan, and execute difficult decisions is crucial for achieving desired outcomes. Mishandled decisions can adversely affect employees and tarnish the corporate reputation, while well-executed ones can pave the way for ongoing success and positive brand perception. Empathy and compassion toward workers should underpin every decision to ensure everyone affected is treated with the humanity and dignity they deserve. Ultimately, we are all human beings entitled to respectful treatment.[159]

Life is filled with difficult decisions, and winners are those who make them. —Dan Brown, American author.

Problem-Solving

Managers often take charge and solve problems single-handedly, assuming that's their role as leaders. They outline the issue, prescribe the solution, lay out the action plan, and set things in motion. Some believe leaders should have all the answers, especially given that they're paid the *big bucks*.

However, the reality is something different. No leader, no matter how experienced or knowledgeable, consistently possesses all the answers or the best insights. Even when top executives communicate problems and solutions, they're not operating in isolation. Collaboration and input from various sources are integral to effective decision-making and problem-solving processes.

Effective managers and leaders often approach problem-solving by involving others in the process. Instead of dictating solutions, they ask questions like, "What are we going to do?" This collaborative approach enhances the quality of decisions and solutions. Engaging various team members' expertise improves performance and fosters employee engagement and growth opportunities. Moreover, when problems are tackled collaboratively, individuals contributing to the solution feel a sense of ownership and pride in the outcome.

I've learned that the best leaders also possess exceptional intuition, which enables them to quickly sift, filter, and analyze the associated details to identify the root cause of an issue, which can then be discussed with others on the path toward resolution. That said, some leaders inadvertently fall into the trap of unintentionally restricting discussions by asking leading questions or steering the conversation toward their predetermined direction. This approach limits the input and contributions of others, hampering the organization's ability to solve problems collaboratively and innovatively.

Ideally, it's far better to present a problem in the most minimalistic way possible, within in a sentence or two. Presenting a problem concisely allows others to contribute their ideas and perspectives without being influenced by the leader's preconceptions. By asking questions and refraining from expressing personal opinions, leaders create an environment where team members can contribute naturally and without bias, leading to richer discussions and more comprehensive solutions.[160]

> *Too many problem-solving sessions become battlegrounds where decisions are made based on power rather than intelligence.* —Margaret J. Wheatley, American writer, teacher, speaker, and management consultant.

Bill Gates is an excellent example of someone with the uncanny ability to cut through complexity and discern the essence of an issue swiftly and deliberately. He has a remarkable talent for distilling vast amounts of data and opinions into clear insights, identifying the key variables that critically matter. Within moments, Gates can formulate a path forward that may elude others involved in the discussion. His capacity to synthesize clarity from complexity sets him apart as a leader in problem-solving and decision-making.[161]

The World Economic Forum recently listed complex problem-solving as the number-one skill for companies, given our trend towards an ever-more complex and uncertain world. Research shows that organizations excelling in problem-solving capabilities achieve up to 3.5 times higher returns to shareholders than those lacking in this area. Prioritizing and developing problem-solving abilities is crucial for companies, as those that excel in this aspect consistently outperform others.[162]

Fortunately, problem-solving is a learned skill and something that's within everyone's grasp. The systematic process described below can be applied effectively to virtually any type of problem:

- Define the problem: This includes boundaries and constraints, a clear statement of the problem to be solved, and is defined by outcomes rather than activities or intermediate outputs. Avoid overly structuring the problem, which can artificially constrain creative solutions. Be specific, measurable, and time-bound wherever possible. Define decision-makers and what success should look like.

- Disaggregation and Prioritization: Most problems are too complicated to solve without breaking them down into logical parts, which helps us understand each of the drivers or causes. Logic trees and effective prioritization result in faster solutions with less effort. Prioritize problems where impact and influence are high.

- Work Plan and Processes: Define each workflow and clarify desired outputs. Assign each task so that everyone knows what they're doing and by when. Avoid scope creep by ensuring that each task ties to an essential objective. Each work plan should span 2-3 weeks maximum to facilitate progress tracking and enable incremental wins that stimulate positive feelings of accomplishment. Focus on the 20% of the problem that yields 80% of the benefit. Revise the work plan as new insights are achieved.

- Seek Breakthroughs: Look for breakthrough thinking rather than incremental improvements. Address and mitigate team biases and effectively employ team brainstorming.

- Analysis: Start small and expand to more extensive analyses only when necessary. Use heuristics, shortcuts, and summary statistics to optimize the analysis approach. Employ the "Sherlock Holmes" approach of asking who, what, where, when, and why, but ask "why" five times more often. Resist the temptation to boil the ocean with unnecessarily expansive and complex analyses when simpler techniques are deemed adequate.

- Synthesize results: Combine your information and findings to answer your questions, construct arguments, or solve problems. Use text, tables, and appropriate visual displays that are easily understood. Consolidate findings and results.

- Communicate: Your conclusions should be presentable in ways that form an engaging story, supported by facts, analyses, and arguments that convince your audience of the merits of your recommended path. Show each graphic as a branch on your revised tree structure where possible. Return to the problem definition to confirm that the initial objectives have been met. Carefully lead the audience from situation to observation and finally to resolution (recommended actions).[163]

Remember that problem-solving is an iterative process rather than a linear one. Even after you've reached your decision point, you can repeat the process as more information becomes available to gain more insight for even deeper understanding or further optimization.

Rookie problem solvers show you their analytic process and mathematics to convince you that they are clever. But the most elegant problem solving is that which makes the solution obvious. —Unknown.

Intuition

Intuition can be defined as the ability to understand something instinctively without the need for conscious reasoning. It is also the perception of truth, facts, or insight.

Ideally, while decisions involve facts, data, analysis, and inductive reasoning skills, they also involve your heart, your intuition, and your gut feelings. Sometimes, data and analysis aren't available, or perhaps you need to decide something more quickly than analysis or data-gathering will allow. In those instances, your heart and gut may be the best tools to guide you.

Scientists have discovered that the heart and brain operate as a unified system, with the heart transmitting more signals to the brain than vice versa. This suggests that the heart may wield a greater influence over our success than the brain. By communicating the body's emotional state to the brain, the heart profoundly affects brain function and decision-making processes. Research has indicated that individuals who follow their hearts tend to experience greater satisfaction in their careers and personal lives.[164]

> *All of my best decisions in business and in life have been made with heart, intuition, guts... not analysis. If you can make a decision with analysis, you should do so. But it turns out in life that your most important decisions are always made with instinct, intuition, taste, heart.* —Jeff Bezos, American entrepreneur, media proprietor, investor, computer engineer, and commercial astronaut.

Your intuition can be considered your inner guidance system, aiding decision-making in various life scenarios. It becomes a powerful tool for navigating uncertainties and gray areas with practice. For example, trusting your intuition can steer you towards better choices if something feels off during an interview or when considering a job offer.

Intuition is a valuable tie-breaker when faced with uncertainty or indecision, especially after thorough analysis. With regular use, intuition becomes more reliable and intuitive. To strengthen it, reflect on your values and convictions, ensuring decisions align with what serves you or your organization best.

To tap into your intuition, consider the following steps:

- Create a quiet space to reflect and meditate on your problem without distractions.

- Take deep breaths and consider your choices, noticing how each feels.

- Pay attention to any red flags that arise and avoid prematurely discounting them.

- Allow the process to unfold naturally without the undue pressure of being right—which can impede the intuitive process.

- Trust in the intuitive process and be patient as insights emerge.

Before you act on your instinctual decision, you'll want to reflect on whether any of several cognitive biases are influencing you. You might also benefit from soliciting feedback from others. Consensus leadership benefits from the opinions of others, which can expose any weakness or bias in our intuition.

After resolving your decision or path forward, embrace it and trust your judgment. Recognize that every decision can be refined or adjusted later on. Move forward with conviction, confident that you've made the best choice possible at this moment in time.[165]

> *Never apologize for trusting your intuition—your brain can play tricks, your heart can blind, but your gut is always right.* —Unknown.

CHAPTER 12

Transitioning Jobs

You can't connect the dots looking forward: you can only connect them looking backward. You have to trust that the dots will somehow connect in your future. —Steve Jobs.

For most of us, work is a constant in our lives. It anchors us and provides meaning and purpose. It's where we learn new skills, hone our abilities, and discover ourselves. We connect with others through work, forge friendships, and sometimes even find love. While your career isn't everything, it plays a significant role throughout its various ups and downs.

Navigating career transitions is a pivotal aspect of professional growth, often requiring courage, adaptability, and a strategic mindset. In today's dynamic job market, career paths are rarely linear, and embracing change can open new opportunities for personal and professional reinvention. Whether you're seeking greener pastures or facing an unexpected job loss, how you handle these transitions can significantly impact your future success and reputation.

Properly managed careers require attention, monitoring, and nurturing. Without care, they can stagnate and decline. By approaching job transitions with resilience and optimism, you can turn challenges into opportunities and continue to grow and thrive in your chosen field. Taking charge of our work lives early on allows us to shape them to our benefit rather than being enslaved by them. It's never too early to start this process.

> *As you start your journey, the first thing you should do is throw away that store-bought map and begin to draw your own.* —Michael Dell.

Non-Linear Career Path

If a clairvoyant had predicted my career path in advance, I wouldn't have believed them. Career change often takes unexpected turns, making it difficult to predict where it will lead. While some things go as planned, many do not. External influences can sometimes motivate change when we're unwilling or unable to initiate it ourselves. Rolling with the punches and turning setbacks into learning experiences or opportunities for career resets builds confidence and resilience.

> *I really think a champion is defined not by their wins but by how they can recover when they fall.* —Serena Williams, American professional tennis player.

According to the Bureau of Labor Statistics, the average worker changes jobs 12 times during their career—and that doesn't include career impacts due to pandemics, market uncertainty, etc. Unlike decades ago, when employees were expected to toe the line within the same company throughout their career, the modern worker views their non-linear career as an asset, not a liability. Many consider working at the same company for decades boring and unfulfilling. The longer we stay, the higher the odds of becoming pigeonholed in a dead-end job.[166]

A non-linear career path isn't the same as indiscriminate job-hopping—it involves intentional, deliberate career moves that involve strategy and planning. Given the ever-changing job market, non-linear career paths are becoming the new normal for these reasons:

- People are working longer. The traditional 40-year career is slowly becoming a thing of the past, as people now work 60 years or longer.

- Priorities and values are changing. While salary remains critical, the modern worker is increasingly motivated by flexible and remote work options, work-life balance considerations, and career development opportunities.

- Skills are key. Employers continue to migrate towards skill-based workforces, expanding jobs to people without college degrees. This provides new opportunities to nontraditional candidates and self-taught career-switchers.

- Pace of change is increasing. Our increasingly global market continues to evolve rapidly, putting a premium on new skills. Employee loyalty diminishes when companies implement layoffs and hiring freezes, contributing to increased stress levels and eventual employee burnout. Companies want flexible workers who can adapt to evolving work situations.[167]

Workers who remain in their jobs for extended periods can suffer financial disadvantage in the long term. Workers who stay with a company for more than two years can face a pay discrepancy of up to 50% compared to those who seek new opportunities. Once viewed negatively, changing jobs regularly is now considered advantageous by many talent experts. Regularly changing jobs can lead to a steeper learning curve, higher performance, accelerated career advancement, and enhanced earnings.

People who change jobs are routinely placed out of their comfort zones, driving them to rapidly acquire new skills and deliver impactful results that benefit a company's profitability. Typically high achievers, their résumés often outshine those who remain in stagnant roles. Research suggests that learning curves plateau after three years of continuous employment. Long-tenured employees may become less engaged, and experience diminished learning opportunities. Statistics indicate that employers derive the least valuable work from individuals who stay with the company the longest.

While the costs of turnover and re-training are valid concerns, forward-thinking leaders view them as part of the expenses incurred in pursuing rapid growth and scaling. They believe that only the best talent can fuel a company's meteoric rise, and such talent often consists of individuals who regularly change jobs. The growth and profitability achieved by staffing a company with top talent far outweigh the incremental costs associated with training and attrition. Moreover, the best companies excel in parting ways with employees effectively; many former employees may return, requiring less training and quickly resuming their contributions to the organization.[168]

It's common to see friends and colleagues remain at the same companies for many years, some even throughout their careers. However, loyalty doesn't always translate into favorable outcomes. Many loyal workers may miss out on lifetime earnings because their managers perceive them as *safe* and not deserving of significant raises, bonuses, or advancements. Over time, these employees may find that their bosses stop making concerted efforts to keep them satisfied and motivated.

At some point, you'll likely face the decision of whether to stay in your current job or seek new opportunities. Staying put might make sense if you're well-compensated and find fulfillment in your work. However, exploring new prospects could be beneficial if you're stagnating from a lack of learning, challenge, or compensation. Even if you're well-paid but unhappy, prioritizing job satisfaction over compensation might be wise. Ultimately, staying in a job that doesn't bring joy could prevent you from discovering a fulfilling and stimulating career elsewhere.[169]

Sometimes, employers force us to change jobs, whether we want to or not. While we hope to leave jobs or retire on our own terms, we might face layoffs or termination for various reasons. Always be prepared for the possibility of losing your job unexpectedly. Exercise sensibility by ensuring that your résumé is always up to date, especially during periods of downturn or volatility in your company or industry. Maintaining a healthy attitude during transitions is essential.

Staying in a job that you dislike or if you feel undervalued is detrimental to both yourself and the company. If you can pursue a fantastic job at a company you admire, don't hesitate or overthink it. Seize the opportunity for your own benefit and career advancement.

> *Getting fired is ok. Resigning is ok. Being laid off is ok. Moving on is ok. What's not ok is staying somewhere you are tolerated and not appreciated. Your life will be much better elsewhere.* —Adam Danyal, digital marketing specialist, author, and tech and gadget influencer.

Losing Your Job

Being terminated from a job often triggers a range of emotions that relate to the traditional grief phases described by psychiatrists: denial, anger, bargaining, depression, and acceptance. However, not everyone undergoes all of these phases, and feelings may blend non-linearly. Facing termination can be emotionally challenging, especially when it doesn't come as a relief. The longer one remains unemployed, the greater the mental toll it can take. Initially, individuals may engage in self-analysis, trying to make sense of the termination and possibly deflecting blame away from themselves.

When caught in the "why me" phase, grappling with questions and self-doubt is natural. However, while analyzing potential causes of failure, there's an opportunity to glean insights that can shape a positive attitude moving forward. Remember, setbacks are just one part of your career journey, and maintaining a positive perspective is essential. Your career is a culmination of successes and setbacks, not defined by any singular event.

Before diving into your job search, consider taking a moment to reconcile with your new reality. Losing a job can be a grieving process, and practicing self-compassion is critical. Treat yourself with the same kindness you would extend to a friend or loved one facing similar challenges.

> *You can't get past a mental block in a punitive environment. And while moving on doesn't necessarily mean choosing the easiest or most pleasurable path, you can always choose the kindest.* —Ellen Hendriksen, author, educator, and clinical psychologist.

Finding distractions can be immensely helpful in times of distress. Spend time outdoors, take a walk, or engage in previously overlooked activities. Treat yourself to a movie, plan a day trip, or indulge in a hobby you've considered. Reconnect with loved ones or foster new relationships.

Feeling down after a setback is natural, but dwelling in despair for too long can lead to chronic pessimism. Share your feelings with a supportive partner, friend, or confidant, but be mindful of negative influences. Surround yourself with those who offer empathy and understanding, and avoid judgmental or critical individuals until you feel emotionally prepared for tough conversations.

While mourning what you've lost is natural, it's also an opportunity to shift your perspective towards the possibilities ahead. Consider the newfound freedom from worries and responsibilities that your previous job entailed. Embrace the joy of being untethered and in control of your future career path.

Maintain a sense of perspective by acknowledging that others may be facing more severe challenges, such as health issues, financial struggles, or abuse. Recognize that your temporary situation can be resolved through your actions and determination. Consider dedicating time to helping those less fortunate—you may find solace and satisfaction in contributing to the well-being of others.

When faced with unexpected unemployment, I embraced various productive activities alongside my job search. I devoted time to home projects, volunteered at my child's school, and explored potential business ventures. Regular walks helped clear my mind and boost my spirits. During one transition, I pursued online courses to obtain a Program Management Professional (PMP) certificate, which proved invaluable in securing my next position. Networking was critical during this time, enabling me to reconnect with friends and former colleagues while advancing my job search.

Take control of your future and make the most of your time off. Stay positive and hopeful, as good things often happen to those who demonstrate resilience in the face of setbacks. Enjoy the present moment, as you may find yourself re-employed sooner than expected. By embracing challenges and setbacks with resilience, you open yourself up to levels of success that were once unimaginable.

> *Getting fired from Apple was the best thing that could have ever happened to me. The heaviness of being successful was replaced by the lightness of being a beginner again. It freed me to enter one of the most creative periods of my life.* — Steve Jobs.

Greener Pastures

Deciding to leave a job can stir up mixed emotions, ranging from fear to excitement. Recognizing these signs is vital for personal and professional growth, whether you feel unchallenged, stuck in a dead-end role, undervalued, or dealing with a toxic work environment. Assessing your situation and considering a change is critical to aligning with your career aspirations and values.

> *Maturity is learning to walk away from people and situations that threaten your peace of mind, self-respect, values, morals or self-worth.* —Unknown.

Struggling in a current job is not uncommon, especially when roles don't match abilities or interests. Promotion doesn't always translate to success, as excelling in one role doesn't guarantee aptitude in another. Recognizing these mismatches is critical for career satisfaction and productivity.

Your career doesn't usually grow and evolve out of chance or passivity. It requires continuous monitoring, contemplation, planning, and action. In the best case, it thrives from the successful implementation of a thoughtful strategy planned and executed by you and your manager in partnership.

Long-term studies consistently reveal that employees more often leave their jobs due to poor management than other company-related issues. A recent study reaffirmed this trend, indicating that 57% of employees left their jobs because of their manager.[170]

Some of the most common traits of poor management are:

- Failing to show respect for other people's work.
- Acting unprofessionally.
- Failing to listen to other people's concerns.
- Failing to demonstrate empathy or compassion.
- Unwilling or inability to coach others.
- Unwilling to engage and inspire their teams.
- Unwilling to have difficult conversations with employees.

Studies have found that leaders who receive the lowest scores from their subordinates often lack competence. This phenomenon aligns with the "Peter principle," which suggests that individuals are promoted to positions beyond their ability level. Consequently, employees may report to a boss who struggles to fulfill their responsibilities, placing the entire team at risk of failure.

Employees often remain in jobs with bad bosses due to various reasons. Some value their work or relationships with colleagues more than their negative interactions with their bosses. Others hope for improvement or leadership changes. Additionally, the psychological concept of "Loss aversion" makes it hard to leave earned achievements like high salaries or prestigious positions. These factors influence employees' decisions to stay despite challenging work environments.

Enduring a toxic work environment can lead to serious health risks, including chronic stress and illness. Despite the fear of change, quitting may ultimately be the best option for those suffering in such situations. However, making that decision requires confidence in one's skills, abilities, self-worth, and courage to take action. Remaining in a hostile work environment can hinder personal and professional growth, preventing individuals from reaching their full potential.[171]

Sometimes, individuals choose to quit their jobs with the mistaken belief that the problem lies with their boss or other external factors when the root cause may be internal. It's crucial to conduct an honest self-assessment to identify the source of frustration and address it directly rather than assuming that switching to a new job or company will automatically resolve the issue. Focusing on self-improvement can often fix the problem and enable individuals to maintain a satisfactory job.

If leaving is ultimately the best choice, endeavor to secure a new job offer before you submit your resignation—those who search for new work while still employed often find that their leverage during compensation negotiation is stronger than if they're unemployed. Transitioning seamlessly from one job to another without an employment gap can also eliminate any loss of income.

Transact the separation process professionally to maintain positive relationships. Provide appropriate notice, submit a formal resignation letter, and exit gracefully. Be prepared for the possibility of being escorted out immediately upon resignation, though hopefully, it won't come to that.

> *Sometimes walking away has nothing to do with weakness, and everything to do with strength. We walk away not because we want others to realize our worth and value, but because we finally realize our own.* —Unknown.

Leaving on Good Terms

When you leave your current job, it's essential to transact the separation process thoughtfully to set yourself up for the best outcome. Likewise, employers should always act professionally, respectfully, and empathetically when terminating an employee. The working world is interconnected, and your reputation matters. People talk, and your actions can have lasting consequences. Remember the famous proverb: "What goes around, comes around."

> *Don't burn bridges. You'll be surprised how many times you have to cross the same river.* —H. Jackson Brown Jr., American author, and inspirationalist.

The most effective employee departure should ideally lead to a constructive exit interview, with the former employer holding a positive view of you and considering rehiring you if the opportunity arises. This might even result in a favorable letter of recommendation or reference for your future job endeavors. Conversely, burning bridges upon departure will negate these possibilities, ultimately harming your future prospects.

My advice is to refrain from using the threat of leaving as a bargaining tool to enhance your work situation or compensation. While it may yield short-term gains, I have yet to see it lead to positive outcomes in the long run. Once you signal your willingness to leave, your employer may perceive you as less committed and engaged, making you vulnerable to being replaced. Even if your boss accedes to your demands temporarily, it could limit your future growth opportunities and result in stagnant compensation over time.

Statistics show that most employees who accept counteroffers leave or are terminated within 12 months. If an employee is leaving for better compensation and their existing package is competitive, it's prudent to refrain from countering their offer. On the other hand, if the departure stems from a lack of challenges or growth opportunities, it should serve as a wake-up call to the employer. Employees seeking growth are worth retaining and investing in.

When you decide to leave, inform your boss before sharing your plans with your co-workers. Doing otherwise is insensitive, unprofessional, and disrespectful. I experienced this firsthand when a star employee announced his departure during my weekly all-hands meeting, causing an uncomfortable atmosphere and straining our relationship. Prioritizing a discussion with your manager demonstrates respect and professionalism. If you've secured a new job offer, avoid boasting about it to your current co-workers to prevent jealousy and negative perceptions about your current employer.[172]

Submitting a resignation letter is important—it formally documents your decision to leave. Schedule a meeting with your manager and refrain from mentioning your resignation until the meeting, whether face-to-face or via video call. Keep the resignation letter brief and direct as evidence of your voluntary departure. Address it to your immediate supervisor and maintain a positive tone, expressing gratitude for the opportunity and support that you were provided. Avoid airing grievances or disclosing details about your new job. Remember, your resignation letter leaves a lasting impression on your employer, shaping how they remember your time with the company. It may also be referenced later if you eventually consider returning.[173]

Workers typically provide at least two weeks' notice when resigning unless they're recent hires. Anything less can be seen as disrespectful to your employer. Providing sufficient notice allows your employer to adjust to the upcoming gap in coverage caused by your departure. For senior employees, offering three or four weeks' notice may be more appropriate, considering their higher level of responsibility and impact on the team.

As you leave your position, it's worthwhile to email your colleagues, expressing gratitude for their support and camaraderie. Describe your experience in favorable terms, highlighting the opportunities you were provided and the enjoyment you found in your position. This action nurtures your active network even after you've left the company, as these contacts may prove valuable in future endeavors, whether in seeking new opportunities or providing referrals.

Some companies are open to working with former employees or establishing a long-term alliance or professional connection. For instance, when I left Trimble Navigation to launch Endgate, my boss offered me a long-term consulting contract, which I maintained for several years. This arrangement mitigated the financial risk associated with transitioning to a startup. It also paved a path back to Trimble as a full-time employee in case Endgate failed.

It pays to remember that speaking negatively about your employer, whether during your tenure or after you leave, is one of the worst things you can do. Such behavior reflects poorly on you and can significantly damage your professional reputation.

> *Don't do something permanently stupid, just because you're temporarily upset.* —Unknown.

Reinventing Yourself

Career change often involves trial and error, adaptability, and flexibility. The process can be daunting, particularly if financial stability is a concern. It demands a willingness to explore different paths and envision potential futures.

Transitioning between careers can be emotionally challenging as you navigate between holding onto the past and embracing the new. It's normal to feel unsettled during this period. Engaging in productive activities that support your transition can help restore your focus and motivation. Investing time acquiring new skills and knowledge relevant to your new career path can be beneficial. Spending time reflecting on your aspirations, exploring various possibilities, and weighing their advantages and disadvantages is well spent. Embracing new experiences, people, and ideas beyond your career change can offer valuable insights into your goals and preferences.[174]

If you wish to reinvent yourself, focus on what you wish for and not on what you fear. —Unknown.

Many individuals feel the urge to reset their careers, driven by evolving interests, market changes, skills obsolescence, or a desire for a less stressful lifestyle. Sometimes, it takes a jolt to motivate change, like the recent global workforce upheaval caused by the pandemic. This has prompted many to contemplate changing companies, exploring new sectors, and undergoing retraining to align with personal passions. Whether seeking change due to internal or external factors, a career reset often involves introspection and strategic planning to navigate the transition successfully.[175]

In times of uncertainty, we often reflect on our life choices and whether they align with our core values. The transition to remote work has also contributed to this introspection by removing certain job perks previously enjoyed in the office. Without these benefits, workers can see their jobs more clearly, prompting reflection on their current situation and empowering them to take control of their destiny.

I began my career as an antenna engineer but quickly transitioned into management roles. Simultaneously, my sideline consulting business led to my co-founding Endgate, a tech firm specializing in millimeter-wave transceivers and antennas for the exploding cellular backhaul market. Roughly nine years later, we merged with Milliwave to form Endwave, which we took public just before the dot-com bust. Next, I served as VP of Engineering at two startups; the second involved innovating the full-body scanners found at airports and government installations worldwide. Eventually, I shifted my focus back to program management, which had always brought me the most career satisfaction. Joining Space Systems Loral as a technical and program advisor, I was soon promoted back into management roles, eventually becoming Department Manager. My final career role as technical program manager (TPM) at Facebook involved leading efforts to innovate proof-of-concept communication systems that enable ultra-low-cost internet in developing countries. Our pioneering efforts, alongside others, seeded and underpinned the new HAPs (high altitude platform) pseudo-satellite-based communications industry.

Looking back, I never expected that my work would take me from shipboard defense electronics to GPS-based surveying equipment, terrestrial cellular communication systems, consumer smartphones, full-body scanners, satellite antenna systems, and HAPs communication systems. The one common thread throughout every market and product was antennas, my original and enduring passion.

If you're facing a shortage of job opportunities in your current field, it's worth exploring how your skills might translate to other sectors. While doing so can expand your job search, some skills are more transferable than others. As you update your résumé and engage in interviews, you'll need to articulate to recruiters and interviewers how you can adapt to different products, markets, or industries. Address any gaps in your résumé, and be ready to discuss them thoroughly during interviews.

Sticking to the familiar may seem like the safe choice, but it could lead to lingering doubts about missed opportunities. My only regrets stem from playing it safe and staying in unfulfilling roles for too long. My greatest career successes have resulted from taking calculated risks and reshaping my professional path from time to time.

Make yourself who you've always wanted to be. —Unknown.

CHAPTER 13

Job Search Strategies

It's never too late to be what you might have been. — George Eliot (Mary Ann Evans), English novelist, poet, journalist, and translator.

I've almost always enhanced my work situation when transitioning from one job to another. Change can evoke feelings of unease and fear. Just contemplating a job switch can stir up thoughts of uncertainty and doubt, and the sheer amount of effort it might require can swiftly dampen one's motivation. However, change also ushers in fresh beginnings and can signal the conclusion of unfavorable circumstances. Change facilitates learning and personal growth and propels us forward.

Positive career change requires a plan, research, updating your résumé and online profile, interview preparation, conducting interviews, and follow-up. It benefits from commitment, resilience, patience, and a positive attitude throughout the journey. Ideally, you'll secure a new job while still employed, but in the worst-case scenario, you'll navigate the job search while unemployed, which can add urgency and stress to the process.

If you are motivated to change jobs, don't delay or agonize over the *what-ifs*. Take the plunge—you'll most likely be glad you did.

If you're offered a seat on a rocket ship, don't ask what seat! Just get on. —Sheryl Sandberg.

Selecting Target Companies

With powerful online search tools, finding suitable companies and jobs is now easier than ever. You can identify leading companies in your chosen market space and find organizations aligned with your values and passion. Many companies offer online job search engines and interview preparation advice. Recruiting firms provide professional search services, résumé assistance, and access to extensive company databases for effective regional job searches.

When considering which companies to target, don't assume you're unqualified for top-tier firms. While leading companies may have rigorous interview processes, even large corporations like Google or Apple require a large pool of motivated individuals for their operations. Many companies, including Microsoft, have transitioned away from grueling interview techniques as they found them ineffective. Research shows that IQ isn't always correlated with success, which has motivated recruiters to favor traditional interviewing methods over torturing candidates with ridiculous brain teasers. While companies like Google seek high IQs for specific roles, they also value sincere, creative, dedicated individuals with a solid can-do attitude for many positions.

Finding a job can be challenging, especially if you filter out legitimate candidate companies because you're afraid you might not meet their standards. Worse yet, many people shy away from companies because of their high application rejection rates.

Avoid these mental traps. Securing an offer involves a numbers game: Casting a broad net increases your chances of landing interviews and your dream job. Be confident, and remember you are as worthy as anyone else to interview at great companies. Have faith in the process and your value. Rejections are part of the journey; stay positive and keep pushing forward. Treat every interview as a learning opportunity that brings you closer to your goal of securing a great offer.

> *One important key to success is confidence. An important key to self-confidence is preparation.* —Arthur Ashe, American tennis player, and activist.

The interview is an opportunity to evaluate your fit for a job and if the job and company align with your needs. During the interview, focus on assessing the company and its culture as much as possible while presenting yourself positively. Pay attention to the following cues:

- Was scheduling your interview easy or difficult? Were you treated well by everyone you dealt with before and during the interview? Did everyone you interacted with act friendly, happy, energetic, and welcoming?

- Were you shown respect during the interview? Did your interviewers show up on time? Did they arrive fully prepared? Did they afford you ample time to ask your questions? Did they answer them freely and transparently?

- Did the interviewers appear desperate to hire you? If so, that could indicate they're struggling to recruit great candidates. You don't want to work at a company that hires mediocre talent.

- Is the work environment positive and inviting? Is it noisy, drab, chaotic, and absent of energy? Are the workers happy, energetic, and interactive, or are they isolated, insulated, and siloed? Can you detect palpable stress in the workplace? [176]

Critically assess each target company to determine if it fosters a positive environment that aligns with your values and will make you a happy and satisfied contributor. For instance, companies with chronically high turnover rates may signal a toxic culture or leadership that undervalues employees. Employee reviews on platforms like Glassdoor can reveal systemic issues within the company. It may be wise to proceed cautiously if you encounter numerous negative reviews or recruiters evading questions about culture or employee satisfaction. Additionally, poorly maintained facilities and outdated equipment may indicate financial struggles within the company.

Listen to your intuition during interviews. If you can't envision yourself thriving within the company, continuing your search is best. Evaluate the caliber of the workforce—are they average or consistently impressive? Look for signs of employee professionalism and knowledge and evidence of a competent executive team steering the company. Consider whether the company is respected, meeting its goals, and if its mission and value statements are clear and compelling. Assess the quality and demand for the company's products or services, as well as the effectiveness of its overall strategy.[177]

> *The only way to do great work is to love what you do. If you haven't found it yet, keep looking. Don't settle. As with all matters of the heart, you'll know when you find it.* —Steve Jobs.

Networking

In today's rapidly evolving business landscape, networking is essential, particularly in the tech industry, where 73% of respondents report being hired due to connections. In the current hybrid environment, 61% of professionals believe online networking can lead to job opportunities. While networking can cause the mildest of introverts to cringe with fear, every interaction you have with someone, whether a co-worker or a friend-of-a-friend, is a chance to practice your networking. It isn't difficult, and practice makes perfect. Embrace your anxiety![178]

> *Networking is not about collecting contacts. Networking is about forming relationships.* —Unknown.

Of the eight jobs I've held across my career, networking led to five of them. For instance, my interview with Facebook might never have occurred without the support of Raj Nijjar, an engineer I worked with two decades prior—his friend at Facebook was willing to refer me internally. Countless individuals have aided my career progression without expecting anything in return. We help one another because it's the right thing to do. Mutual support fosters collective growth and success in our professional journeys.

Interestingly, networking with *weak* ties, individuals from your past with whom you've lost contact, can often be more valuable when applying for jobs than your strongest connections. In the example mentioned earlier, a friend of a past colleague was willing to submit my résumé based on a positive referral from a trusted friend. This highlights the importance of nurturing diverse networks for unexpected opportunities and connections.

I've found LinkedIn to be a tremendously powerful tool for networking when fully utilized. For instance, when targeting a specific company, you can search for LinkedIn members working there. Sorting through profiles can help identify common threads or connections who might offer referrals or advice. For example, searching for workers who are alumni from your same school can facilitate outreach due to shared history. Similarly, reaching out to former colleagues employed at your target company can be beneficial. Remember to express gratitude for any support and return the favor if the opportunity arises later![179]

Some individuals hesitate to utilize their networks during a job search. They may believe their résumé suffices or feel reluctant to impose on friends or former colleagues. However, in my experience, searching for new employment demands significant effort and persistence. I never hesitated to leverage every available tool and connection to maximize success and minimize the duration of my search process to the degree possible.

> *The time to build a network is always before you need one.*
> —Douglas Conant, American business leader, author, keynote speaker, and social media influencer.

Don't rely solely on one website for my job search. While LinkedIn is the largest job-hunting platform, employers increasingly use other social media platforms like Facebook and Instagram to find candidates. Depending on your posting histories, cleaning up your social media presence may be necessary by removing any content that recruiters may view unfavorably. Consider also seeking assistance from professional recruiters or agencies to aid in your job search. Typically, you won't have to pay recruiters upfront; they collect fees from your next employer on the backend. The American Staffing Association offers a searchable online directory of recruiting firms by location, field, and job type.[180]

While compiling a long list of possible target jobs online is often straightforward, the challenge becomes differentiating your résumé from others submitted. How do you get it noticed and placed at the top of the recruiter's stack? Weak contacts can help you identify job openings you're unaware of and point you to unannounced or pending positions. This gives you a first-responder advantage when these postings are released, provided you're prepared to submit your application promptly.

Since many screening interviews are now conducted virtually, enhancing your digital communication skills is more critical than ever. Practice being professional on video, optimizing your camera and background to appear polished and engaged.

If you have difficulty securing a permanent position, consider temporary work while continuing your search. Temporary positions can serve as a pathway to permanent employment and usually offer benefits such as insurance and paid time off. Additionally, use your temporary contract work to strengthen your résumé.

Ultimately, networking is crucial when searching for work because it opens doors to opportunities that may not be publicly advertised. Building connections with industry professionals can provide valuable insights, referrals, and guidance. A strong network increases visibility and helps you stand out in a competitive job market.

> *The richest people in the world look for and build networks. Everyone else looks for work.* —Robert Kiyosaki, American businessman, and author.

Your Résumé and Online Profiles

I've reviewed thousands of résumés over the years, ranging from exceptional to genuinely awful. While a great résumé doesn't guarantee an interview, a bad one can prevent it. Your résumé and online profiles serve as your first impressions for recruiters. Their sole purpose is to engage the recruiter or hiring manager long enough to generate interest and prompt them to reach out to learn more. They shouldn't be exhaustive accountings of everything you've ever done, but rather summary highlights that capture the reader's interest. These tools are critical in your job-hunting arsenal and must be nearly perfect.

> *A résumé should not be a kitchen sink of your entire career; rather a focused narrative describing why you're a solid fit for your targeted role at the company.* —Matthew Warzel, career coach, and outplacement expert.

Your résumé should be concise, organized, easy to read, and tailored to each role you apply for. It should depict your career progression without unexplained gaps and link job responsibilities with accomplishments. While job descriptions are secondary, meaningful achievements underscore your potential. Highlight personal accomplishments that showcase your unique contributions and tangible impacts. Avoid exaggeration, but confidently present your skills. Instead of clichés, use action verbs to convey the things *you* accomplished or influenced personally.[181]

Perfecting your résumé is now more critical than ever, with many companies using automated résumé-filtering algorithms to handle their high volume of applications. These algorithms are designed to reject résumés that contain certain mistakes.

Here are some guidelines to improve your résumé's effectiveness, potentially increasing your chances of landing an interview:

- Typos: If you're unskilled at spelling, proper grammar, punctuation, and sentence structure, engage someone who can expertly review and edit your résumé before submissions.

- Lies: Lying or exaggerating about your qualifications can remove you from contention, especially given the relative ease of online fact-checking.

- Length: A résumé isn't intended to replace the interview. Keep details concise; you can elaborate in person. Longer résumés raise error risks and rejection chances, so aim for brevity. Stick to one page per ten years of experience, up to a maximum of two pages.

- Formatting: Prioritize clarity over style. Keep it neat with one font, no smaller than 10 points. Use white paper, black ink, and half-inch margins for printed copies. Follow employer instructions for formatting, as it can change across platforms. Present accomplishments in bullet points, and list experience in reverse chronological order, focusing on the last 15 years. As you get older, consider omitting the year of your college degree to avoid age bias. Avoid informal language, text abbreviations, and emojis.

- Confidential Information: If you've handled confidential information, chances are you've agreed to an NDA or similar protection contracts. Employers avoid candidates with any hint of conflict of interest or carelessness in protecting past employers' sensitive information. Mishandling of sensitive information signals to potential employers a risk with their data.

- Customize: Tailor your résumé to each job opportunity. Use the detailed job description to help you align your résumé for that particular role. This usually requires minor editing, but remember to avoid copying the job description verbatim, as doing so could trigger the employer's review algorithm, which could block you from consideration.[182]

- Contact info: Include your telephone number and professional email address. Some recruiters like to see your LinkedIn profile link on your résumé, and some expect applicants to include their Instagram and Twitter handles. It is no longer necessary to include your physical address.[183]

- Remote-specific skills: Showcase skills that validate your ability to work independently and examples of demonstrated adaptability and resiliency.

- Gaps: Briefly address any gap in employment history. Reference any part-time or contract work performed during the gap or any education or career development you pursued.[184]

- Objective: Some recruiters prefer an "objective" paragraph outlining the ideal role you seek, while others don't. Consider replacing it with a lead-in summary section, briefly describing your critical skills and experience level. This summary draws the reader into your résumé.

- Photos: Résumé photos are a thing of the past. I can't recall seeing a photo on a résumé in the last ten years. It is best to include your photo in your online profiles instead.[185]

- Exaggerating: For recent graduates or those with minimal experience, don't overselling yourself. Using terms like "seasoned" or "expert" can seem unrealistic. Be truthful and realistic about your background and experience. Initiative, accomplishments, hard work, self-awareness, and honesty are more valuable in catching recruiters' attention than exaggerated claims.[186]

- Clarity: Strive to be concise about your qualifications. While you may have diverse skills and experiences, avoid portraying yourself as a jack-of-all-trades. Clearly define your identity, the role you seek, and why you're qualified. This clarity enhances your résumé's impact.[187]

Maintaining an active LinkedIn presence fuels career success. It is a powerful networking tool within your industry and increases your visibility, potentially leading to job opportunities. Keep your profile updated, regardless of your job search status. Share recent accomplishments, industry news, and relevant articles to engage your network. Invite past and current connections to expand your network. Interact with others' posts by liking, commenting, or reposting, and join relevant online groups to strengthen connections with like-minded professionals.[188]

Your online profile picture significantly impacts profile views. Ensure it presents you professionally without being overly formal. Use a current photo suitable for your industry, avoiding selfies or personal-event pictures—an amateurish photo may detract from your profile. Additionally, activate "job notifications" to promptly respond to online job postings, increasing your chances of a favorable response.[189]

You are not your resume, you are your work. —Seth Godin, American author, blogger, speaker, and former business executive.

Application Timing

It's helpful to optimize your job application timing and method for maximal success. Experts recommend applying for jobs in mid-January when companies gear up to achieve their new year goals. After the holidays, budgets are finalized, hiring approvals are secured, and funds are allocated for recruitment. Conversely, hiring tends to slow down at the end of the year as companies prepare for holidays and budgets become exhausted. Another favorable time to apply is October—hiring activity typically surges after employees return from summer vacations, and companies aim to fill open positions before the year-end.

Experts suggest that submissions made between 6-10 a.m. are more likely to result in callbacks or selections than those sent in the evening after 7:30 p.m. Therefore, targeting early morning hours for application submissions can enhance your chances of securing a response from the recruiter.

Tuesday mornings, rather than Monday, might be the best time to apply for a job. The longer you wait to apply to a new job posting, the lower your odds of receiving an interview invitation. Whenever possible, respond to job postings within 96 hours of being posted.

> *Sometimes opportunities float right past your nose. Work hard, apply yourself, and be ready. When an opportunity comes, you can grab it.* —Julie Andrews, English actress, singer, and author.

Recruitment Automation

Progressive companies use technology to improve recruiting and hiring experiences and increase overall efficiency, particularly in performing mundane and repetitive tasks. This, in turn, frees up their staff, enabling them to create and drive higher personal impact.

Artificial intelligence, bots, and automated tools are revolutionizing the recruiting landscape. These technologies streamline hiring by automating high-volume and time-consuming tasks such as candidate sourcing, interview scheduling, applicant screening, and communications. Automated assistants, including chatbots, simulate human conversations through text or voice commands, providing candidates with a seamless experience that mimics interacting with a human recruiter.

While some may be wary of automation tools initially, it's important to understand that they can prove invaluable for the job seeker. Recruitment automation can improve your search experience by speeding up application responses and matching you with relevant job opportunities more effectively. They can also enhance your chances of being matched with roles that align with your skills and preferences. By reducing human error and bias, they create a more transparent and accessible hiring process, helping you to stand out based on merit rather than traditional gatekeeping.

As a job seeker, you'll want to do some activities online to increase your chances of being discovered and leverage these various automation tools to your benefit. If you shy away from social media, you might be disadvantaged in today's job market. Sourcing apps scour websites and social media for the best job candidates. Therefore, enhancing your exposure within digital domains will improve your odds of landing a great job.

Online tools are beginning to replace the résumé, and many companies even accept LinkedIn profiles in place of traditional résumé. When you submit your online profile link, make sure that you update your privacy settings so that your critical information, including contact details, is visible to all viewers.

It's important to remember that some companies use lie-detection tools during pre-employment screening to monitor the honesty of candidates' responses. Therefore, it's essential to always be candid and truthful in your interview responses, whether online or in person.[190]

Interview Preparation

Preparing for your interview, whether a telephone pre-screen or an in-person meeting, is essential for success. Tailor your preparations to the specifics of each job position, and brush up on subject areas that may have grown stale or that you need to improve. Research the company, its mission, press releases, current projects, and planned pursuits. If you're provided the names of those interviewing you, research their backgrounds to understand their roles, interests, and accomplishments. Personalizing your questions and comments based on your research can set you apart from other candidates and show the interviewers that you've done your due diligence.

> *The strongest factor for success is self-esteem, believing you can do it, believing you deserve it, and believing you can get it.* —Unknown.

Some companies publish interviewing guides to help candidates make the most of their interviews. For example, Amazon recommends that candidates adopt the STAR method (situation, task, action, and result) to answer behavioral-based interview questions.

Thankfully, interview preparation is now more straightforward than it used to be. In the past, job candidates often fretted over notorious curveball questions designed to throw them off balance, a practice embraced by companies like Microsoft—these questions, often mind-puzzles, aim to identify extraordinarily gifted or creative thinkers. However, researchers ultimately concluded that brainteaser puzzle questions contribute to costly miss-hires and fail to enhance recruiting effectiveness.

Nowadays, websites like Glassdoor.com offer candidates probable interview questions in advance. Some recruiter platforms even provide examples of recommended answers. For instance, I was surprised by the extent of information and guidance Facebook recruiters provided me before my multiple rounds of interviews. While they didn't share actual interview questions, they clearly defined the role, responsibilities, and expectations, both technically and managerially. The pre-interview phone discussion with their recruiter, Usha Rag, allowed for an informal chat before the formal interviews, providing further insight and guidance that I found particularly informative. Usha was highly personable, engaging, and supportive, diffusing any tension I might have experienced.

There's also been a noticeable shift away from questions about a candidate's past job performance, as they're seen as poor predictors of future success. Those questions can lead to embellishment by good storytellers, even if their roles are minor. Instead, companies are leaning towards questions that reveal a candidate's problem-solving skills and future-oriented thinking. Recruiters are interested in candidates' ability to forecast industry trends, outline plans, and adapt to change. They also place great emphasis on innovation and learning.[191]

Some experts suggest you can nail your interview by honing your improvisational skills. They claim that improv success depends more on preparation than being a quick thinker. The key is to avoid overthinking questions or responses, which can lead to getting tripped up. It also involves listing typical questions likely to be asked and preparing brief but effective responses to each one before the interview. Rehearsing your answers while paying attention to your voice and expressions can further hone your performance.

Never underestimate the importance of interview preparation. Preparedness is critical to making a strong impression and demonstrating your genuine interest in the role. It helps you articulate your skills confidently, align your experience with the company's needs, and handle challenging questions with poise, ultimately boosting your chances of success.

A job interview is not a test of your knowledge, but your ability to use it at the right time. —Unknown.

Rewire Your Brain

If you're struggling to land a job offer after multiple interviews, a lack of confidence might hinder your success. Others can often sense someone's lack of confidence through body language, expressions, or subtle cues. Resolving confidence issues before interviews is essential to avoid undermining your chances.

First and foremost, let go of any shame associated with losing your previous job. Job loss can happen to anyone, regardless of their position or circumstances. What's most important is how you handle your current situation and the attitude you embrace moving forward. Dwelling on past failures only serves to create a false self-image.

If you've been trying to secure a job for a long time and bills are piling up, it's natural to feel desperate or adopt a self-pitying mindset. Neither of these attitudes is helpful or constructive. Remember that you have valuable skills, experience, and abilities that employers need and desire. Turn the tables around and take charge of interviewing *them*. Approach your job search from a position of power, not as a victim.

Treat yourself with kindness and compassion during a prolonged job search, just as you would support others facing similar struggles. If you are sulking or drawn into the darkness, find some distractions. A change of scenery or a walk in the fresh air can be enough to provide a new and positive perspective.[192]

> *The probability of rejection is 100% if you don't even apply. If you're not getting rejections, you're probably not trying hard enough. Instead, wear these rejections as a badge of honor to remind yourself that you're reaching for the stars.*
> —Unknown.

Keep At It

A recent survey of 1,000 job applicants found that, on average, successful applicants applied for 10-15 jobs and received between 6 and 10 rejections. The average respondent started losing confidence in themselves after the fifth rejection, and 64% pivoted to a different type of job based upon their loss of confidence during their search. On average, the survey respondents took at least three months to find their *dream* job. Of course, the more focused your search and specialized your expertise, the longer your job search might take.[193]

> *When someone tells me 'no', it doesn't mean I can't do it, it simply means I can't do it with them.* —Karen E. Quinones Miller, American journalist, historian, author, and community activist.

I've always viewed the job search as a numbers game, much like dating. Employers rarely knock at your door; you must put yourself out there. The more interviews you have, the better your chances. Don't expect your first application or interview to land you a job. Keep searching, even after a positive response, until you find the right fit. Patience and perseverance are keys to success in the job search.

Avoid overthinking your answers or trying to tailor them to what you think the interviewer wants to hear. Be authentic and let your true self shine. You want to work for employers who value you for who you are. Companies that play mind games or set unreasonable barriers during interviews may not be worth your time.

Maintain a positive mindset during your job search and avoid dwelling on negative thoughts. Rejections are not personal and do not reflect your value or abilities. Remember that finding the right job takes time, and embrace the search as a learning opportunity to improve your situation.

Rough patches in life are temporary. Enjoy what free time you have while you can. Courage, confidence, resilience, patience, and humility will serve you well and position you to win.[194]

> *If opportunity doesn't knock, build a door.* —Milton Berle, American actor, and comedian.

Qualifications

Job seekers commonly undermine their search efforts by excessively filtering out job postings that they feel are beyond reach. They might not check every requirement box or allow doubt to cloud their judgment. Research shows that women are more likely to underestimate their competence than men and avoid applying to a job posting unless they meet 100% of the requirements.

While some job qualifications listed in postings are firm requirements, others are merely *guidelines*. Much of the job-specific knowledge is learned after being hired, as companies often use custom tools and proprietary know-how that job candidates will not have been exposed to previously. Don't overlook job postings simply because you feel under-qualified; not meeting every requirement doesn't mean you shouldn't apply.

> *What would you do if you weren't afraid?* —Sheryl Sandberg.

Great leaders anticipate that candidates new to a role will grow into their positions. They appreciate energetic individuals who ask questions, seek mentors, and have a desire to learn. New employees are expected to make mistakes as they acclimate to their roles.

It can be helpful to search for jobs that will stretch you. If you're over-qualified for a job, then although you'll hit the ground running, the job may not lead to growth or satisfaction, resulting in stagnation or disappointment. Job postings should be treated as guidelines rather than a strict set of requirements that every candidate must possess. Having some of the skills a job requires is essential, but job seekers should open themselves to more than just those positions for which they're already overqualified.[195]

As you prepare your resume or conduct an interview, guide recruiters to see how your skills, knowledge, and experience prepare you for success in the new role, even if not all checkboxes are ticked. Understand the gaps and how you'll address them. If they're insurmountable, it's wise to move on and focus on roles that are more within reach.

If you're completely qualified for the job you apply for, you aimed too low. —Art Markman, American psychologist, educator, and author.

Know Your Worth

Many companies today will not hire candidates who they consider to be *overqualified*. However, they fail to consider that overqualified individuals can do things better and faster than underqualified or barely qualified employees. Hiring highly qualified employees offers a cost and efficiency gain that companies often overlook or undervalue.

Job seekers should believe in themselves and appreciate the value they bring to the lucky organization that hires them. Know your worth, and research the typical compensation range for your expertise and experience. Ask for and expect to be compensated fairly for the value and impact you bring to an employer. Learn to stand up for yourself and to say "no" to lowball offers. Be bold and ask for the salary that you deserve.[196]

The minute you settle for less than you deserve, you get even less than you settled for. —Maureen Dowd, American columnist, and author.

When a recruiter asks for your salary target, they often seek to determine your minimum acceptable amount or your current/past salary, potentially disadvantaging you in negotiations. Stay calm and confident, and avoid becoming adversarial. Encourage them to disclose the approved salary range to maintain negotiation leverage. If pressed, assert your worth and suggest a realistic figure at the higher end of the market range to begin negotiations.

Remember that salary is often only one component of your overall compensation package. The value of stock options, for example, can be worth far more than your salary, depending on the company and its market performance.

Understanding your worth when interviewing is essential for both personal confidence and effective negotiation. Knowing your value allows you to clearly present your skills, experience, and accomplishments, positioning yourself as a strong candidate who meets or exceeds the role's requirements. It empowers you to advocate for fair compensation and benefits, ensuring you don't undervalue yourself in the hiring process. By knowing your worth, you can approach interviews with self-assurance, make more informed decisions about job offers, and avoid settling for less than you deserve.

Personal Branding

Your "personal brand" is an amalgamation of your skills, attitudes, beliefs, and abilities, combined with the impression you leave on others. In business, your brand influences how others feel about you as a contributor and your perceived value to the organization.

When you create a brand that communicates your unique value as a contributor, your special attributes become part of your reputation—which can help attract opportunities in work and life that align with your authentic self. If you fail to craft a personal brand intentionally, others may create inaccurate, biased, or incomplete perceptions of you.

When you set out to build your personal brand, follow these steps to increase visibility and clarify your value proposition:

- Define your goals, values, and purpose. Consider your value to others, skills, and abilities, and ask yourself how you'd like to be thought of by others.

- Consider your existing brand and contemplate how you'd like to modify and improve it. For example, through education or other achievements, you could strengthen your resume where your brand is weak. Or perhaps you can remove gaps in your brand through networking and social media efforts to establish and communicate your expertise more expansively.

- Socialize your brand through application and repetition. For example, consider presenting at conferences or symposia. Writing papers for journals can establish and reinforce your credentials and expertise. Become an influencer or promoter on social media.

- Iterate and adjust continuously. Your brand isn't a one-and-done pursuit. Just like your resume, it adjusts and evolves alongside your career.[197]

- When evolving your personal brand, focus on outcomes. The outcome you want to achieve will inform the actions you'll need to take to achieve it.

- Solicit feedback from colleagues, mentors, and stakeholders when assessing your brand and value. Sometimes, we succumb to personal biases when self-evaluating, so objective feedback from others can provide a much-needed calibration when building our brand.

- Celebrate others. Our personal brands shouldn't be one-sided and wholly self-serving. Recognize and celebrate others' achievements while building our own brands. Remember that recognizing others, humility, and treating others graciously are hallmarks of great leaders.[198]

Personal branding is the art of shaping how you present yourself to the world. When you master it, you can transform your career by aligning your values and skills with your professional goals. Crafting a genuine, strategic brand positions you as a standout candidate in a competitive market.

Everyone has a personal brand, by design or by default. — Lida Citroën, personal branding expert, author, and speaker.

Phone Interviews

Phone interviews are often a candidate's first interaction with a potential employer, making them a crucial step in the hiring process. They provide an opportunity to showcase your communication skills, professionalism, and enthusiasm for the role, all while allowing the employer to assess your qualifications and fit for the position. It's essential to prepare thoroughly for a phone interview by researching the company, reviewing the job description, and practicing responses to common interview questions.

We've all heard stories of the unfortunate few who have been exposed for being less than fully dressed during video conferences. How would you feel if, after working hard to secure a phone interview, your interviewer somehow noticed that you were wearing only a shirt?

It's important to dress appropriately for interviews, whether in person or via video conference. Aim to match or slightly exceed the company's typical dress code. If unsure, don't hesitate to ask the recruiter for guidance beforehand. They're usually supportive and want you to succeed in the interview process.

For video interviews, set up your camera to capture a neutral background, like a bare wall, to keep the focus on you and your qualifications. Anything visible in the camera's frame could affect how the interviewer perceives you, so keeping it professional and free from distractions is best.[199]

Phone interviews conducted without video can pose unique challenges compared to video interviews. Both parties may struggle to connect deeply without visual cues like facial expressions and body language. In such situations, candidates must rely on their tone of voice, inflections, and energy to convey enthusiasm and engagement. Speaking in a monotone voice can suggest a lack of energy and interest. It's helpful to sit up straight and engage actively in the conversation to overcome this tendency. Listen attentively, speak clearly and confidently, and let your natural personality shine through to make a positive impression.

Video interviews offer the advantage of providing visual cues, allowing candidates to supplement their verbal responses with appropriate facial expressions and body language. Engaging actively by smiling, laughing, and maintaining eye contact with the camera can telegraph genuine interest in the conversation. Avoid distractions and focus on the interviewer's words to ensure effective communication and a positive impression.

Some companies are adopting advanced technology for phone screen interviews, such as the "asynchronous" interview format. Candidates receive pre-recorded interview questions and record their video responses as though a live interviewer had asked them. This approach streamlines the pre-screening process for hiring companies, conserving valuable interviewer time, especially for companies with high-volume hiring needs.

Automated interviewing offers several other advantages, including reducing candidate nervousness typically associated with traditional phone interviews. Recorded responses can be viewed by everyone on the hiring team, which drives transparency and uniformity. Moreover, all candidates receive the same questions in the same order, ensuring fairness and consistency. Pre-recorded questions also afford candidates time to prepare thoughtful responses, enhancing the quality of their answers compared to spontaneous phone interviews.

However, automated interviewing has its drawbacks. Some candidates may feel uncomfortable recording themselves, and the lack of follow-up questions limits the depth of the interview. Additionally, automated interviewing lacks the opportunity for two-way conversation, which hinders the company's ability to promote itself effectively. That said, automated phone interviewing is likely here to stay, at least for some companies. Job seekers would do well to accept and embrace this new normal and treat it like any other form of interviewing. Approach it seriously, prepare judiciously, and strive to do your level best.

The 1-on-1 Interview

Interviewing can be nerve-wracking, whether you're confident or not. But if you can focus on the moment, do your research, fully prepare, and answer each question concisely and with clarity without being overly verbose, you'll stand out amongst the many other candidates. While most interviews are 1-on-1, occasionally, you might face a panel of simultaneous interviewers.

For example, during one particular interview for a VP position, I encountered a panel of executives seated across from me, firing off questions and diving deeper into each other's inquiries. It felt more like an inquisition than a respectful exchange. Despite the intensity and intimidation, I kept my composure and confidence, eventually securing an offer. While the experience was intense and exhausting, being prepared and confident in my qualifications made it bearable and even exhilarating.

Every candidate should pay particular attention to how they present themselves when interviewing. Human brains are well-designed to size up other people rather quickly. Even minor issues can become major impediments.

> *When presenting yourself, remember that impressions matter. The whole picture has to be right. Others will be watching for all sorts of clues and cues that tell who you are. Be on time. Be authentic. Be prepared.* —Stephen Schwarzman.

Consider the following as you prepare for your interview:

- Your teeth can indicate your general age, health, smoking, eating, and drinking habits. Grinding your teeth could indicate certain psychological and personality traits.

- If you or your clothes smell of cigarette, cigar, pipe, or marijuana smoke, that can be an immediate turn-off to many non-smoking interviewers.

- Dressing appropriately and attending to personal hygiene are fundamental.

- Poor grammar can be an immediate turn-off for many interviewers. It can also expose or accentuate your sociological background or education level.

- Your self-confidence indicates how you feel about yourself and can impact relationships. If you don't feel good about yourself, you might lack the positive emotional energy to focus on others in the workplace.[200]

Below is an abbreviated list of suggestions on how to nail your interview:

- Arrive on time, in an excellent physical and emotional state, and with an optimistic attitude. Don't overcaffeinate—arrive fully rested. Avoid the rush by planning to arrive early. Wear comfortable clothes and make sure you're hydrated. Account for unexpected traffic or parking delays when you arrive at the interview location (don't risk being late).

- Prepare for your interview. Research the company and interviewers, and have your notes and questions ready.

- Project confidence, positivity, and optimism. Engage in a give-and-take conversation to learn about the company and have your questions answered. Remember, nervousness is normal, but don't let it define you. While self-deprecation can be appreciated, it should be limited during interviews. This is your time to highlight your strengths, not undermine yourself.

- Pay attention to signals of company culture, pride, and passion. If interviewers lack warmth, respect, or enthusiasm, reconsider their suitability as employers.

- Be honest, and don't exaggerate your answers. Research shows that, on average, candidates tell two to three lies (or fibs, if you will) in a 10-to-15-minute interview. People tend to dodge discussions around deficiencies in their résumés or might blame their failings on somebody else to distract or pivot from the topic. Most candidates exaggerate or conceal at least something in a job interview. Younger applicants tend to deceive more because they have less experience to draw upon. Hiring managers also lie—they want to sell candidates on their fabulous corporate culture, whether true or not. Always maintain your integrity and character. Own your history and background, and market yourself in the best way possible.[201]

- Avoid using jargon or technical terms to appear overly confident in areas where you lack expertise. Instead, be honest about your weaknesses and demonstrate a willingness to learn and grow in areas critical to the company.

- Breathe and remain calm, especially if you're thrown some curve balls. Your tone can be as impactful as your words.

Interviewers want to see that you are thoughtful, creative, respectful, and courteous.

- Ask questions freely, but strive for balance. As a candidate, you'll naturally inquire about the job, position, or company. Interviewers should provide an opportunity for questions, and you should not hesitate to ask. If the interview ends before you can ask them, get your answers before accepting any offer.

When asking questions during an interview, consider how the interviewer might perceive them. Questions should demonstrate your preparedness, research, and interest in the position. Avoid inquiries that could inadvertently signal negative traits. For instance, instead of asking about overtime, inquire about typical hours. Similarly, avoid early questions about compensation or authority, as you may come across as greedy or power-hungry. Instead, focus on questions about stretch goals or opportunities for advancement. Asking about the interviewer's job satisfaction can demonstrate emotional intelligence and likability, as people enjoy discussing themselves and appreciate genuine interest from others.[202]

Behaving respectfully and showing interest, passion, optimism, and curiosity are pluses. Listening attentively and allowing the interviewer to finish their questions before responding is essential. Candidates who habitually cut off interviewers before they finish asking questions may inadvertently disqualify themselves; interrupting others suggests a lack of interest in listening and can be disruptive, disrespectful, and inconsiderate.

Interviewers commonly find questions about candidates' technical skills, experience, and accomplishments straightforward to navigate. If you're passionate about your work, your enthusiasm will naturally shine through in your responses. However, expect questions about your soft skills as well, which can be more challenging as they require introspection. Honesty and transparency are essential. Avoid overthinking or hesitating too long before responding, and refrain from being overly clever or glib in your answers.

It's helpful to prepare for questions that interviewers commonly ask and to present yourself in the best light possible. The following suggestions aren't meant to be prescriptive—use your best judgement in each case:

- Motivation: Emphasize your excitement about the new company's opportunities rather than criticizing your current or past employer. Interviewers want to see that you're leaving for positive reasons and will assess if they can provide what you seek to inspire your performance. Prospective employers typically avoid hiring those who speak negatively about their current or past employers.

- Failures: When asked about your biggest failure, concentrate on what you learned, take responsibility, and discuss your actions to address the situation. Avoid blaming others and be truthful, recognizing that everyone makes mistakes. Employers ask this to gauge your attitude toward risk and innovation. Emphasize how you learn and grow from failure.

- Weaknesses: When asked about your biggest weakness, be honest and choose a minor weakness that won't hinder your performance in the job you're seeking. Avoid cliché responses like "I'm too detail-oriented." Clearly state your weakness, discuss steps you're taking to address it and share the positive outcomes of your efforts. This demonstrates self-awareness and a proactive approach to self-improvement.[203]

- Teamwork: When responding to teamwork-related questions, provide examples of your experiences collaborating with others and working as part of a team, particularly in challenging situations. Discuss how you've resolved team issues, motivated colleagues, or navigated challenging project constraints. Illustrating your ability to work effectively in a team environment enhances your candidacy. Avoid taking sole credit for successes, and demonstrate humility in recognizing team achievements.

- Customers: If asked about serving customers, you'll want to describe how you represented your company in a positive light and overcame challenges to deliver exceptional customer service.

- Time Management: If asked about time management, discuss how you balanced multiple competing demands, effectively prioritized, remained organized, and completed those tasks on time.

- Communications: If asked to describe your communication style, you might explain how you use different communication methods that you excel at as necessary to perform your job.

- Adaptability: When addressing questions about adapting to change or dealing with ambiguity, share examples of how you've overcome adversity or quickly pivoted your efforts when faced with unexpected situations. Highlighting instances where you maintained a positive attitude while navigating uncertainty can demonstrate your ability to adapt effectively.[204]

- "Tell me about yourself": The interviewer is primarily interested in your professional qualifications and experiences, not your personal life or unrelated topics. Use the interview time to address significant gaps in your résumé or highlight what sets you apart from other candidates. Share examples that showcase valuable character traits such as persistence, empathy, courage, and creativity, which align with the company's values. If relevant, mention any volunteer work or personal passions that reflect your commitment to social causes and community involvement.[205]

- Pride: If you're asked to describe an accomplishment you're most proud of, narrow it down to something relevant. Feel free to provide an example from previous jobs or outside of work that provides the interviewer insight into who you are. Tie it back to how it can be applied to the company you're interviewing.

- Fit: When asked why you think you're a good fit for the position, remember that employers seek candidates aligned with their organization and values. Describe how your background matches up to the expected job role and responsibilities. Alternatively, explain how the company's mission aligns with your passion, which will fuel your impact, contribution, and commitment.

- Biggest Challenge: If you're asked to describe your biggest challenge, the interviewer is likely assessing your problem-solving skills and how you handle stress. Respond with a specific work example that illustrates an obstacle and how you overcame it.[206]

After your interview, sending a follow-up email is recommended. According to a recent survey, 68% of hiring managers consider a post-interview thank-you email consequential. It could be the deciding factor if you're in a tie with other candidates. Request each interviewer's name and email address during the interview. Send individual, customized notes within one or two days after the interview. Remind them who you are and how you'll contribute to the company. Your letter should be brief, direct, and engaging, no more than a short paragraph or two. If the interviewer voiced a concern about your qualifications or if you struggled to answer a particular question, use this opportunity to follow up and fill in any gaps.

While you must impress interviewers with your positive attributes, it's equally important to eliminate any reasons for them to exclude you as a candidate. Avoid basic mistakes, maintain a positive attitude, and don't present yourself as *average*. Instead, exude positivity, energy, and passion. Put your best foot forward until you've completed the interview. Treat the hiring process like a game—learn the rules and tilt the outcome in your favor by exhibiting the proper behavior and abilities.[207]

> *Job interviews are like first dates. Good impressions count, awkwardness can occur, outcomes are unpredictable.* —Unknown.

Articulating Creativity

Employers value your ability to generate solutions and solve problems, which should be evident in your résumé and during interviews. Creativity is demonstrated by your history of addressing challenges others may have missed or by employing unique approaches to problem-solving. During interviews, provide context for your creative solutions, highlighting the impact and value they brought to projects or organizations. Discuss your significant challenges, your response, and the outcomes achieved. Emphasize whether your solutions could be scaled or applied to similar problems, contributing to broader corporate objectives and positive impact for the company.

When discussing instances of your creativity, acknowledge that creativity often emerges from collaborative team efforts. Recruiters understand the significance of teamwork in fostering innovation. Therefore, give credit where it's due and recognize your teammates' contributions while highlighting your own role.

Creativity isn't limited to any particular group or function. Creativity within companies can exist and should be encouraged *everywhere*. Regardless of your profession or the role you seek, everyone can articulate examples of how their creativity has brought value and impact to their employer.

Highlighting examples of your unique creativity outside of work can also be valuable during an interview. Sharing experiences where you've exhibited creativity in personal endeavors can further demonstrate your innovative thinking and problem-solving abilities to potential employers.

[Steve Jobs] didn't expect innovation out of just one group. He expected it everywhere in the company. When we were running operations, we tried to be innovative in operations and creative in operations, just like we were creative elsewhere. We fundamentally had to be in order to build the products that we were designing. —Tim Cook.

Ageism

Navigating the job market as a *seasoned* (otherwise known as "old") worker has its challenges. Ageism remains a prevalent bias, which perpetuates misconceptions about older workers, such as lacking adaptability, innovation, or tech-savviness. It's relatively easy to recognize signs of ageism, such as layoffs or buyouts targeting older employees, a lack of challenging assignments or promotions for them, and descriptions of older workers as "stuck in their ways" or "lacking energy."[208]

Age bias can vary depending on geographical location. Recent studies have shown that ageism is more prevalent in specific regions of the United States, particularly in the southeastern and northeastern states like New Jersey, the Carolinas, and Florida. These states also tend to have higher percentages of adults with poor health and increased per capita Medicare spending, contributing to overall health disparities even before the onset of the COVID-19 pandemic.

Researchers suggest that states with a significant population of retirees may experience more tension between younger and older generations regarding government spending on housing, medical facilities, and social networks. This tension could influence hiring decisions, especially when younger recruiting managers perceive older workers as a financial burden. Combating ageism requires self-awareness regarding language, attitudes, and assumptions across all levels of society.[209]

Not long ago, funding startups founded by 20-somethings was all the rage. However, a recent study examining 2.7 million new companies found that founders under age 30 had the highest startup failure rate, at 53%. 50-year-old founders have almost twice the probability of founding an extremely successful company as a thirty-year-old. Further, a 60-year-old startup founder is three times as likely to found a successful startup as a 30-year-old startup founder and is 1.7 times as likely to found a startup that winds up in the top 0.1% of all companies. This recognition has led investors and founders alike to appreciate the value of retirees, who bring experience and mature guidance to startups in need of adult supervision.[210]

It's interesting how human aging impacts our cognitive abilities. Starting in our 20s, our brains begin to shrink, affecting reaction times and learning. However, our brains adapt to these changes through a process termed the Scaffolding Theory of Aging and Cognition (STAC), proposed in 2009. STAC suggests that the aging brain forms scaffolding to support cognitive function as we age. Recent research indicates that as gray matter diminishes in the left hemisphere, the brain compensates by utilizing the right hemisphere. These adaptations may enhance leadership abilities by improving problem-solving skills, especially in interpersonal or abstract contexts. Psychologists suggest that for many, leadership abilities may peak in their mid-50s due to cognitive enhancements from scaffolding. Notably, seven out of the ten largest companies on Fortune's 2018 list were led by CEOs aged between 50 and 60.[211]

Further, age does not diminish our capacity for creativity or innovation. For example, a 2008 Northwestern University study found that the average age of scientists achieving work leading to a Nobel Prize was 39, and the average age of U.S. patent applicants was 47. These findings emphasize that excellence can emerge at any age. Some individuals demonstrate remarkable abilities early in life, while others may shine later. Therefore, when evaluating candidates for hiring or assessing potential, it's essential to focus on critical skills and capabilities rather than age. We remain fluid and dynamic throughout our lives and should never underestimate our potential for growth and achievement as we age.[212]

Fortunately, in the aftermath of the pandemic, there has been a noticeable resurgence in employers acknowledging the significant value and contributions that senior, experienced professionals bring to companies. There's also been a growing trend of hiring retirees, as leaders recognize the benefits of engaging experienced older consultants who possess extensive networks and can quickly integrate into projects. According to the Bureau of Labor Statistics, individuals 65 and older represent the fastest-growing segment of the labor force, reflecting a shift towards longer careers and delayed retirement.

Personally, while I experienced ageism while interviewing later in my career, I was ultimately able to secure employment at Facebook at age 57, when the average age of its workforce was 29 years old. As Facebook's leaders broadened their focus beyond software to hardware design and advanced communications solutions, they recognized the importance of leveraging the expertise of experienced professionals like myself. This shift in mindset marked a notable evolution from earlier sentiments expressed by Mark Zuckerberg regarding the capabilities of younger individuals: "Young people are just smarter... Why are most chess masters under 30?"

> *Subject matter expertise is the antidote to ageism.* —Carol Fishman Cohen, author, speaker, and career consultant.

If you're encountering challenges in securing interviews or job opportunities due to your age, you might improve your prospects by targeting companies with forward-thinking leadership that values experience and advanced skills. Stay proactive in keeping your experience and knowledge up to date, ensuring they remain relevant and valuable to potential employers. Engage with the latest books, periodicals, blogs, and industry newsletters, and attend relevant conferences and conventions to stay informed about industry trends and developments. Demonstrating current knowledge and initiative during interviews can help counter concerns about being obsolete, out of touch, or overqualified for a position.

Remember that successful companies focus on what people know and what they can achieve rather than how old they are. While ageism is real, it doesn't need to be a death sentence for an older person's career. Ultimately, expertise trumps ageism.[213]

Age tends to melt away when skill rises to the top. —Don Raskin, author, and career coach.

When You Receive an Offer

When you first receive a job offer, the next steps are crucial. It's best to avoid immediately accepting or countering a verbal salary offer with your target amount. Instead, politely ask to await the written offer before discussing terms—a legitimate offer should be formalized in writing. While the urge to accept immediately may be strong, remember that you have significant leverage with an offer in hand. The company has already invested time and resources in vetting you, which confirms their serious interest. After you've received your written offer, it is the opportune time to negotiate aspects of your compensation package. Though most companies carefully structure competitive offers, there's often room for negotiation to finalize the deal.

Your salary at every company somewhat depends on what you made prior. Think of your raises as being compounded over time, such that by the end of your career, you'll have made substantially more money overall for even slight increases along the way. Therefore, it's important to negotiate your salary whenever you have a chance, particularly early in your career.

> *I wish I would have known that what you negotiate at your very first job will affect the salary of all your future jobs.* — Anna Runyan, American entrepreneur, executive, and podcaster.

When reviewing your offer, explore it holistically; your base pay is only one of several components. You might investigate opportunities for extra paid time off or flexible work arrangements. If you have specific needs like relocation, bring them up for discussion. Signing bonuses can provide recruiters upfront flexibility without altering salary standards. Justify your negotiation by emphasizing the value you'll contribute to the company's objectives. However, asking for more without a compelling justification can be viewed unfavorably.[214]

When negotiating, refrain from apologizing, as it may imply hesitation. Avoid using negative language like "no" and instead opt for positive expressions like "I'd prefer" or "I'd be more comfortable with." Aim for the best possible offer before acceptance, being clear about your expectations and limits. Rather than using "want," emphasize what the company "needs" and how you can fulfill those requirements. Remember, your value is sought after and comes with a corresponding price tag.[215]

Beyond negotiating your compensation package, you should also consider the following questions before you accept:

- Is this the job that you've been looking for? Consider how the role fits into your long-term career plans and aspirations. Is your gut or intuition trying to warn you that something doesn't feel right?

- Am I compromising or being too quick to accept? When you're anxious to start making a salary again, jumping on the first offer you receive can be tempting. Don't settle for a mediocre job simply for a paycheck when continuing your search might lead to the job of your dreams.

- Are there any conditions to your offer? Some offers might require a drug test, security clearance, reference checks, or a requirement that you sign an NDA or non-compete agreement. If you feel that you're at risk of failing any pre-conditions or can't sign their required agreements or contracts for any reason, you should discuss this with the recruiter before accepting the offer. It is best to deal with issues upfront, transparently, and in good faith.[216]

If faced with a lowball offer, remain calm and optimistic about the potential for a positive resolution. Recognize that low offers can stem from various factors, such as budget constraints or an expectation of negotiation. Appreciate the underlying value of the offer, and take time to gather your thoughts before responding. Request time to consider the offer and avoid committing on the spot. When ready to discuss, opt for a phone or in-person conversation to convey sincerity effectively. Maintain professionalism and express gratitude while being clear about your needs. Often, a compromise can be reached for a mutually beneficial outcome. However, if an agreement isn't possible, the choice is yours to accept or thank them graciously and promptly resume your job search.[217]

> *There is no job that is so great that you deserve to be paid less.* —Devin Bramhall, content marketing consultant, writer, and storyteller.

Before accepting an offer, ensure all your concerns are addressed. For instance, if you have upcoming travel plans after joining, disclose this beforehand to avoid surprises for your new manager. Springing such plans at the last minute can disrupt your new organization and strain relationships. Offer to take unpaid time off if needed to demonstrate responsibility and consideration. This proactive approach sets a positive tone for your employment.

When you agree to a final offer, accept it confidently and approach your new job with total commitment and enthusiasm. Now is the time to deliver on what you've promised. If, on the other hand, you decide to reject the offer so that you can pursue something better, stand by your decision with confidence and do not look back.

> *When someone offers you an amazing opportunity and you're not sure if you can do it, then learn how to do it later.* —Richard Branson, British entrepreneur, adventurer, and business magnate.

First Weeks on the Job

Once you've landed a new job, you should be proud to have successfully navigated the interview process and grabbed the gold ring. On your first day, remember this famous expression:

> *You'll never get a second chance to make a good first impression.* —Unknown.

The first few weeks on a new job are critical for setting the tone and establishing your place within the team. This is the time to make a strong, positive impression, learn the company culture, and build relationships with colleagues and supervisors. It's essential to show initiative, ask thoughtful questions, and actively listen to understand the expectations and workflows. By demonstrating a willingness to learn and contribute early on, you'll lay the foundation for long-term success. Remember, your efforts in these early stages will be noticed and appreciated, setting you up for a thriving career in your new role!

Whenever I've started a new job, I've pulled out all the stops to exceed my employer's expectations. I showed up early and stayed late. I energetically accepted all assignments and searched for additional ways to make a more significant initial impact. I endeavored to participate in every team-building event and social gathering I was invited to. If co-workers asked for support or advice, I would drop whatever I was doing and dive in to help. In my experience, this is a winning strategy for "noobs."

In contrast, some new employees make a rocky start from day one. I remember hiring a senior manager who, on paper, appeared impressive and highly recommended by his spouse, a high-level manager in the same company. Despite my initial hesitation following his interview— something didn't feel right—I proceeded with an offer based on the positive reviews provided by other interviewers. Shortly after joining, he sent a derogatory letter to HR and copied me and my superior, criticizing perceived deficiencies in HR's onboarding process. His aggressive and confrontational behavior persisted over time, along with performance issues that he failed to correct, ultimately leading to his dismissal. This experience underscores the importance of trusting one's instincts when red flags arise during interviews. It also highlights the need to approach your new job positively and optimistically rather than wielding a flame thrower shortly after onboarding.

Ideally, when you join a new company, you should be supported, encouraged, and inspired by your new employer. Your team should welcome you with open arms and be optimistic about the potential contributions you'll make. As the newest employee, you should welcome your new job opportunity with energy, commitment, and dedication. Endeavor to learn, contribute, and provide valuable impact whenever possible, always embracing a consistent can-do attitude. Your future success is limitless when you present a positive initial impression and follow that up with continuously impactful performance and an enthusiastic attitude.

Be yourself. Everyone else is already taken. —Oscar Wilde.

CHAPTER 14

Management and Leadership

He who is not a good servant will not be a good master. — Plato, ancient Greek philosopher.

Management and leadership can be fulfilling and impactful career choices. As a manager or leader, you can inspire greatness in others and significantly contribute to the organization's success. These roles allow you to influence employees, enhance their performance, advance the company's goals, and foster growth in their professional and personal lives.

> *Leadership is an action, not a position.* —Donald McGannon, American broadcasting executive, and attorney.

When contemplating advancement to a management or leadership role, it's important not to underestimate the potential workload and stress. Leadership can be difficult, self-isolating, challenging, intimidating, and demanding, especially at the highest levels. For example, a recent study shows that CEOs work roughly 63 hours a week on average, including weekends and while on vacation. Further, a CEO's work life isn't necessarily glamorous—it can be gritty, exhausting, and often thankless. And as a manager, forget about sitting in a big leather chair in a fancy office, handing down decisions that your staff will carry out while you rake in piles of cash. Leaders and managers work hard, make tough decisions, and even deliver information that can upset many people. As with most things in life, transitioning into leadership carries advantages and disadvantages, so it makes sense to adopt a realistic view as you contemplate your path to advancement.

As a young manager, I underestimated the workload and responsibilities of the role. In addition to my engineering and program oversight duties, I juggled personnel oversight, performance reviews, budgeting, staffing plans, and product strategies. The added responsibilities and the pressure to deliver on corporate objectives often led to overwhelming stress. Over time, however, I learned to manage my workload more effectively by being proactive, delegating tasks, establishing boundaries, and improving my time management skills.

Most successful leaders are characterized by empathy, vision, and high emotional intelligence. They engage and inspire others, fostering collaboration and creativity within the organization. However, leadership is not for everyone, as it requires specific skills, aptitudes, and predispositions that not all individuals possess. Leadership is a unique role that demands a combination of innate qualities and learned skills to drive success.

Unfortunately, alongside great leaders, some exhibit destructive behaviors such as bullying, intimidation, and egotism. These individuals often prioritize their own opinions and agendas over the well-being and contributions of their team members. Some may shy away from accountability or conflict resolution, leaving difficult issues unresolved. Others thrive on conflict and competition, fostering a toxic work environment filled with politics and backstabbing.[218]

Achieving greatness through the efforts of others is the hallmark of leadership success. If you can't see yourself thriving in this pursuit, then management or leadership might not be the right fit for you, and that's perfectly fine. Management isn't for everyone, and fortunately, many other equally fulfilling and upwardly mobile career paths can bring success, happiness, and satisfaction to those who aren't so inclined.

> *Leadership is about making others better as a result of your presence, and making sure that impact lasts in your absence.*
> —Sheryl Sandberg.

Manager vs. Leader

The distinction between a "manager" and a "leader" can be subtle, and often depends on the organization's structure and culture.[219] Generally, managers focus on implementing plans and achieving objectives through the coordination of personnel while also promoting stability. Leaders, on the other hand, set the strategic direction, inspire the workforce to follow it, champion change, prepare the organization to adapt, and support employees as they navigate the transition. While managers tend to focus on operational aspects, leaders emphasize vision, innovation, and adaptation to change.

The difference between managing and leading lies in their approaches and sources of authority. Managers guide their teams toward achieving specific goals, monitoring progress, and assessing the value produced. They derive authority from above via their position in the organizational hierarchy and have people reporting directly to them. In contrast, leaders create value themselves and through their followers, extending their influence broadly. They earn authority from below through the trust and support of those who follow them. While managers oversee and coordinate the efforts of the individuals on their team, leaders create circles of influence across various organizations and stakeholders. Leaders influence, inspire, motivate, and enable people across the organization to create a significant impact that fosters overall success.[220]

Your title makes you a manager, but your people will decide if you're a leader. —Bill Campbell, American business executive, leadership coach, and mentor.

Are managers also leaders? Do leaders also manage? Of course, where overlaps exist. Great managers *lead* by inspiring their teams and setting tactical and strategic directions for their teams, organizations, and programs. Managers administer, plan, organize, coordinate, and focus on performance. Managers can also define a vision for their teams, align it with the company's broader goals, and ensure it resonates throughout the organization. It's difficult to overstate a great manager's impact on an organization and its workers.

Leaders *manage,* to ensure that their teams follow them towards their vision of success. They innovate, inspire, motivate, and focus on people and vision. However, most managers focus on execution and tasks, whereas leaders focus on vision, purpose, aspirations, and strategy. Leaders help organizations and people grow, while managers execute plans and improve performance and processes.

While leadership provides direction, inspiration, and a compelling vision, management ensures that plans are executed efficiently and effectively. Without effective management, even the most inspiring leadership may falter in achieving tangible results. Conversely, robust management without effective leadership may lack vision and fail to inspire and motivate teams. The optimal approach for organizations is to balance strong leadership and management, recognizing that both are necessary for sustained success. The harmonious integration of these two aspects drives organizational achievement.

Not everyone excels at both leading and managing. Companies often prepare employees for executive positions as leader-managers. As businesses become more competitive and volatile, they require better management to avoid chaos and to enhance their focus on quality, consistency, and profitability. Major transitions and rapid change or adaptability are often necessary for companies to survive and compete effectively in today's fast-paced business environment, which demands better leadership. Coping with complexity and change dictates a complement of management *and* leadership.

While managers are often associated with control, problem-solving, and process manipulation, leaders are perceived as more enigmatic and credited with crafting visionary paths for organizations. Yet, creating a vision isn't mystical; it involves exhaustive data collection, analysis, and drawing logical or insightful conclusions. Leaders are strategic thinkers who are fearless in taking calculated risks to propel their organizations forward.

Visionaries aren't always groundbreaking innovators; they often amalgamate existing ideas in novel ways to achieve objectives. Originality matters less than how well the vision serves stakeholders' interests—customers, shareholders, employees, and society. Equally crucial is its translation into competitive and compelling plans and strategies. A common error in organizations with solid management but weak leadership is the reliance on long-term planning instead of a clear vision and strategy. Without vision, plans become mere guidelines, leading to nowhere significant.

The other critical aspect of leadership is alignment and motivation. Aligning people provides a sense of direction and empowers everyone in the organization in a way that organizing rarely does. Motivating people is unique from *controlling* them. Motivation ensures that workers will have the focused energy to overcome obstacles and resist diffuse activity. Motivation satisfies the human need for achievement and provides a sense of belonging, self-esteem, recognition, and control. However, motivating workers requires diverse methods and tools employed by skilled individuals with appropriate behaviors. The more significant the desired change, the more challenging the motivation task becomes.[221]

In my experience, the best leaders I've worked with haven't just offered guidance, praise, resources, and feedback—they've actively joined me in tackling challenging issues and completing critical tasks. Instead of simply judging, they coached and engaged with me. Their actions spoke volumes, demonstrating tangible investment in our shared goals.

Managers and leaders complement each other effectively when they collaborate. Great leaders recognize the value of their managers' insights and knowledge, especially regarding customer interactions and operational realities. By tapping into this information, senior executives gain a deeper connection with managers who contribute to the refinement of corporate strategy and vision. Inclusive leadership teams involve a broader range of stakeholders, allowing for a more comprehensive organizational vision to emerge. Sometimes, innovative visions originate from lower-level leaders and managers, driving growth within their business units and influencing the broader company direction.[222]

Tell me and I forget. Teach me and I remember. Involve me and I learn. —Benjamin Franklin, American writer, scientist, inventor, statesman, diplomat, printer, publisher, and political philosopher.

Leadership Styles

Great companies owe much of their success to their exceptional leadership and talented employees they attract and lead. Leadership, however, is an art, not just a science, requiring a unique set of skills, abilities and behaviors for success. Leadership excellence isn't a novel concept, and it extends beyond the business realm—historical figures like Lincoln and Washington serve as powerful examples. Their leadership legacies offer valuable lessons for those aspiring to lead, inspiring us to forge our paths while drawing from their remarkable examples.

> *Leaders are right, a lot. They have strong judgment and good instincts. They seek diverse perspectives and work to disconfirm their beliefs.* —Jeff Bezos.

Navigating conflict, uncertainty, and critical decisions is inevitable as a leader. There are diverse approaches to leading teams, resolving conflict, and making decisions, each requiring specific skills. Some styles may feel more natural than others, depending on the situation, the people involved, and their personalities. Mastery often comes through repeated practice and exploration of different styles and approaches. Over time, leaders refine their skills by applying various methods to different scenarios.

While the "Golden Rule" of treating others as you want to be treated serves as an inspirational guiding principle for leaders, effective leadership occasionally requires bending that rule in certain situations. Diverse personality types respond differently to communication and motivation strategies. Influential leaders understand the nuances of individual preferences and adapt their approaches accordingly to stimulate their team members' desired actions and responses.

Below is an abbreviated list of common leadership styles. Each style provides certain advantages, disadvantages, strengths, and weaknesses. They're commonly applied and communicated in different ways and circumstances for optimal effectiveness. Recognizing and understanding these styles can help you to lead your employees more effectively:

- Affiliative: Affiliative leaders embody the principles of servant leadership, prioritizing the growth and well-being of individual employees and the team as a whole. They focus on fostering harmony across departments, resolving conflicts, and promoting cooperation among team members.[223]

- Amiable: Amiable leaders are patient, sympathetic, and kind. They are usually easygoing and likable, but their tendency to avoid conflict can be a leadership weakness.

- Analytical: Analytical leaders are deeply thoughtful or contemplative. They're serious, purposeful, set high standards, and are orderly and organized. They may be perfectionists and often tend to over-analyze things.

- Autocratic: Autocratic leaders make all the decisions without necessarily consulting subordinates or team members. Rarely effective, this style should be applied sparingly to avoid alienating the team.[224]

- Charismatic: The charismatic leadership style highly depends on the leader's charm and charisma, self-motivation, passion, and confidence. Successful, charismatic leaders can rally a strong band of supporters who will follow their lead.

- Democratic (Participative): Democratic leaders inspire participation and collaboration among team members, fostering creativity and innovation. However, decision-making processes may be slower due to consensus-building efforts.

- Driver: Drivers are confident, detail-oriented, and efficient strategists but may struggle with the interim steps to achieve goals. They are determined and productive but can also be insensitive and unsympathetic, rushing decisions and avoiding accountability for failures.

- Harmonizing: Harmonizing leaders focus on worker's emotions more than tasks and goals. They form emotional bonds with workers that create loyalty and feelings of belonging. This leadership style results in heightened trust and can stimulate innovation. It is commonly employed during periods of abrupt transition, trauma, or unrest.[225]

- Laissez-faire: Laissez-faire leaders delegate responsibility to team members, allowing them to work independently with little interference. However, promoting autonomy and creativity can also create ambiguity and a lack of direction.

- Producer: These leaders focus on getting results. They set high standards for performance and expectations for success. They may not provide details on the *how* but will focus more on the *what*.[226]

- Transactional: Transactional leadership involves incentivizing and rewarding personnel for precise work performed. Transactional leaders are commonly found in sales and marketing organizations. This approach may result in work performed at the minimum level, as required to meet a specific objective.

- Transformational: These charismatic leaders create a thriving work culture based on strategic vision and intellectual stimulation to initiate positive change. They focus on setting high goals and strict deadlines to achieve exceptional results.

While many leaders employ a variety of styles suited to different circumstances, the "Driver" style has been the default for too long. However, it is losing favor in the modern workplace as workers reject constant direction and control. Progressive leaders now focus on inspiring and earning the trust of their teams. They encourage risk-taking and creativity by surrendering control and empowering their workers, pushing authority down the ranks.

Exceptional leaders empower and mentor their workers to become leaders themselves, fostering leadership at all levels. They prioritize active listening to understand their workers' concerns, objections, and suggestions. They also understand that trust is the cornerstone of successful leadership today. When leaders and workers trust each other, transparency and honesty are allowed to thrive. People feel safe admitting mistakes and failures because they know they won't be scapegoated or punished.[227]

Beyond leadership style, influential leaders possess these and other skills and competencies for success:

- Organizational performance: Leaders inspire organizational performance and clearly understand how their role drives an organization's Mission and Vision.

- Strategic planning: Leaders demonstrate competence in strategic planning, which enables them to succeed across their many goals and objectives.

- Fiscal stewardship: Leaders optimally utilize and deploy available resources and budgets to meet organizational objectives. They also ensure adequate capital is available to fund every phase of their company's evolution.

- Relationship building: Leaders build positive relationships internally (employees, board members, and the executive team) and externally (customers, community, and other stakeholders). Leaders create partnerships between people throughout the organization.

- Branding expertise: Leaders exemplify the organization's brand. They look and act the part and uphold the company's brand identity internally and publicly. They serve as corporate spokesperson to motivate investors, employees, and the board to feel pride in their company's work and contribute as a team.[228]

Encouraging your team to take ownership and contribute their best ideas (*managing by objective* rather than micromanagement) can lead to remarkable results. Some of my teams' most significant technological advancements occurred when I stepped back and allowed others to innovate freely. Witnessing the growth and success of others through mentoring and coaching is incredibly rewarding. Nurturing a safe, fun, and inclusive work culture that encourages innovation, creativity, and work recognition can lead to incredible outcomes for the company and its employees.

> *When you're a leader—no matter how long you've been in your role or how hard the journey was to get there—you are merely overhead unless you're bringing out the best in your employees. Unfortunately, many leaders lose sight of this.* — Dan Cable, business educator, author, and management scholar.

Leadership Adaptation

As teams and businesses grow and evolve, leaders adjust their approach accordingly. Initially, adapting your leadership style and strategies in response to changing circumstances, challenges, and the evolving needs of your team or organization can feel bewildering—you might feel as though you're losing control as you navigate the unfamiliar. You might also fear the prospect of fully entrusting new managers to lead efforts that you were previously responsible for. Adapting involves flexibility, emotional intelligence, and the capacity to learn from new information and feedback. Managing at scale involves striking a balance between diving deeply into technical or management issues and delegating to others while maintaining an appropriate level of oversight.

Leading a large organization often means that the intimate personal relationships found in smaller teams give way to more topical connections. Unfortunately, this shift can create barriers for team members who may feel uncomfortable approaching you directly with issues or concerns. Moreover, they may perceive you as intimidating solely due to your position within the organization. In response, leaders must redouble their efforts to maintain a welcoming and supportive demeanor, encouraging open communication and rewarding those who freely share ideas, issues, and concerns.

As your organization expands, the demands on your time multiply with countless meetings, emails, texts, and calls, which can lead to overwork and burnout if left unchecked. Success hinges on mastering effective prioritization, time management, and minimizing distractions. Leaders of large organizations excel at focusing on high-value tasks, filtering out noise, prioritizing ruthlessly, and delegating responsibilities. They understand that perfection is unattainable and prioritize what truly matters. People-centric skills are critical, as leaders recognize that success depends on their team's efforts.[229]

As a leader, creating a unifying vision and environment is essential to maximize team potential. This involves bridging cross-functional gaps, fostering collaboration, and inspiring others to excel. Building trust and navigating complex relationships are vital aspects of leadership. It starts with articulating and embodying the organization's vision and demonstrating empathy and respect in all interactions. Without this foundation, teams may default to disarray or misalignment.[230]

> *The conductor of an orchestra doesn't make a sound. He depends for his power, on his ability to make other people powerful... to awaken possibility in other people.* —Benjamin Zander, English conductor, musical director, and educator.

As entrepreneurs lead their companies through growth phases, they encounter diverse challenges. For instance, during the launch of Endgate, I didn't have any direct reports and was, therefore, our antenna designer, business unit director, and proverbial corporate bottle-washer. With the company's expansion, my focus shifted from antenna design to recruiting top talent, evolving our technology roadmap, liaising with customers, investors, strategic partners, and patent attorneys, and expanding our product portfolio. Delegating design tasks became necessary as I mentored subordinates and oversaw organizational growth. This prompted multiple adjustments to our organizational hierarchy to better support our evolving needs.

At other companies, when I led much larger organizations, it became essential to cultivate additional managers to oversee their respective groups. As the organization expanded, I recognized the necessity of decentralizing decision-making and empowering others to take charge. This required a shift in my focus towards developing and trusting other managers, even when their methods differed from mine. Adapting to this reality meant accepting that other managers would implement their own processes and leadership styles. My attention transitioned to ensuring that the overall outcomes were positive and goals were met—the "what" instead of the "how."

Leadership adaptation is essential for navigating changing environments, fostering innovation, and ensuring organizational agility. By embracing flexibility, continuous learning, and empathy, leaders can effectively steer their teams through challenges, inspire confidence, and drive sustained success in dynamic business landscapes.

Leaders don't create followers, they create more leaders. — Brigette Hyacinth.

Servant Leadership

As a manager or leader, it's essential to understand that your primary role is to serve your team, not the other way around, if you want to achieve success. You and your company succeed through your employees. You aren't in charge of them—your team is in charge of you.

Servant leadership, while often recognized for its focus on empowering and supporting others, carries subtle yet powerful advantages that extend beyond traditional leadership styles. At its core, it prioritizes the growth and well-being of team members, fostering an environment of trust, collaboration, and innovation. Building mutual respect is crucial, and this often comes from working *in the trenches* with your team and engaging them in group and one-on-one settings as appropriate.

It's perfectly fine not to have all the answers; admit to it outwardly when you aren't sure, and then do whatever it takes to get the answer. Others will respect you for your honesty and transparency. And when you make your employees feel important and valued, they will exceed your basic expectations.

> *True leadership is when people follow you when they have a choice not to.* —Jim Collins, American business and leadership researcher, author, speaker, and business consultant.

When hoeing new ground or navigating uncertainty or ambiguity, embrace other experienced leaders and solicit their support and guidance whenever possible. They've been there and can help you avoid reinventing the wheel at every turn. Setting a positive example is essential—your team will emulate your behavior, so you'll want to model the qualities and behaviors you wish to instill in them.

Many managers still rely on power and fear to motivate their teams, hindering productivity and morale. In contrast, servant leaders share the company vision and inspire employees to contribute and enhance it collaboratively. To foster a healthy work environment, fear must be replaced with psychological safety, which enables open collaboration and innovation. Trust encourages transparency, truth, respect, and accountability among team members.

Servant leaders actively listen to their employees' inputs, valuing their perspectives and insights. They demonstrate a genuine passion for their work, their team, and the growth of their organization. By meeting the needs of others and removing obstacles, they enable rapid, unhindered progress. They foster a culture of continuous learning and development among their employees, which fuels future success for both individuals and the company.[231]

The lesser-known nuances of servant leadership include a deep emphasis on empathy, and humility, which create a culture where individuals feel valued and more willing to contribute their best work. To accomplish servant leadership, a leader must consistently put the needs of the team above personal ambitions, offer guidance without micromanaging, and empower others to make decisions. By creating opportunities for growth and development, leaders can cultivate a strong, motivated team that drives long-term success for both individuals and the organization.

> *Exceptional leaders understand that employees aren't just part of the company—they are the company.* —Unknown.

Words Matter

The saying "Actions speak louder than words" underscores the importance of follow-up and follow-through, emphasizing deeds over promises. However, effective leadership also hinges on how leaders communicate and the language they employ when conveying their messages. Communication is a foundational element of effective leadership, highlighting its pivotal role in achieving success.

Occasionally, we find ourselves spellbound as we listen to the potency of a well-delivered speech. For example, Amanda Gorman's stirring address during President Biden's inauguration captivated the nation, showcasing the transformative power of inspirational speech.

Great leaders and orators can uplift and motivate us, especially during challenging times, through the sheer force of their words.

The power of our words cannot be overstated, especially for leaders. Great speakers understand the importance of clarity, empathy, courage, and integrity in their communication. They recognize that words lead to action—they take the time to consider the impact of their messages on others. Courageous leaders prioritize truthfulness over ambiguity, ensuring their words are clear and respectful. By being deliberate and mindful in their communication, they foster understanding and trust among their team members.[232]

> *The very best leaders I know wrestle with words until they are able to communicate their big ideas in a way that captures the imagination, catalyzes action and lifts spirits.* — Bill Hybel, American author, and church figure.

Language matters and the power of words can be palpable when expressed with expertise. Words are a reflection of our character. By following a few essential guidelines, we can transform an otherwise average presentation into one that is truly inspirational:

- Avoid using contractions. Words such as "can't," "won't," and "shouldn't" are negatives. When you replace "we can't achieve x without..." with "we can achieve x with...," you transform your statement from a possibility of failure to the expectation of success.

- Convey power. Replace "try" with "do": Words like "try" and "want" are weak and convey a lack of commitment or uncertainty. Instead, embrace the usage of words that signify control and influence, like "do," "can," and "will."

- Use words that influence. Instead of using low-impact words like "just," "kind of," and "maybe," use their assertive counterparts like "I believe," "approximately," or "exactly."

- Imply choice rather than compulsion. Avoid using terms like "I have to" or "I need to," as they imply that an outside force is compelling you to do something. Instead, use terms that indicate confidence and purpose, such as "I want to," "I've chosen to," or "We will."

- Avoid the term "probably." Leaders appear weak when unsure of themselves—the word "probably" implies a 50-50 chance of failure. If you're uncertain of something, admit it deliberately.

- Choose words that an eighth-grader would understand. Consider your audience and use big words sparingly and only when appropriate.[233]

- Prioritize clarity above all else to ensure everyone easily understands your message. Simplifying complex ideas enhances audience engagement and comprehension.

- Understanding your audience's perspectives and emotions enables you to tailor your language accordingly. Empathetic communication fosters inclusivity and rapport.

- Words have the power to ignite passion and drive change. Aim to inspire and uplift your audience, leaving them with a sense of purpose and motivation.

- Every word carries weight. Consider the impact of your language, ensuring that each phrase contributes meaningfully to your overarching message.

In leadership, the impact of words shapes the work culture, inspires action, and builds trust. By choosing words carefully, fostering open communication, and demonstrating empathy, managers, and leaders can cultivate a positive work environment where clarity, motivation, and collaboration thrive.

> *The truth is, leaders rise and fall by the language they use. Sometimes whole visions live or die on the basis of the words the leader chooses for articulating the vision.* —Bill Hybel.

Empowerment

Plenty of managers thrive on telling others what to do. Perhaps they bask in the feeling of power or believe that their authority and position have earned them the right to order their subordinates around. Others may lack essential trust in their workers, afraid they won't make quality decisions or do the right things when left unattended.

Employee empowerment involves granting workers the autonomy to make decisions in their daily tasks while recognizing their competence and fostering trust in their judgment. It emphasizes the belief that employees can make sound business choices and should be empowered to manage their responsibilities and approach their work in ways they see fit while taking ownership of the outcomes.

Influential leaders recognize that promoting creativity and productivity requires giving employees the freedom and autonomy to generate and pursue their own ideas. Empowering employees to innovate and create boosts their morale and engagement and strengthens their commitment to the organization.

Richard Branson of Virgin is a prime example of a leader who champions this philosophy. He credits employee empowerment for the emergence of new business ventures within Virgin through "intrapreneurship," which has led to deeper market penetration. By providing freedom instead of constraint, Virgin creates springboards for ambitious employees.

> *People are fundamental in driving the success of a business. If you treat your staff like the smart and capable adults they are—and give them the choice to make informed decisions—you will cultivate an environment in which everyone can flourish.* —Richard Branson.

Empowerment requires leaders to treat culture-building as a critical and continuous priority, which only occurs with deliberate purpose.

CEOs lead the charge by embedding their ethics and vision into the culture, ensuring every member understands what is expected and how tasks should be approached. When corporate visions and values are clearly communicated, employees feel empowered to contribute to the business's success without management's constant oversight and approval. Values should be consistently reinforced through all aspects of the organization, including rewards and promotions. It's important to entrust the great individuals you took pains to find and hire and encourage them to apply their skills and talents to grow the business on the right path.[234]

I transitioned from being a control-oriented manager to an adept delegator early in my career. As a young manager, I initially expected underperformance among my team members. Consequently, I adopted a controlling leadership style to preempt missed deadlines or program failures. However, I gradually extended greater autonomy to my employees while I observed their performance. Surprisingly, they most often exceeded my expectations, showcasing creativity and self-motivation when given space to thrive. This pattern persisted across different companies and team compositions, further shaping my leadership approach. I learned to adjust my level of oversight based on individual expertise and self-direction, granting maximal freedom to seasoned professionals while providing more guidance to junior staff. Many leaders undergo similar learning curves to optimize team effectiveness, refining their styles through trial and error.

> *The ultimate use of power is to empower others.* —William Glasser, American psychiatrist, and author.

Leadership Growth and Maturity

Management and leadership proficiency usually improves over time, with both training and experience. While teachable, many effective strategies and techniques require experimentation, practice, and repetition to build *muscle memory*. However, it's noteworthy that even seasoned leaders can find themselves making rookie mistakes from time to time.

Some common errors include:

- A failure to demonstrate organizational values.
- Taking excessive and unfamiliar risks.
- Prioritizing self over others.
- Lacking strategic vision.
- Lacking a moral compass.
- Micromanaging others.
- Employing fear-based management styles.
- An unwillingness to take responsibility for failures.[235]

When leaders fail to adapt, learn, and refine their skills, their actions can corrode workplace morale and culture and stifle employees' creativity, efficiency, and adaptability. This can undermine engagement and trust and, in the most severe cases, lead to an organization's downfall.

In my early days as a manager, I was overly confident, headstrong, and blunt in my approach. My focus was solely on results, achievement, and impact, often overlooking the well-being of my team. It took time, experimentation, and trial and error for me to realize the importance of emotional intelligence in driving organizational success. I understood that motivating with kindness and rewards is effective, and encouraging a positive work environment where workers feel respected, appreciated, and valued leads to better performance and retention. Like any skill, leadership improves as we learn from our mistakes and adapt our methods accordingly.

As we grow in our leadership roles, we develop the ability to navigate challenges with greater agility and resilience. Leading through periods of significant change demands a calm and confident demeanor as we inspire and motivate others through uncertain times. Experienced leaders embrace complex challenges as opportunities for new solutions, demonstrating resilience in adversity.

Leading cross-functional efforts demands a mature approach to oversee and guide the contributions of a diverse collection of experts and stakeholders. It involves influencing and navigating multiple teams and their activities, building relationships and bridges across various functions. For instance, cross-functional technical leaders often collaborate with teams spanning legal, sourcing, policy, security, infrastructure, and others, each with diverse components and concerns. Effective leadership in such contexts involves managing a broad spectrum of issues, data, and perspectives to achieve strategic and tactical objectives.

Experience plays a crucial role in leadership, yet numerous talented young leaders exhibit exceptional leadership skills early in their careers. While these individuals may achieve early success, they, like all leaders, continue to refine and improve their methods over time. Leading self-directed personnel in favorable conditions is relatively straightforward for many. However, exceptional leadership is tested when navigating challenging teams, pursuing ambitious objectives, and managing within significant cost, schedule, and performance constraints. Such situations separate exceptional leaders from the rest.

Steve Jobs, Bill Gates, and Mark Zuckerberg are prominent examples of successful leaders who achieved remarkable feats in their younger years. Nevertheless, each has openly acknowledged and reflected upon their early leadership failures or missteps, expressing regret over certain aspects of their initial approaches. As time passed, they underwent significant personal and professional growth, refining their leadership methods, techniques, and tactics to enhance their long-term effectiveness. Their reflections serve as valuable lessons, highlighting the importance of continuous improvement and evolution in leadership.

Gates, for example, rarely took breaks from work in the early days of Microsoft. He's since admitted that, at the time, he didn't believe in vacations or weekends. He pushed everyone around him to work extremely long hours. In fact, he used to overlook Microsoft's parking lot every day to observe who was leaving early and staying late. Fortunately, he eventually decided that such scrutiny wasn't sustainable or appropriate. Once he became a husband and father, he found that excessive work intensity wasn't conducive to performing effectively at work and enjoying a great life.[236]

You are not a slacker if you've cut yourself some slack. — Bill Gates.

Wise leaders continually evolve, recognizing that they don't possess all the answers. Embracing a growth mindset, they actively seek wisdom from others and remain open to learning opportunities in every situation. When faced with positive and negative outcomes, they reflect deeply, analyzing what transpired, what contributed to success or failure, and how they could have acted more effectively. They assess their behavior and tactics, identifying areas for improvement and considering alternative approaches for future situations. They also evaluate their emotional responses and strive to maintain composure and clarity amidst challenges rather than succumbing to anger or fear. Through this ongoing process of introspection and adaptation, exceptional leaders cultivate resilience and wisdom, continually refining their leadership approach to navigate diverse scenarios with skill and insight.

After weathering each successive challenge, it's valuable to reaffirm the belief that every event unfolds for a purpose, and every setback can pave the way for a fresh start. Past decisions or outcomes don't dictate the future. Recognizing mistakes as part of the human experience, it's unproductive to demand perfection from oneself or others. In moments of doubt or regret, maintaining perspective is essential—acknowledging imperfections and extending kindness and compassion to oneself is necessary. When others stumble, empathy prevails, as we've all encountered similar learning opportunities on our personal journeys.[237]

> *A truly great boss is hard to find, difficult to part with, and impossible to forget.* —Alex Beame, American writer, and journalist.

Managing Superstars

Throughout my career, I've made it a priority to recruit top-notch employees. The collective brilliance of my teams has enabled us to achieve remarkable feats and accomplishments. However, managing "superstars" presents its own set of challenges. The dynamics of a team can significantly influence its overall success, with superstars capable of either enhancing or impeding organizational performance.

Research indicates that star contributors, while valuable, can inadvertently hinder effective collaboration within teams due to their egos. Moreover, the presence of a creative star may unintentionally stifle the creativity of other team members, as they may feel intimidated or overly reliant on the star's ideas and contributions. This reluctance to contribute can also stem from a fear of saying something *stupid* and appearing foolish. Additionally, team members may become less inclined to contribute when they depend on the superstar to develop the exceptional ideas and perform most of the heavy lifting.

Creating a culture of psychological safety is crucial for maximizing superstars' potential while empowering their teammates. When team members feel safe to express their ideas and opinions without fear of judgment or reprisal, it reduces the intimidation factor often associated with star contributors. Additionally, encouraging the superstar to speak last in discussions can help prevent their dominance and allow space for other team members to contribute their perspectives and ideas freely. This approach fosters a more inclusive and collaborative environment where all team members can thrive and contribute to the team's success.[238]

Superstars often exhibit strong personalities and high expectations. While they can bring unparalleled contributions to the team, they may also possess egos that match their talents, making collaboration and team dynamics more complex. It's not uncommon for superstars to exert influence over their work environment and relationships, sometimes leading to conflicts or tensions within the team. However, with effective leadership and a supportive team culture, it's possible to harness the potential of superstars while mitigating the negative impact of their behavior on team dynamics.

I've observed that most employees, regardless of their inherent talents, respond well to positive behavioral role models. Mentoring superstars in effective interpersonal interactions can yield positive outcomes. Some may find that their abrupt or abrasive style hinders their growth and advancement. You can demonstrate how successful interactions can lead to desirable results by modeling clear and respectful behavior. Seeing the effectiveness of this approach in others can often prompt superstars to adjust their own behaviors for better outcomes.

I've often advised superstars to understand that technical greatness alone isn't sufficient; superior skills must be coupled with positive behavior. Bullying or inappropriate conduct can negate their exceptional abilities or even result in termination. Furthermore, consistency and transparency are often essential for high performers who dislike ambiguity. It's important, therefore, to ensure clear and consistent communication, especially when goals or requirements may change. Sharing the broader vision of our pursuits allows high performers to understand how their contributions fit into the larger mission. This fosters a sense of ownership and commitment to the endeavor.

For high performers who thrive on recognition, make it a priority to showcase their achievements publicly. Presenting work to others allows high achievers to shine and be recognized for their excellence, which is essential for their motivation and engagement. Design reviews, project out-briefs, proposal preparation, and customer presentations are excellent ways of creating impact and value while spotlighting the exceptional contributions of team personnel.

High performers usually do their best work when they're provided the freedom to innovate with minimal managerial oversight. Eliminate noise and distraction from their efforts to enable them to work in an environment conducive to deep thought and concentration. Take steps to minimize low-value and mundane tasks that interrupt their essential work, either by offloading or removing them. This approach enables high performers to focus on tasks that drive innovation and excellence.

Creating an environment where high performers collaborate with other high performers fosters creativity and innovation. Ideas build upon each other in such settings, enhancing creativity and collective improvement. While individual brilliance is valuable, the collaborative efforts of capable team members can make unique ideas even better. Encouraging this dynamic and collaborative environment yields tremendous collective achievements that everyone can take pride in.[239]

> *Leadership is not about forcing your will on others. It's about mastering the art of letting go.* —Phil Jackson, American former professional basketball player, coach, and executive.

Micromanagement

Micromanagement is generally described as a management style that involves an excessive degree of control and oversight. It is usually practiced when leaders demand tight command and control, which was the default mode of most managers for years. However, research shows that micromanagement diminishes trust in workers' capabilities and commitment and reduces productivity, innovation, and morale.

Micromanagers are prone to criticizing others' work—they focus on finding fault and rarely acknowledge exceptional effort. They insist on tasks being done *their* way and become agitated when deviations occur. Obsessing over insignificant details, they assert dominance by appearing superior. Micromanagers often hover and disrupt critical workflow with excessive status checks and interventions. Some even take pride in their controlling tendencies, believing perfectionism justifies their behavior. In extreme cases, they'll retrieve work from others to *fix* or properly finish it themselves.[240]

> *Micromanagement is a complete waste of everybody's time. It sucks the life out of employees, fosters anxiety, and creates a high stress work environment.* —Brigette Hyacinth.

Executives are not immune to micromanagement tendencies. They may excessively monitor deputies' adherence to plans or insist on approving every detail, diverting valuable time and energy from more critical and impactful endeavors. Moreover, executives who micromanage can also complicate their business "exit strategy" if potential buyers convince themselves that the business they're interested in acquiring can't operate without its deeply enmeshed founder or CEO. Delegating responsibility and fostering autonomy among leadership tiers is essential for organizational sustainability and growth.

A CEO who avoids a month-long vacation out of fear that the business cannot function without them may inadvertently harm both the company and its employees. Leaders should trust their team's capabilities and set an example for work-life balance. Many CEOs must delegate more, control less, and groom potential successors. This necessitates self-confidence, trust, and a willingness to subordinate personal ego. Each team member should be an expert in their domain and capable of managing autonomously. Effective CEOs prioritize big-picture concerns over minor details.[241]

If you are micromanaging, take the time to reflect on your leadership style. Trust in your team's abilities and strengths, even if they work differently than you. Provide clear assignments, expectations, and deadlines, then empower your team to excel in their own way. Avoid fixating on unnecessary details and focus instead on results.

Remember, there's often more than one way to achieve a goal, and yours may not always be the best.

> *Micromanage the process, not the people.* —Joe Apfelbaum, business strategist, and executive.

If you work for a micromanager, always strive to meet deadlines and consistently exceed task expectations. Regular communication with your manager to clarify assignments and expectations is critical. While it may be tempting to under-communicate to avoid micromanagement, this can worsen the situation. Increasing communication provides your manager with a sense of control and visibility, which can help build trust. As your manager observes your continuous reliability and achievement, they may reduce their oversight and increase delegation.[242]

But before we reject the notion of micromanagement altogether, it may actually be necessary in certain situations where heightened scrutiny, drive, or oversight is needed. When applied judiciously, the potential for adverse effects can be mitigated. However, it's crucial to recognize when such close supervision is appropriate and when it risks stifling productivity and morale.

While employees resent *constant* monitoring, managers must gauge their team's capabilities to determine when closer supervision is warranted. When workers need help or additional guidance or motivation, an effective manager will deeply engage, clarify, inspire, and focus, then step back to allow the worker to own their work and produce the desired results and work product. Micromanagement isn't about doing the job for others but ensuring they have the support needed for success. Some people naturally require more oversight than others, and a manager who disengages to avoid micromanaging can encourage failure.

Additional oversight or direct engagement can also be necessary when the business is going through a transition or a pivot, which requires intense focus and guidance. Once the team is on a solid path, step back and provide them the freedom to excel. Likewise, stepping in to resolve an issue is warranted if your team isn't collaborating or cooperating effectively. When working towards a fast-approaching deadline, managers can inject themselves to lead a temporary sprint to succeed.

Great managers prioritize results and performance over policing employees' occasional social interactions or personal tasks during work hours. Recognizing that workers are social beings with outside interests and obligations fosters a healthy corporate culture. Encouraging employees when they occasionally need to attend to personal needs, even during work hours, promotes loyalty and engagement. This approach can yield long-term benefits for both individuals and the organization.

Never tell someone how to do something. Just tell them what needs to be done, and they will amaze you with their ingenuity. —George S. Patton, American Army general.

Delegation

Delegation is an essential leadership skill that fosters team confidence, corporate growth, and work-life balance. Leaders who struggle to delegate may become bottlenecks as they resort to micromanagement, which signals a lack of trust in their teams and an unwillingness to prioritize strategic tasks. Effective delegation empowers teams to take ownership of tasks and enables leaders to focus on scaling the business and other high-impact initiatives.

> *No person will make a great business who wants to do it all himself or get all the credit.* —Andrew Carnegie, Scottish-American industrialist, and philanthropist.

Successful delegation hinges on building a team with diverse skills that complement your abilities. Prioritize those tasks that you'd like to retain that are aligned with your strengths and expertise, and delegate those to others who are better equipped to handle them. Alternatively, delegate challenging tasks while providing coaching and support to provide learning and growth opportunities for your team.

When you delegate, you might occasionally find your delegee struggling or requiring more training or oversight than you expected. However, these are normal aspects of the delegation process. Address these challenges promptly while maintaining open communication with your delegees and encouraging them to seek guidance when needed. While delegation has its share of risks and drawbacks, its benefits greatly outweigh the negatives. Without delegation, leaders risk becoming overworked and unable to focus on critical tasks essential for personal and organizational success. Delegation isn't merely optional; it becomes an indispensable aspect of effective leadership.

> *Delegation requires the willingness to pay for short term failures in order to gain long term competency.* —Dave Ramsey, American personal finance personality, radio show host, author, and businessman.

Your workers are your single greatest asset. Monitor their work and coach them as required. Don't disengage, but rather stay attuned and connected. Light but continuous oversight is necessary for effective delegation until your delegee attains competence at performing the delegated task. Your delegees should clearly understand their assignments, objectives, and expected outcomes. They must *own* their assignments and feel personally committed to and responsible for completing them effectively.

> *Surround yourself with great people; delegate authority; get out of the way.* —Ronald Reagan.

Leadership Trust

Trust forms the cornerstone of effective leadership. In business, we rely on our leaders to uphold ethical standards and act as moral guardians of our organizations. Similarly, in politics, we entrust our leaders with the responsibility to uphold the Constitution and prioritize the collective interests of all citizens over personal agendas or partisan affiliations. Leaders must align with our accepted values and principles, consistently demonstrating them through their conduct and decisions. Trust in leaders fosters confidence and unity, driving positive outcomes for businesses and societies.

> *Character makes trust possible, and trust is the foundation of leadership.* —John C. Maxwell.

Trust is not given lightly; it must be earned through actions and behaviors. Honest and transparent communication and reliability in fulfilling commitments are essential to building trust. Effective leaders cultivate trust among their superiors and subordinates, although striking this balance can be challenging. They must be able to offer and receive honest feedback, make difficult decisions when necessary, and consistently exhibit supportive and empathetic leadership. By embodying these qualities, leaders can inspire confidence and loyalty among their team members, fostering a positive and productive work environment.

I've observed that weak, unethical, or untrustworthy leaders rarely operate alone—they prefer to surround themselves with similar personalities and behaviors. The presence of one leadership problem within a company hints at deeper, hidden issues. When you encounter a company with accounting irregularities or unethical management practices, it's worth wondering what else might be festering below the surface.

> *There is seldom just one cockroach in the kitchen.* —Warren Buffett.

Corporate scandals, such as Enron Corp., WorldCom, and more recent examples of corporate misconduct, confirm that ethical lapses and governance failures are recurring challenges that investors and regulators must remain vigilant against. I get alarmed when politicians attempt to eliminate or water down ethical guidelines or standards or gut America's corporate and financial guardrails, such as regulations and whistleblowers.

Instead of doing what they can get away with, great leaders operate within the confines of the law while adhering to the highest ethical and moral standards. They take the high road and do what's *right*. They resist the temptation to stray in pursuing power or profits, and instead earn our enduring trust by embracing stewardship and corporate citizenship. They treat their shareholders as partners, practice accounting transparency, and provide understandable and timely managerial explanations throughout their tenure.[243]

Kevin Quirk, a brilliant prior colleague of mine, once reflected upon how his father infused in him the importance of trust and behavior while he was growing up:

> ..we all get to control whether our word is our bond, whether or not we engender trust through honesty, whether we treat everyone with respect, and whether we're leaders or pretenders. There is only one thing in life that you truly control, and that is your word.

Trust is the cornerstone of effective leadership. It enables collaboration, empowers teams, and drives organizational success. Leaders can earn and sustain trust by consistently demonstrating integrity, transparency, and reliability, fostering a culture of engagement, loyalty, and high performance within their teams and across the organization.

Recognition and Appreciation

Confident bosses never fly solo. They acknowledge that their own successes are a consequence of team efforts. They don't need the glory—they know what they've achieved, both independently and through the efforts of others. They stand back and celebrate their accomplishments by letting others shine.

While recognition and appreciation are often used interchangeably, it's worth clarifying their nuances. In simple terms, recognition relates to *what people do*, whereas appreciation relates to *who they are*. Recognition and appreciation are given for different reasons, and employees require both to be engaged and motivated.

> *A person who feels appreciated will always do more than what is expected.* —Unknown.

Recognition and appreciation are powerful tools regardless of your role—peer, friend, leader, or subordinate. Consider how you felt the last time you received a compliment or acknowledgment for your work. Recognition validates our efforts and gives them meaning, making us feel valued and appreciated. Our achievements may feel empty without recognition, leaving us questioning their significance and impact.

Receiving recognition from someone who competed against you and lost is profoundly meaningful. It reflects a level of graciousness that transcends competition. Similarly, being acknowledged by industry leaders or highly successful individuals in your field instills a sense of importance, value, and uniqueness. It validates your achievements, recognizes your excellence and expertise, and affirms your identity and potential at a deep level. The innate desire for recognition is powerful and fundamental to human nature.

When presented with the opportunity to congratulate someone for their contribution or achievement, you face a choice: You can remain silent out of jealousy or spite or because you don't want them to enjoy what you couldn't achieve. Alternatively, you can reach out and acknowledge their success. Some worry that acknowledging someone else's win might highlight their own lack of success by comparison, as they view *winning* as a zero-sum game. However, providing praise holds more power than receiving it. When you recognize others, you all rise together. Offering accolades allows you to share in the glory of achievement. Being part of a collective win is far more fulfilling than being a lone winner in isolation, where competition is cutthroat.

> *When you give praise, you are acknowledging that someone else doesn't have to lose for you to succeed.* —Tim Denning, Australian entrepreneur, blogger, author, and coach.

Even if you dislike or have competed against the recognized recipient, acknowledging them can disarm and diffuse any animosity, even if only temporarily. Your recognition has the power to alter the dynamics of your relationship. Displaying this skill can earn you respect, even from your detractors. With practice, it can become a powerful habit that enhances your career trajectory.[244]

The most confident leaders and managers often recognize and reward outstanding contributions through monetary rewards or career advancement. Unfortunately, I've witnessed cases where deserving workers were overlooked for recognition because their managers fell short. In some instances, I could influence those managers or provide recognition on their behalf, but in others, I couldn't intervene. It's disheartening to see top performers passed over while others receive accolades and promotions for mediocre performance or, worse, credit for the work of their colleagues.

You are your own best advocate when it comes to receiving recognition and rewards for your achievements. It's sometimes necessary to "manage up" your successes to prevent your career from stagnating. However, it's important to be mindful of how you promote yourself to avoid being perceived as arrogant or having an inflated ego. Toot your own horn sparingly and only when your performance speaks for itself and is beyond reproach.

By demonstrating the following behaviors, it's possible to increase the odds that your work and impact will be recognized by leadership:

- Show your commitment to the company by investing in professional growth. Read books, subscribe to journals, or take relevant courses to expand your skills. Stay informed to tackle new challenges effectively. Immersing yourself in relevant literature enhances performance and contributes to company goals.

- Regardless of your role, strive to be the best. Familiarize yourself with performance metrics and analytics relevant to your area. Understand how your work aligns with the organization's objectives. Embrace accountability, avoid scapegoating, and exhibit self-awareness when addressing challenges.

- Do what you say you will do. Whatever you commit to, do it well and meet or exceed your objectives. Leaders recognize dependable employees with a track record of getting tough jobs done on time. They appreciate reliability and consistently high-quality work. These people can be entrusted with challenging assignments and increasingly higher levels of responsibility.

- Develop your strategic thinking skills to complement effective execution. Generating compelling plans that align with organizational objectives requires foresight and creativity. Practice strategic thinking by exploring new opportunities that contribute to broader goals.

- Exercise your creativity as you formulate execution plans or strategies. Leaders appreciate innovators.

- Improve your communication skills, whether writing documents, making presentations, or having difficult conversations with peers, subordinates, or leadership.

- Expand your organizational interactions by engaging with influential individuals from diverse departments. Collaborate cross-functionally to broaden your impact and contribution. Engaging with colleagues outside your immediate area enhances your visibility and effectiveness, fostering opportunities for growth and collaboration.

- Set an excellent example for others to emulate, regardless of your position. Encourage and recognize others, and don't force attention upon yourself.[245]

- Learn and embrace new tools, such as AI, to improve your effectiveness and increase your impact at work. Automate tasks wherever possible to free up time for additional endeavors.

Research indicates that employees thrive when praised three times more often than criticized. Coupling appreciation with incentive rewards significantly boosts morale and productivity. Tangible forms of recognition, such as spot bonuses or public acknowledgment in meetings, can effectively motivate and engage employees. Additionally, emailing a superior to commend an achievement is a simple yet meaningful gesture that fosters a positive work environment.

Praise and recognition should ideally be given promptly upon success or achievement. It should be specific, tied explicitly to an achieved objective, or better yet, a stretch goal. While verbal acknowledgment is essential, tangible tokens of appreciation further underscore the significance of the accomplishment. Providing meaningful gifts demonstrates genuine care for our employees and acknowledges their valuable contributions.[246]

Every team develops unique personalities and preferences, shaping its local culture and achievement standards. Thus, it may be necessary to tailor recognition programs for each distinct team, especially if they are geographically dispersed. Each office or team should be free to recognize its members in ways that resonate with them as long as the process remains fair and equitable in distributing rewards across all teams. Moreover, companies should consistently acknowledge and celebrate achievements from cross-functional, multi-team efforts throughout the year. Embedding this practice into the company's culture fosters a tradition of recognition and celebration.

Don't scrimp or cut corners when offering gifts as rewards for achievement. Ensure that they are meaningful, appropriate, and of high quality. Gifts that are cheap imitations or knock-offs tend to devalue the award and lessen the impact.

Recognition and appreciation are vital in cultivating a motivated and engaged workforce, as they acknowledge contributions, boost morale, and foster a positive organizational culture. By implementing genuine and timely recognition practices, leaders can inspire loyalty, drive productivity, and create an environment where employees feel valued and motivated to excel.

Accountability and Ownership

Confident leaders embrace the possibility of being wrong and demonstrate accountability for their decisions. They are secure enough to step back from losing propositions rather than stubbornly persisting. They focus on discovering *what's* right rather than insisting on *being* right. Additionally, they take ownership of mistakes and failures while deflecting praise onto others when things go well.

> *Leadership consists of nothing but taking responsibility for everything that goes wrong, and giving your subordinates credit for everything that goes well.* —Dwight D. Eisenhower, American statesman, military officer, and 34th president of the United States.

"Do what you say you will do" is a foundational leadership principle. Regrettably, many individuals underestimate the importance of keeping their word. Accountability involves taking responsibility for one's actions, promises, and commitments. Yet, despite this, many leaders falter in honoring their word, sending signals to others that they cannot be relied upon or trusted. This inconsistency erodes trust and undermines their credibility and predictability.

In today's world, we're witnessing a decline in the value placed on accountability, honor, and character. Our society is becoming more entrenched in emotionally charged and divisive interactions characterized by blame and hostility. As a result, the traditional definition of accountability is being reinterpreted, with many accepting compromised ethics as the new norm. This trend reflects a concerning shift from the principles of integrity and responsibility essential for a healthy and ethical society.

Leadership experts agree that it's important to listen to a leader's words and observe their actions—the talk *and* the walk. To earn trust, it's crucial to demonstrate integrity and be true to one's word. Leaders who exemplify this behavior set a powerful example for the entire organization, inspiring others to follow suit and fostering a culture of trust and reliability.[247]

Scapegoating is one of the most damaging forms of mismanagement, particularly for team morale. Those who resort to scapegoating often try to shift blame onto others to protect themselves or as a substitute for genuine corrective action. It creates a toxic atmosphere where individuals feel unfairly targeted and undermines trust and collaboration within the team.

I've witnessed this destructive style of management on multiple occasions. When faced with missed performance goals or project deadlines, some managers resort to blame-shifting rather than addressing the underlying issues. I recall a specific instance where a corporate executive refused to approve our program schedule and demanded unrealistic timelines instead. When we inevitably fell behind, he unjustly accused our high-performing subcontractor of underperformance to deflect from his overruling our original plan. This behavior disregarded our subcontractor's valuable expertise and support and threatened to sever a crucial partnership for our project. It was a clear display of unchecked power and misplaced blame.

Effective leaders recognize that assigning blame and penalizing high-performing contributors never yields positive results. They understand that program delays can arise despite stellar team performance and expert management. Therefore, it's crucial to establish realistic plans, set reasonable expectations, and incorporate sufficient margin and contingency into schedules and budgets to accommodate unexpected challenges while actively managing risks. Exceptional leaders stand by their teams in the face of adversity while addressing underperformance through training, mentorship, or removal if necessary. I've always encouraged project managers to communicate program plans, status updates, risks, and schedules widely and regularly to ensure transparency, prevent surprises, and drive alignment amongst the team, leadership, and stakeholders.

Embracing a transparent and accountable approach may initially feel daunting, but it can empower and earn you respect. In my experience, this approach has often defused tension and garnered the deep respect of executive leadership. Exceptional leaders value honesty, accountability, and learning from mistakes. They appreciate team members who take responsibility for challenges and issues and offer timely and effective solutions.

Leaders who embrace responsibility and accountability prioritize setting clear goals and expectations while preparing for potential challenges. By accepting responsibility, they reject the notion that success or failure is purely a matter of luck or circumstance beyond their control. They acknowledge that plans may deviate but remain steadfast in adapting and overcoming obstacles. They've *lived* the reality captured in the saying: "Nothing ever goes according to plan."

Taking ownership of mistakes or failures is critical when you're accountable for a task or project. As the leader, you are responsible for any issues involving vendors, team members, subordinates, or others. After acknowledging the problem, outline your plan for corrective action, recovery, and next steps, and then take proactive steps to ensure a successful outcome.[248]

We all make mistakes occasionally and say things that we later regret. The civilized response is simple: apologize. Yet, why does extending an apology seem so challenging for many? Perhaps we don't want to appear weak or lack the self-confidence to *own* our mistakes. Or, possibly, we struggle with empathy or refuse to accept accountability. When we fail to take ownership of a mistake, we miss the opportunity to repair damage, heal wounds, and reset relationships on a more positive footing for the future.

The solution is straightforward:

- Apologize sincerely. Recognize that your actions (or lack thereof) directly affected others. Through apology, all parties can begin the healing process and move forward.

- Avoid scapegoating. Avoid shifting blame elsewhere. Don't resort to empty apologies that deflect responsibility (i.e., "I'm sorry you're upset").

- Listen intently. Allow the person to express their feelings, concerns, and perspectives without interruption. You can demonstrate empathy and understanding by actively listening to their point of view.

- Make amends. Take proactive steps to prevent repeating the same mistake. Don't merely aspire to do better; implement concrete corrective measures that drive actual change.

- Learn and grow. Reflect on the situation and identify what led to the wrongdoing. Use it as an opportunity for personal growth and commit to learning from the experience to avoid repeating similar mistakes in the future.

- Provide time and space. Understand that rebuilding trust takes time—provide the other person the space they need to process their emotions and heal from the situation. Be patient and respectful of their pace.

- Forgive. If you receive a genuine, sincere apology, acknowledge and accept it. We all seek to avoid or resolve conflicts, and apologies are the most effective path.[249]

Owning up shouldn't be confused with the constant need to apologize. Some individuals say "I'm sorry" excessively, which diminishes its meaning. Over-apologizing for situations beyond your control can diminish others' respect for you, as it may suggest a lack of confidence. Moreover, it devalues the impact of future apologies and can become irritating when overused.

Owning up necessitates humility. Conversely, the opposite behavior involves covering up our deficiencies, mistakes, or underperformance, which manifests as defensiveness. "Cover your ass" (CYA) often perpetuates itself in a chain reaction; if superiors practice it, subordinates are likely to follow suit. CYA tendencies frequently coincide with stonewalling, where necessary conversations about underlying issues are blocked. Unfortunately, many employees feel unable to engage in open and honest dialogues about sensitive topics within their workplaces, indicative of a stonewalling culture. Breaking this cycle is challenging yet worthwhile.[250]

Leadership accountability and ownership are essential for fostering trust, driving results, and promoting a culture of responsibility within organizations. By owning decisions, actions, and outcomes, leaders set a positive example and empower their teams to strive for excellence and achieve collective goals effectively.

> *Implementing extreme ownership requires checking your ego and operating with a high degree of humility. Admitting mistakes, taking ownership and developing a plan to overcome challenges are integral to any successful team.* — Jocko Willink, American author, podcast, and naval officer.

Motivation and Engagement

Motivating and inspiring workers is a top priority for leaders and managers. Motivated employees think more creatively, work harder to meet and surpass expectations, and hold themselves and others accountable for results. They exhibit a passion for their work and actively seek learning and growth opportunities, which can fuel higher advancement and success. Motivated workers feel more engaged and connected to the company and their colleagues, which drives the business forward.

> *Employee engagement is an investment we make for the privilege of staying in business.* —Ian Hutchinson, employee engagement speaker and expert.

Despite its importance, employee motivation remains a significant challenge for many managers. Recent polls indicate that only 13% of workers worldwide feel engaged at work. The remaining disengaged, frustrated, and perhaps disgruntled employees consume a disproportionate amount of corporate time, energy, and resources and risk undermining motivated employees and corporate cultures.[251]

So why is motivating employees such a challenge? Perhaps managers pay too little attention to their employees' mental state and personal difficulties and fail to recognize legitimate concerns as they continue to grow and propagate. Sometimes, well-intentioned managers ask their employees all the wrong questions, or their workers aren't sufficiently self-aware to recognize and articulate their frustrations or concerns.

Motivation isn't something that you do *to* people. People ultimately *choose* to be motivated. Leaders play a crucial role in creating the conditions that encourage employee motivation. Genuine, meaningful, and sincere efforts from leaders are essential, as employees can easily discern insincerity or token gestures. Effective recognition goes beyond occasional compliments; it should be specific and describe how the accomplishment positively impacted the company. Public recognition allows others to witness and amplify the message. Acknowledging any sacrifices made by employees further enhances the credibility of gratitude. A genuine and recognition-rich environment fosters employee motivation and encourages them to do their best.[252]

Motivated employees thrive when their work is relevant and meaningful. They seek to contribute to a company's positive societal impact and align their efforts with its vision and strategy. For many, joy arises from fulfilling work that benefits the company, colleagues, customers, or community. Cultivating joyful experiences fosters a shared sense of purpose, commitment, and pride within organizations.

Leaders are essential in ensuring all employees feel heard, recognized, and acknowledged consistently. Great leaders authentically encourage joy in the workplace through sustained efforts in diversity, inclusion, harmony, apprenticeship, and engaged leadership.[253]

> *People often say that motivation doesn't last. Well, neither does bathing—that's why we recommend it daily.* —Zig Ziglar, American author, salesman, and motivational speaker.

Fear vs. Inspiration

It's striking how many managers and leaders resort to using fear as a tool to drive employee performance. While some may appear friendly or approachable on the surface, they readily revert to instilling fear in their workers when faced with pressure or deadlines. Others show little concern for how they are perceived—they embrace a raw and unfiltered approach and even take pride in their reputation for cutthroat behavior.

Research consistently finds that fear-based leadership is ineffective in the long term. While it may produce immediate results, it fosters toxicity and high employee turnover rates. Managers relying on fear tactics are often driven by insecurity and resentment toward those questioning their decisions or authority. They use coercion to maintain control and suppress dissent. For some, their professional identity may be their sole source of personal power, and they recognize its fragility. Alternatively, they may lack the self-esteem needed to empower and uplift their employees, fostering a culture of compliance rather than confidence. Some individuals are ill-suited for leadership roles and lack the necessary character and temperament.

> *People don't leave bad companies, they leave bad managers.*
> —Marcus Buckingham, English author, motivational speaker, and business consultant.

Fear-based managers may demonstrate one or more of the following behaviors at work:

- They fear-monger. Fear-based managers may tend to teach *at* you. Watch for the telltale signs of *my way or the highway*.

- They label their enemies. Fear-based managers quickly assign labels to their co-workers, e.g., friend or enemy, predator or prey. They fear those they meet until they establish that they can control or bully them.

- They're trophy collectors. Fearful managers are constantly finding ways to stoke their egos because they're otherwise unable to feel good about themselves. They amass trophies such as job titles, big budgets, large staff, professional credentials, patent counts, etc.

- They're resistant to learning. Fearful managers don't want to learn new things and don't want their workers to learn anything they don't already know. These managers want to be the de facto source of information within their organizations and seek to ensure that nobody tips over the apple cart by learning something new on their own.

- Metric-centric. Fearful people love measurements, metrics, and KPIs. They weaponize (and even manipulate) data to judge or subjugate others to maintain their perceived superiority. They will embrace petty and meaningless metrics when necessary to accomplish their objective.

Many companies are becoming more proficient at identifying and weeding out fear-based managers. They're also embracing a more humanistic leadership approach to avoid employee turnover. When interviewing, pay attention to telltale signs that can expose fear-based managers.[254]

> *Leadership is based on inspiration, not domination; on co-operation, not intimidation.* —William Arthur Ward, American motivational author, speaker, and college administrator.

Inspirational leaders, by comparison, employ various behaviors and techniques to motivate their workers. The following are some typical examples:

- They provide autonomy and flexibility, entrusting their employees to utilize their unique abilities to do their best work.

- They reward outstanding performance through positive reinforcement.

- They invest in their workers and encourage them to learn and grow through training and increasingly challenging assignments.

- They instill purpose in their workers' roles. When everyone feels a part of something meaningful and worthwhile and believes their jobs matter, they remain motivated to excel continually.

- They seek input from their workers on decisions, large and small. Everyone wants to be heard and appreciated, and when managers ask for their opinions, this creates a sense of belonging, which makes them feel like they matter.

- They set a positive example for their workers. When everyone on the team sees their manager as someone who works smart, meets deadlines, and takes their job seriously, others will emulate their positive behavior. Attitude is everything, and effective managers recognize that.[255]

In leadership, inspiring others through vision, empathy, and encouragement cultivates a culture of growth and innovation, whereas leading through fear can stifle creativity and erode morale. By embracing inspiration over fear, leaders empower their teams to overcome challenges with resilience, creativity, and a shared commitment to achieving organizational success.

Success is not just what you accomplish in life, it is about what you inspire others to do. —Unknown.

Goals

Setting goals and helping employees meet them are among leaders' most rewarding pursuits. Effective goal-setting can fuel a company to new heights. If done poorly, employees can become demotivated, disillusioned, or worse.

Goals serve as crucial guides, steering individuals, teams, and organizations away from stagnation and mediocrity toward meaningful endeavors and accomplishments. Aligned goals focus efforts and foster motivation, driving individuals and teams to learn, develop, and perform at their best. They instill purpose and direction, fueling progress and growth across all levels of an organization.

Psychological studies consistently affirm that the most motivating goals are clearly defined and time-specific. While goals can be tied to behavior or outcome, behavioral-based goals tend to be more effective in motivating workers. Workers can become overly fixated on results, whereas behavioral change can yield long-term benefits and sustainable progress.[256]

> *While a fixation on results is certainly unhealthy, short-term goals can be useful development tools, if they are balanced within a nurturing long-term philosophy.* —Josh Waitzskin, American former chess player, martial arts competitor, and author.

Some individuals resist setting goals, especially stretch goals because they are reluctant to be measured against them and held accountable. They may fear negative repercussions, whether financial or reputational, if they fall short. Often, they cite risk and uncertainty as valid reasons for resisting challenging goals, questioning why they should be held to standards that may not be achievable through no fault of their own. This mindset can lead to overly simplistic and meaningless goals or easily attainable deadlines. People who set goals that are easy to achieve hope that a near-perfect record of goal completion will lead to positive performance evaluations, bonuses, or salary adjustments. However, setting trivial goals can result in subpar performance, ultimately failing to achieve the desired project and organizational outcomes.

Effective managers offer a blend of objectives when setting performance goals, ranging from those with high confidence and predictability to challenging or stretch goals. Some adhere to the Three C's Rule:

- Common: Commonality ensures alignment toward a shared goal.

- Compelling: When a goal is compelling, it inspires the necessary energy and commitment to achieve it.

- Cooperative: Cooperative goals necessitate teamwork for successful accomplishment.[257]

Setting moderate goals ensures that employees can demonstrate achievement and build confidence and pride. Stretch goals also fuel the employee's growth and development. They encourage stepping out of comfort zones, exploring new challenges, and discovering potential passions. Achieving these goals can lead to a profound sense of accomplishment.

In my experience, the best goals are designed to challenge and inspire excellence. They should motivate employees to deliver exceptional results and help the team, organization, and company meet their objectives. Stretch goals should be ambitious enough to make individuals or teams slightly nervous or uncomfortable. Even if stretch goals aren't fully met, striving for them usually leads to higher achievement than would have otherwise occurred. Managers should avoid penalizing employees for missing their stretch goals. Remember that stretch goals are designed to be challenging to meet. Therefore, they should only be considered *upside* metrics, which can only *elevate* a worker's performance review when positive achievement is demonstrated. Stretch goals, when missed, should never lower a worker's performance review, as that could lead to undermining the individual or team's motivation to strive for future stretch goals.

> *The greatest danger for most of us is not that our aim is too high and we miss it, but that it is too low and we reach it.* — Michelangelo, Italian sculptor, painter, architect, and poet of the High Renaissance.

"SMART" goals are a widely used framework for setting clear, achievable objectives. Each component of SMART—Specific, Measurable, Achievable, Relevant, and Time-bound—plays a crucial role in effective goal-setting:

- Specific: Goals should be clear and detailed, outlining precisely what is to be accomplished. This prevents ambiguity and helps maintain focus on a defined outcome.

- Measurable: Incorporating measurable criteria allows progress to be tracked. This ensures that goals can be evaluated, providing motivation and a clear indication of success or areas for improvement.

- Achievable: Goals should be realistic and attainable based on available resources and constraints. Setting achievable targets prevents discouragement and keeps morale high.

- Relevant: The goal should align with broader objectives and priorities. Relevance ensures that the goal matters and contributes meaningfully to overall growth or success.

- Time-bound: Every goal should have a deadline or timeframe for completion. This creates a sense of urgency and helps maintain momentum by setting clear expectations for progress.

Each element ensures that goals are well-structured, realistic, and focused, increasing the likelihood of successful outcomes.

Setting priorities and daily goals requires focus and discipline. Identifying the primary objectives that need to be accomplished each day and week is essential. Breaking them into smaller tasks allows for a sense of progress and momentum, which fuels continued performance. Conversely, overwhelming yourself with an extensive list of goals can drain your energy and confidence, making the workload seem insurmountable.[258]

A goal properly set is halfway reached. —Zig Ziglar.

Regular monitoring and assessment of goal progress are essential to ensure that teams and employees stay on track toward achieving their objectives. In cases where goals require adjustment, management approval is necessary to prevent individuals from manipulating the goal process. For personal employee goals, each employee should be involved in developing or supporting the development of their goals to ensure their buy-in.

Setting goals is crucial for providing direction, motivation, and clarity in personal and professional endeavors. By defining clear and achievable goals, individuals and organizations can enhance focus, track progress, and ultimately achieve greater success and fulfillment.

Connect With Your Team

Building strong relationships is fundamental to effective management. To inspire your team, nurturing healthy interpersonal connections with your teammates is essential.

> *Lack of connection starts contention and leads to conflict. Great leaders reduce conflict and create connections. Connections lead to trust.* —Mareo McCracken, author, and sales and growth expert.

An exceptional relationship is rooted in honesty and trust, which enables people to resolve disagreements and differences productively. Each party is committed to the other's development and growth rather than self-interest. When you lower your guard to expose your authentic self, people will most likely find you to be more likable and interesting. Curiosity about others fuels engagement and deepens bonds.

In the business world, the faster you can trust one another, the sooner you can collaborate and build a productive team and organization. There's no exact formula for success, as working relationships continuously evolve. Simply initiating the process of improving a relationship can lead to tangible progress—you never know what's possible until you take the first step.

Post-pandemic, we continue interacting with many coworkers through Zoom and other virtual tools. With many feeling a heightened need for deeper connections, managers have a unique opportunity to strengthen these relationships. More than ever, investing in building meaningful connections with employees and coworkers is essential.[259]

I've always made it a point to socialize regularly with my teams, whether during lunch breaks, dinners, beer bashes, team-building offsites, or business trips. I tend to steer clear of business discussions while bonding, focusing instead on non-work-related chats, which stimulate energy and engagement. Creating an environment where team members feel comfortable opening up and connecting on a personal level can lead to stronger bonds and a more positive team dynamic overall.

I've found that the most successful and enjoyable companies spend time, money, and energy encouraging friendship and deep worker connections. At ARGOSystems, we embraced a vibrant social atmosphere. Company-wide, we had weekly Friday beer bashes with live bands, organized ski trips, camping adventures, and themed parties. Many enduring friendships were formed through these interactions, contributing to our positive work environment. Amidst our hard work, we supported each other, decompressed during stressful times, and celebrated victories together.

At Endwave, we cultivated a similar culture, organizing events that brought our team closer together. We often enjoyed after-hours activities with our spouses and significant others. One of my annual traditions was a water ski trip to the nearby Delta, followed by a barbecue dinner and poolside relaxation at my house. We celebrated important milestones together, attending each other's weddings and bachelor parties. During work crunches, we united to work nights and weekends, ensuring we met our deadlines. These personal connections were integral to our productivity and success.

Forming personal connections with co-workers can lead to lasting friendships that transcend the workplace. These deep bonds foster co-operation, collaboration, and a sense of security among team members. When conflicts arise, resolving them becomes easier and more direct when individuals share strong connections. Such relationships help dissolve the "us versus them" mentality that can prevail in organizations characterized by tribalism or departmental solidarity.

While nurturing relationships with co-workers is vital, managers must balance fostering deep connections and maintaining professional boundaries. Leaders must be able to address issues objectively, especially with problematic team members. Employees should recognize and respect their manager's authority. Further, it's important to avoid showing favoritism, as perceptions of unfair treatment can impact performance evaluations and opportunities for advancement. Respecting personal boundaries and maintaining professionalism while fostering friendliness is key to creating a positive work environment.

> *If you are going to be a leader, you are not going to please everybody. You have to hold people accountable. Even if you have that moment of being uncomfortable.* —Kobe Bryant.

While managers are primarily evaluated on their team's performance, results, and impact, more attention is now being given to assessing *how* they lead their teams. The following questions can help with such assessments:

- How satisfied are your subordinates?
- Are they being treated respectfully?
- Are you effectively inspiring them?

- Are you taking an active role in demonstrating recognition and appreciation for their work?

- Are you actively supporting their career planning and pursuits?

The best leaders understand that *how* their workers are treated, motivated, and inspired is central to their engagement and performance. But while employee opinions matter, management isn't a popularity contest—keeping everyone happy continuously is a lofty aspiration for most leaders. Striking a balance between achieving objectives and fostering positive relationships is one of many keys to effective leadership.

Multigenerational Teams

Managing across generations can be a real challenge, especially when there's a significant age gap between the manager and their team. How does the manager engage, collaborate, and relate with others when they feel they have so little in common? Unfortunately, when we are fundamentally un-relatable, we can fall into the trap of using harmful stereotypes or blaming solvable problems on each other instead of working to understand and appreciate the differences that distance us. The key to success lies in embracing an attitude of appreciation for the diversity within our teams, whether age-related or otherwise. There's valuable insight to be gained from understanding the preferences, habits, and behaviors of colleagues from different generational backgrounds when we're willing to learning from them.

Strength lies in differences, not in similarities. —Unknown.

There are currently five generations in the workforce. Each exhibits unique personality traits and values:

- The Silent Generation (born 1925 to 1945).
- Baby Boomers (1946 to 1964).
- Generation X (1965 to 1980).
- Millennials (1981 to 2000).
- Generation Z (2001 to 2020).

Many individuals, including behavioral experts, have developed generalizations for each of these groups of workers, aiming to outline their behavioral tendencies. Regrettably, many discussions tend to focus on these stereotypes as negatives rather than taking the time to recognize that the significant differences we all have are positives and something worthy of understanding, valuing, and accepting.

When dealing with age-related stereotypes and discrimination, we should put ourselves in the shoes of those who are being discriminated against. Consider that those who are threatened or marginalized by age-based stereotypes become less able to commit to their current job, pursue long-term professional goals, and are less adjusted psychologically, given their lack of engagement or immersion into their team and culture. When we seek to overcome our biases, we commit to educating ourselves on the realities different generations have faced throughout their careers. Understanding those nuances is essential to acceptance, which is critical for any manager.

Individuals who feel marginalized or threatened by age-based stereotypes may struggle to commit to their current job, pursue long-term professional goals, or fully engage with their team and company culture. Overcoming our biases involves educating ourselves about the diverse realities different generations have experienced throughout their careers. This understanding is critical to fostering acceptance, an essential quality for any manager.

Respecting boundaries is essential, especially when managing diverse age groups. Each generation brings unique beliefs and values to the table. For instance, topics like diversity, equity, and inclusion (DEI), mental health, and gender roles are now openly discussed in the workplace, whereas they were once considered taboo. Younger workers are generally more progressive about social issues and are comfortable discussing them at work. Conversely, older workers may be less inclined to engage in these discussions for fear of judgment. Personal feelings matter, and managers must approach sensitive topics carefully and empathetically. While not everyone may agree, they should understand why specific issues are valued within the organization. Race, gender relations, and marriage equality may elicit diverse responses across generations.

The healthiest work cultures make employees feel comfortable when asking for help, taking risks, and sharing ideas. They ensure that employees experience psychological safety at all times. When addressing DEI issues and policies, legal, moral, and strategic perspectives must be considered. It's important to explain to employees why these challenging topics are being dealt with in the workplace and how they tie to the organization's values and the overall mission. Focus on common norms shared by the team and minimize the differences. Avoid favoritism and underscore the value of diversity, highlighting the diverse experience base that a multi-generational team brings to the organization.[260]

Each generation has unique lessons to teach and insights to share. Everyone has valuable experiences and knowledge to contribute. For example, younger individuals may lack extensive experience but compensate with energy, intellect, creativity, and inspiration. Amazing things can happen when workers are valued and appreciated for their diverse contributions, and differences are seen as strengths, not weaknesses.

A Calming Force

Working for a manager with a hair-trigger temper is challenging. Almost anything can set them off, and the tension in the room rises once they're angry. Their anger seems to spread, leading to arguments and discomfort among the team. While they may think their outbursts display power and influence, they often appear weak and out of control. These are not the traits you want in a leader along your career path.

> *Self control is strength. Calmness is mastery. You have to get to the point where your mood doesn't shift based on the insignificant actions of someone else. Don't allow others to control the direction of your life. Don't allow your emotions to overpower your intelligence.* —Morgan Freeman.

Experienced leaders are invaluable when guiding teams through tough times. Younger workers often worry and react strongly to unexpected challenges, but seasoned leaders bring a positive perspective and unwavering optimism. Their calm demeanor and problem-solving approach help soothe frayed nerves and refocus energies on adapting and overcoming obstacles. Maintaining emotional calm across the team stabilizes stress levels, boosts morale, and enhances overall performance.

Participating in or leading a complex program or long-term corporate pursuit is akin to running a marathon, not a sprint. Confidence and calmness are crucial enablers during difficult periods at work. In contentious and stressful meetings, especially with senior management, I've often challenged myself to be the calmest person in the room. While others may try to stoke emotions, I refrain from joining the skirmish. Instead, I offer controlled, restrained, and confident responses or advice. This often helps lower the temperature in the room and fosters a more productive interchange among participants.

Words carry consequences and profound power, underscoring the importance of thoughtful speech and projecting purpose and empathy. Impulsive words risk derailing our message and objectives. By focusing on our speech and temperament, we become more mindful and considerate communicators. Cultivating kindness and calmness in our conversations fosters stronger connections and relationships.

Once words are spoken, they cannot be retrieved. Losing one's temper often leads to regret later on. Instead, take time to reflect for a day or so. If your sentiments remain unchanged, communicate them calmly and respectfully. Additionally, angry emails may find their way to unintended recipients, so anticipate the broader audience before hitting send.[261]

Leadership calmness is helpful when navigating turbulent situations with clarity, resilience, and decisiveness— it also fosters stability and confidence among teams. By embodying composure and emotional intelligence, leaders can effectively manage crises, inspire trust, and steer their organizations toward sustainable growth and success.

You can always tell someone to go to hell tomorrow. —Tom Murphy, American broadcasting executive.

Laughter is Healthy

Humor has the potential to benefit businesses substantially. When applied appropriately, humor can enhance a customer's perception of value, which can lead to an increased willingness to pay for products or services. Research indicates that when leaders use humor at work, they're 23% more respected, their teams are 15% more satisfied with their job, and workers find their bosses to be 27% more motivating and admirable. Humor is a sign of emotional intelligence—which can be a competitive advantage and lead to increased employee retention, higher levels of innovation, and improved teamwork.

Work can often become stressful, especially when deadlines approach. How individuals respond to this pressure varies greatly. While some maintain a calm demeanor, others may internalize their stress until it erupts explosively. Humor and laughter are pivotal in alleviating tension and providing perspective when dealing with complex challenges and painful setbacks. Leaders who exhibit a keen sense of humor tend to be more approachable—their behavior fosters cheerful environments where authenticity and creativity thrive. Humor facilitates deeper connections among colleagues, cultivating trust and respect while promoting a sense of shared humanity through laughter.[262]

Numerous studies have underscored the advantages of laughter in professional settings. Physiologically, laughter triggers the release of endorphins, which stimulate circulation and aid in muscle relaxation, ultimately reducing stress's physical symptoms. Remember, though, that workplace humor should always be respectful and non-threatening. Teasing employees or sharing off-color jokes can create a toxic environment and should be avoided. No one should feel pressured to laugh at jokes that make them uncomfortable or turn them into unwilling targets. Instead, opt for self-deprecating humor, which humanizes leaders and fosters connections with colleagues and employees. The key is to keep humor clean, decent, and professional while enjoying the lighter side of work life.[263]

I've always appreciated and embraced humor in the workplace and at home. It is a powerful bonding agent, bringing teams together in a way that nothing else can. The memories of a great laughter session can be revisited repeatedly, especially when new material is scarce. Laughter offers a temporary escape from the daily grind, allowing people to let down their guard and enjoy the moment. It adds a vibrant spark to any story and serves as a reminder that work doesn't have to be serious and dull. After all, everyone is drawn to those who bring joy and laughter into their lives—I know I am.

Thankfully, humor is a skill that can be cultivated through minor adjustments in behavior and mindset. Considering humor's substantial benefits, company leaders should prioritize laughter, fun, and play during team-building activities, especially off-site events. A well-balanced blend of work and play fosters a more vibrant and cohesive team dynamic, ultimately contributing to camaraderie and success.

> *A sense of humor is part of the art of leadership, of getting along with people, of getting things done.* —Dwight D. Eisenhower.

Penny-Wise and Pound-Foolish

Some leaders show poor judgment in their corporate spending habits. Excessive frugality can negatively impact workers and their organization, including innovation, collaboration, job satisfaction, work culture, productivity, team building, and customer relations.

For example, at one company where I worked, the leadership team decided to forego providing bare employee essentials like free coffee, tea, water, or snacks. Their behavior illustrates a lack of consideration for employee well-being and morale, especially in an environment like Silicon Valley, where such perks are commonplace.

Some managers become agitated over expenditures on tools and lab supplies. They may implement strict policies to lock up certain items to ensure they're tightly monitored and controlled against theft or unauthorized use.

By comparison, decades ago, Bill Hewlett, the co-founder of Hewlett-Packard, encountered a locked stockroom while working on a personal project at the HP lab one weekend. A manager had decided that an open stockroom was a "license to steal" and padlocked the door. Bill immediately ordered the lock to be cut and left a note with instructions never to lock the stockroom again. He believed allowing employees free access to company parts, even for personal projects, would foster their passion, technical skills, and curiosity—they would likely learn valuable lessons, which might, in some way, ultimately benefit the company. I completely agree.

> *Without trust we don't truly collaborate; we merely coordinate or, at best, cooperate. It is trust that transforms a group of people into a team.* —Stephen Covey, American educator, author, businessman, and motivational speaker.

Whenever I was responsible for test labs, I made it a point to classify specific tools and supplies as "consumables," acknowledging that they would naturally wear out, get lost, or be misplaced. I ensured budgets were allocated to replenish these supplies regularly. Occasionally, some items would migrate from my department to another, thus unintentionally benefiting others across the company, which I felt was entirely reasonable.

Some penny-pinching leaders hesitate to invest in team-building activities, but I firmly believe such investments are crucial for a company's continued success. These activities, ranging from beer bashes to company picnics, foster camaraderie and strengthen bonds among team members. They also improve customer and vendor relations, as inviting them to corporate events can enhance these connections. I encouraged my team to be generous hosts during business trips, balancing hospitality with fiscal responsibility. Nurturing relationships through such activities is one of the most valuable expenditures a company can make.

Pleasure in the job puts perfection in the work. —Aristotle, Greek philosopher, and scientist.

Likewise, I've advocated for expansive in-person attendance at offsite design reviews and other critical program events. Bringing your team together with strategic vendors, contractors, partners, and customers builds essential relationships, which enhances collaboration and long-term success. The benefits gained easily offset the incremental travel expenses, making it a worthwhile investment. Offsite attendance, especially when gatherings are held at desirable locations, is also a great way of recognizing and appreciating your team's contributions.

It's not the money that matters. It is how you use it that determines its true value. —Unknown.

Effective leaders are wise and prudent in their spending approvals. If your leadership team doesn't see the value in funding activities that boost productivity, loyalty, passion, collaboration, and corporate pride, they're failing their employees and stakeholders.

While financial constraints are inevitable, exceptional leaders prioritize investments that yield long-term benefits and avoid instinctively tightening the corporate purse strings. Constrained budgets can and should influence spending habits, but there are always ways of achieving your objectives when you apply a degree of creativity and dedication. Companies don't need to be rich to be fun—they just need to be led by those adept at making every dollar count without torturing their workforce in the process.

Passion, Strengths, and Superpowers

"Follow your passion" is a famous saying, often directed at young people. However, this advice can feel overwhelming. It places undue pressure on them to pinpoint a single interest to pursue, even before they understand what they enjoy doing. This approach can result in frustration and disillusionment. Additionally, it discourages the exploration of diverse interests and experiences, which is crucial for personal growth during schooling and beyond.

> *One of the huge mistakes people make is that they try to force an interest on themselves. You don't choose your passions; your passions choose you.* —Jeff Bezos.

What exactly is "passion," and how do we find it? Many believe that their passion lies in activities they find enjoyable. However, research sheds further light on this topic. It suggests that passion is rooted in one's values and the impact they create for themselves or others. Simply engaging in activities for pleasure may not be sustainable in the long run. Pursuits that align with your values and allow you to make a meaningful impact are more likely to endure. Passion intertwined with *care* is a crucial combination.

Passions can be dynamic, evolving gradually as your values and interests shift. If you're unsure about your values or passions, exposing yourself to various work opportunities can aid your search. It's also worth considering that passion may not be something you stumble upon but rather cultivate. Tailoring your job to include tasks that spark your curiosity can be beneficial. Alternatively, pursuing your passion outside of work might be the most viable option if such adjustments aren't feasible.[264]

Many individuals follow their passion only to realize they've entered the wrong career or made poor strategic choices. We shouldn't allow our emotions and desires to override practicality and realism. For instance, if we persist in a passionate but failing endeavor, we should reassess the influence of our emotions. While miscalculation is common, reexamination is too seldom practiced. Investing more resources into a lost cause simply because of sunk costs is not a valid justification.[265]

Discovering passion in our work often proves impractical in the long term. Who would handle the essential tasks that nobody desires if everyone pursued their passions? As we age, the demands of paying mortgages, buying food, and covering educational expenses become more pressing. While a fortunate minority may indulge in work they adore and earn substantial incomes from it, most of us strive to find slivers of satisfaction in less fulfilling activities while earning our regular paychecks.

Many inexperienced entrepreneurs believe that starting a business will lead to passion-filled work. However, while the storefront may suggest success, behind the scenes lies the reality: the toil of everyday work, the less glamorous operations, the challenges of financing and meeting payroll, and other necessary but unexciting tasks that sustain their business.

Entrepreneurs often mistakenly believe that passion precedes entrepreneurial effort, yet it's often the reverse. Entrepreneurial passion intensifies with increased effort. The more entrepreneurs invest in their startups, the more enthusiasm they develop. Small victories fuel more significant effort, leading to greater success and more profound passion. Successful entrepreneurs seize compelling opportunities, addressing widespread needs through hard work and dedication. By taking action while others wait, they acquire invaluable experience, skills, and expertise essential for building thriving businesses, leaving bystanders merely observing from the sidelines.

When exploring your passion, it's vital to maintain realistic expectations and prepare for inevitable challenges along the journey. Look beyond mere enjoyment and consider expanding your passions to encompass broader aspects of life. Your passion might stem from providing for your family, employees, and customers or achieving financial stability for a comfortable lifestyle and memorable experiences. The key is recognizing that constant passion isn't necessary; contributing value to the world, community, or loved ones while earning a living is a meaningful pursuit in its own right.[266]

> *Working hard for something we don't care about is called stress. Working hard for something we love is called passion.* —Simon Sinek, British-American author, and inspirational speaker.

Employers play an essential role in enabling employees to explore their passions and grow professionally and personally through new skills and opportunities. While the adage "employees quit because of bad bosses" is often reiterated, we sometimes overlook that employees also leave unsatisfying *jobs*. Individuals depart when their roles lack excitement, fail to leverage their strengths and skills fully, and offer limited opportunities for growth and learning. Many harbor unfulfilled passions due to the demands of work and home, with only a fortunate few securing jobs aligned with their interests. For the majority, however, their passions linger and languish, but they don't go away.[267]

Effective managers delegate diverse tasks to each employee and closely monitor their performance on each assignment. They observe how individuals tackle tasks, identifying those completed swiftly, effortlessly, and with enthusiasm. Recognizing these unique talents or "superpowers" marks the initial step in cultivating a team of experts who leverage their strengths or passions. Employees who are enabled to work in areas where they excel are likely to derive greater satisfaction from their roles.

The term "superpower" refers to identifying a person's natural strength. Identifying strengths can be challenging since we often downplay or undervalue what comes effortlessly to us, almost reflexively, like breathing. When your boss recognizes a task that aligns with your strengths and assigns it to you, you might feel underutilized or undervalued because it feels easy. However, the ease stems from your natural talent, an inherent advantage that should be leveraged.[268]

Identifying a worker's superpower and investing effort to develop it to an expert level often leads to a blossoming of passion. You naturally improve when you dedicate time and energy to something you enjoy and excel at. People don't usually quit activities they're skilled at because being the best at something is inherently enjoyable.

At Facebook, I witnessed firsthand how company leaders actively encourage employees to seek out and recruit others to form working groups for exploring exciting new projects through their renowned *hackathons*. These hacks could span a day, a month, or even longer, providing opportunities for employees to engage in activities they are passionate about. Employee transfers between various operating groups are also encouraged, which fosters skill acquisition and personal growth. Facebook has reaped substantial benefits from promoting such endeavors, evident from their hackathons' multitude of inventions and products. It exemplifies a startup mentality persisting within a large corporation, continually igniting creative sparks and passionate work across its workforce.

> *If the flower does not bloom, fix the environment in which it grows, not the flower.* —Alexander Den Heijer, inspirational speaker, trainer, and writer.

Of course, the hack culture isn't exclusive to Facebook; Google also advocates for its employees to dedicate approximately 15% of their time to pursuing personal projects. This encouragement reflects a corporate strategy that values employees trusting their curiosity and prioritizing their insights alongside the company's objectives—a form of corporate seed-funding for innovation. However, this approach thrives only when employees are granted freedom from their primary responsibilities to explore their passions, unencumbered by micromanagement.[269]

Regrettably, many companies merely pay lip service to allowing employees to explore their passions and move around within the organization. Their fixation on deadlines and efficiency often undermines efforts to support a dynamic workforce. I've witnessed this firsthand at multiple companies, where employees express interest in new assignments or projects only to encounter resistance from unsupportive managers who fail to approve transfer or sharing arrangements. Too often, incumbent managers refuse to release employees, citing potential disruptions to their current pursuits. This leaves employees feeling disillusioned, trapped in dead-end roles, and discourages others with similar aspirations from seeking more engaging opportunities within the company.

When managers become the primary impediment to talent mobility or workforce flexibility, examining the incentives driving their behavior becomes necessary. Fostering a culture of mobility requires reevaluating how managers are recognized and rewarded. Performance objectives should incentivize the rotation of personnel, particularly high-potential talent, and be integral to managers' performance evaluations. Outstanding organizations offer substantial internal recognition and compensation to managers who excel in developing their team members and providing growth opportunities. Such companies cultivate an environment where mobility is not just encouraged but expected. In this context, the best managers become talent magnets who attract employees eager to advance their careers and explore their passions under their guidance.[270]

> *People say you have to have a lot of passion for what you're doing, and it is totally true... you've got to find what you love. And that is as true for your work as it is for your lovers. Your work is going to fill a large part of your life, and the only way to be truly satisfied is to do what you believe is great work. And the only way to do great work is to love what you do... Don't settle.* —Steve Jobs.

Debate and Groupthink

As a manager, you'll likely find yourself in many meetings. You may eventually loathe meetings as a matter of principle, believing they waste valuable time. However, in many instances, meetings are both necessary and effective. Embracing diverse opinions and fostering creative exchanges within meetings can bring a wealth of knowledge, perspectives, and clarity to complex issues, resulting in higher-quality outcomes. However, meetings can also go awry for various reasons, such as when differing perspectives are stifled, and groupthink takes hold, leading to poor decision-making and a lack of innovation.

"Groupthink" is characterized by groups of individuals making irrational or suboptimal decisions to conform, particularly when dissent is discouraged or perceived as impossible. It often arises when group members prioritize harmony and cohesion over critical thinking. Decision-making under pressure exacerbates groupthink, leading participants to suppress doubts and concerns in favor of consensus, even if it means disregarding ethical or moral considerations. Groupthink can also manifest when a dominant leader exerts influence over the group or members engage in bullying to uphold group identity. Additionally, it occurs when participants lack sufficient knowledge about the topic, leading them to defer to individuals who appear more informed or assertive.

To combat groupthink, it's crucial to identify the situations and conditions that enable it to occur. When groups feel threatened, they may adopt an "us versus them" mentality. This can prompt members to accept group consensus and perspectives that don't necessarily align with their personal views. Additionally, groupthink often arises in rushed decision-making scenarios. To mitigate this risk, adequate time should be allocated for thorough discussion and deliberation, allowing every member to contribute in a safe environment where dissent is welcomed. Educating workers about common cognitive biases and empowering them to recognize and resist them can reduce the likelihood of groupthink.

The important thing about groupthink is that it works not so much by censoring dissent as by making dissent seem somehow improbable. —James Surowiecki, American journalist.

Effective leaders tend to set the meeting stage, launch discussions, and then step back to allow participants to debate the issues themselves. Often, it becomes helpful to appoint an individual as the group's *devil's advocate*, who will argue against the consensus, highlight potential flaws, or call out groupthink as it occurs.

Research consistently finds that dissent fosters enhanced creativity, increased innovation, and decreased groupthink within organizations. Diversity in demographics and thought further diminishes the likelihood of groupthink; when members bring varied backgrounds, beliefs, and personality traits to the table, a wealth of unique ideas emerges, driving innovation and mitigating homogenous thinking.

Additionally, rewarding workers for their independent thought and natural creativity reinforces a culture that values diverse perspectives and encourages innovation.[271]

Countless times, I've convened meetings where it initially seemed everyone had already formed their opinions, only to witness those perspectives shift during lively debates. Consequently, I've learned to avoid the trap of micromanaging meetings to rush toward consensus. Instead, it's more effective to establish meeting parameters, encourage full participation, and lightly moderate discussions to maintain focus without stifling creativity.

Allowing discussions to evolve organically encourages deeper engagement and often yields unexpected insights or inspiration. The magic of collaborative dialogue lies in its ability to generate unforeseen outcomes, leaving participants with a renewed appreciation for teamwork and a shared sense of accomplishment.

> *It is better to debate a question without settling it than to settle a question without debating it.* —Joseph Joubert, French moralist, and essayist.

Speaking Truth to Power

Speaking truth to power can be fraught with risk, depending on the personality, integrity, confidence, and behavior of the person in power. It's important to be thoroughly prepared and rehearsed in your messaging, armed with a well-supported rationale, and supported by facts and data. Before broaching potentially unfavorable truths with individuals in positions of power, it's crucial to anticipate their potential reactions. I can attest to several unfortunate examples of how my candid upward feedback to leadership was met with contempt.

Recognize the risks involved, carefully assess the judiciousness and significance of your action, and proceed with utmost caution.

> *Leaders who don't listen will eventually be surrounded by people who have nothing to say.* —Andy Stanley, Leadership Author, Speaker, and Pastor.

Effective leaders actively seek out and surround themselves with free and independent thinkers who offer unfiltered opinions and advice. They rely on such input to inform their thoughts, actions, and decisions. Conversely, ineffective leaders surround themselves with individuals who lack independence—they favor sycophants who offer nothing but flattery and unwavering loyalty or fealty. Among the worst leaders are those who feign appreciation for critical advice but react angrily or seek retribution upon receiving it.

> *When we speak truth to power, we are ignored at best and brutally suppressed at worst.* —Jeremy Hammond, American activist.

Workforce silence often signifies a failure to foster an environment that encourages truthful and transparent feedback—leaders who intentionally or inadvertently cultivate a culture of fear promote silence among their team members. Over time, employees learn that voicing critical or honest opinions, especially regarding executive behavior or performance, may result in swift retaliation. When workers feel psychologically unsafe, they become hesitant to speak up, offer comments, or pose challenging questions. Consequently, they remain silent, even when the CEO invites honest and truthful comments from employees. This is evident when colleagues avoid eye contact and retreat into silence, seeking safety through avoidance.[272]

> *Intellectuals may like to think of themselves as people who 'speak truth to power', but too often they are people who speak lies to gain power.* —Thomas Sowell, American author, economist, political commentator, social theorist, and educator.

Effective leaders cultivate safe and trusting cultures by addressing the various social factors that trigger threats in their employees' minds. For employees to perform at their best and take risks, such as speaking transparently to leadership, leaders must create the following conditions:

- Respect and appreciation: Workers need to feel that their opinions and contributions are valued.

- Predictive cause and effect: Employees must know they'll be supported and treated fairly when they speak or share their thoughts.

- Control: Workers need to feel that they have control over their lives and work.

- Psychological safety: Employees should feel secure expressing their thoughts and opinions without fear of ridicule or retribution. Leaders must create an environment where open dialogue is encouraged, and differences are respected.

- Emotional safety: Team members should feel emotionally supported and valued by their colleagues and superiors. Leaders should foster empathy, compassion, and a sense of belonging within the organization.

- Intellectual safety: Employees should feel comfortable exploring new ideas, challenging assumptions, and experimenting without fear of criticism. Leaders should promote a culture of curiosity, innovation, and continuous learning.

- Physical safety: Workers should feel physically safe in their work environment, free from hazards or threats to their well-being. Leaders must prioritize workplace safety and ensure appropriate measures are in place to protect employees from harm.

- Fairness: Workers must believe they'll be treated fairly and equitably in every situation.

The best leaders exhibit empathy and genuine curiosity. They want to be told the truth about their performance issues and legitimate worker concerns. They want to be called out when they make mistakes so that they can learn and become better. Their persistent curiosity will draw out the information they seek from employees when they feel safe to share.

Surround yourself with people who will reflect the good and bad back to you. —Michelle Obama, American attorney, author, and former First Lady of the United States.

Managing Up

Managing up is a crucial skill that enhances business outcomes and furthers career growth. It involves proactive communication and advocating for oneself within the organizational hierarchy. While in an ideal world, bosses would be competent, effective, and attentive to their employees' needs, reality often falls short of this ideal. Therefore, it becomes incumbent upon individuals to take ownership of their career development by actively managing their relationships and interactions with supervisors and higher-ups.

The perfect employee is the one who motivates their boss as much as their boss motivates them. —Unknown.

Many believe that excelling in their job will naturally lead to better assignments, promotions, and recognition for their performance.

However, some may work for a toxic or ineffective boss who shows little interest in their career satisfaction, trajectory, or well-being. Sometimes, bosses may be clueless about their employees' contributions or fail to recognize exceptional work. They may also neglect to mentor employees or contribute to their career planning, instead piling on additional tasks without providing opportunities for growth, position changes, or salary increases.

Workers at all levels should take control of their careers and seek the support of their bosses to achieve their objectives. Here are some critical steps to consider:

- Set clear goals. Define your career objectives and communicate them effectively to your boss.

- Promote yourself. Proactively advocate for opportunities that align with your career goals and aspirations. Ensure your boss recognizes your output and impact when you perform well or over-perform. This takes a degree of finesse to avoid bragging or alienating others.

- Perform consistently. Strive to meet or exceed goals, keeping your boss informed of progress. Be honest and realistic, under-promise, and over-deliver.

- Communicate effectively. Practice clear and concise communication with your boss, informing them of your progress and any challenges you may encounter. Truth and transparency are the best approach whenever things derail.

- Take initiative. Always be prepared, and do your homework or research. Take ownership of your projects and initiatives, demonstrating leadership and initiative. If you don't know something, admit it.

- Develop skills. Continuously develop and enhance your skills to remain relevant and valuable to the organization.

- Build relationships. Cultivate positive relationships with your boss and other key stakeholders within the organization. Build a solid professional network within and outside the organization to explore new opportunities and stay informed about industry trends.
- Support decisions. Support your boss's decisions, even if you disagree. Avoid passive-aggressive behavior, and never say, "I told you so," if a decision proves wrong.
- Don't complain. Instead of complaining about decisions or situations, offer a different perspective or an even better solution.
- Take charge. If your boss is toxic, incompetent, or clueless, consider seeking new opportunities outside the organization or with another company. Taking action against an underperforming boss can be risky and may result in undesirable outcomes.

Managing up is more than just dealing with bad bosses; all managers benefit from employee insights, especially when they may not be aware of certain aspects. Workers should enhance communication and provide honest, productive, and professional feedback. Effective managing up involves influencing decision-makers, which can be daunting but is integral to career growth. Ultimately, it enhances business impact and personal success. Making your boss look good fosters a positive atmosphere and encourages them to listen to your ideas in the future. Positivity begets more positivity.[273]

Sleep to Perform

Sleep is widely recognized as crucial for health and happiness, and it significantly impacts work performance across all roles and responsibilities. Recent studies have highlighted that insufficient sleep can diminish a leader's perceived charisma, lower motivation levels, and hinder their ability to manage stress effectively.[274] Other research revealed that poor sleep habits result in American businesses losing up to $411 billion annually in productivity.[275]

Consistency in sleep patterns is more critical than the amount of sleep for optimal work performance. This involves adhering to a regular bedtime every night, disconnecting from electronic devices, and allowing the body and mind to unwind from daily demands. Effective leaders recognize the significance of sleep and its impact on performance and encourage their employees to prioritize restful sleep. This not only enhances corporate performance but also reduces sickness and absenteeism, as sleep is known to be vital for immune function.

Recent research by the American Thoracic Society underscores the critical role of sleep in enabling our bodies to form memories, repair muscles, and release essential hormones that regulate appetite and growth. Sleep is a restorative process vital for health and repair, and insufficient sleep is linked to obesity, injury, accidents, and various health issues. Particularly for entrepreneurs, lack of sleep adversely impacts happiness, productivity, alertness, and reaction time. If that's not enough to grab your attention, another study discovered that individuals who sleep less than 6 hours per night face a 13% higher mortality risk than those who sleep 7-9 hours per night.[276]

Information and products designed to enhance sleep quality are available to improve sleep habits. We should all heed the advice of experts and prioritize the well-being of our bodies and brains.

> *The one thing that is everything and requires nothing is sleep.* —Tony Horton, American fitness trainer, author, and former actor.

Change Management

Change is critical for every company's growth and evolution. It's the engine that drives progress and innovation. Without change, businesses can become stagnant, lose their edge, and eventually collapse. However, managing change effectively can unite employees toward a common purpose and propel the company forward.

Change is inevitable. Progress is optional. —Tony Robbins.

Change Management encompasses the strategies and approaches required to introduce and execute changes within a company's operations. It involves meticulous planning, seamless implementation, and ongoing monitoring of activities before and after the change to ensure successful integration and sustained effectiveness.

Change can occur at every level within the organization:

- Individual change relates to procedures, policies, or processes that depend on those who create, maintain, and utilize those tools. Effective individual change management requires understanding how people are motivated to change and a commitment to taking the necessary measures to enact it.

- Organizational change involves broad changes at the company-wide level. It requires identifying teams and individuals who will be affected, clearly communicating deliberate intent, and then training on implementing the change sustainably.

- Enterprise change reshapes every facet of an organization, touching upon leadership, teams, projects, procedures, roles, processes, and organizational structure. This level of change demands full acceptance and commitment, which fosters the flexibility necessary to forge a more efficient and goal-oriented organization.

- Transitional change involves shifting from one operational state to another. For instance, it occurs during a merger between companies. Transformational change represents the most profound shift, where a company opts to overhaul its practices, alter its direction, or venture into new markets.

Any significant change, regardless of its nature, poses challenges. Institutional change, in particular, demands cooperation and collaboration across all levels of an organization. Ideally, change should be pursued and executed with minimal disruption to critical ongoing activities to ensure a smooth transition process.

When change initiatives falter within an organization, it's typically attributed to human factors. Change must combat momentum, inertia, and entropy. Resistance often stems from employees who either fail to recognize the advantages of change or prefer the familiarity, comfort, or personal benefits of the status quo.

Modifying or replacing entrenched systems or processes that are outdated, inefficient, or do not fit current business conditions can be challenging. Leadership may also inadvertently sabotage the change process by failing to create and communicate a compelling vision, mobilize and assign adequate staffing or funds, or otherwise champion the specific efforts required to accomplish meaningful, impactful, and sustained change.

Implementing improvement or change initiatives effectively and consistently is inherently challenging and prone to mishaps. Poorly executed initiatives can result in workers' lack of support and commitment or even active resistance or sabotage. Conversely, successful change efforts can lead to transformative improvements, revitalizing competitiveness and profitability. Without a commitment to continuous improvement, companies risk falling into irrelevance and eventual extinction.

Change is hard because people overestimate the value of what they have—and underestimate the value of what they may gain by giving that up. —James Belasco and Ralph Stayer, transformation experts, and authors.

Change success hinges on several key factors:

- Goals and Objectives: Top leadership conceives and communicates concise corporate change goals. All employees should easily remember and understand these objectives, clearly articulating their rationale and justification. This ensures that everyone, from bottom to top, comprehends their critical role in driving meaningful change within the company, facilitating prioritization and support.

- Motive: Leadership persuades the workforce that change is imperative and inevitable, making it clear that maintaining the status quo is unacceptable and non-negotiable. Only then will employees fully embrace the understanding that change is no longer optional.

- Objectivity: Improvement or change initiatives should flow from the bottom. Middle managers and leaders should resist the temptation to call balls and strikes prematurely when selecting project pursuits. Leadership should develop and then clearly communicate the project selection criterion based on an objective formula, where defined and measurable metrics are utilized and subjective biases are avoided.

- Encouragement: Once initiatives are selected, endorsed, and financed, it's essential to empower the employees leading the efforts to concentrate on their tasks without fear of the abrupt termination of their projects.

- Approval Process: Simplify the project approval process. Project ideas should undergo swift evaluation and either be accepted or rejected without excessive bureaucracy or endless revisions. Employees are discouraged from proposing ideas when the approval process is overly burdensome. Requiring multiple iterations for perfection is counterproductive and stifles innovation.

- Commitment: Leadership backs up its words with financial support, which entails decentralizing budgets across teams to facilitate change.

- Experimentation: Employees are encouraged to experiment with various initiatives to empower and fuel strategy. Meaningful change and improvement are often incremental and organic.

- Workload: Economically constraining those individuals who are driving change or failing to allocate time for initiatives is a surefire way to dampen enthusiasm. Overloading already stretched employees with additional change-specific tasks further disenfranchises those crucial to driving improvement.

- Competition: Initiatives must not be allowed to compete against each other. Each person's or team's pursuit should not detract from another's efforts. Evaluations should consider the holistic impact of initiatives, ensuring they collectively contribute to overarching goals. This necessitates close coordination, collaboration between groups, and the avoidance of sabotage or surprises.

- Process Elimination: Instead of solely prioritizing the addition of new processes, it's essential to dedicate time and effort to evaluating existing processes for potential elimination or replacement. The focus should be on modifying, streamlining, or eliminating current processes unless their current usage can be thoroughly justified. Challenge the status quo and strive to simplify, streamline, and retain only what is truly beneficial, critical, necessary, and justifiable.

Focus on creating the desired change; the initiative *process* must not overshadow the improvement itself. It should be concise, transparent, and straightforward, ensuring employees don't see it as a burden. The focus should be on implementing actual change and improvement, not bureaucracy, command and control, status, or proposal work that is perceived as a tax on the workers' time and energy. Review, approve, authorize, empower, and then step out of the way.

> *Eighty-five percent of the reasons for failure are deficiencies in the systems and process rather than the employee. The role of management is to change the process rather than badgering individuals to do better.* —W. Edward Deming, American engineer, statistician, professor, author, lecturer, and management consultant.

Change is difficult, and sometimes exceedingly so. Altering habits, which are inherently sticky and persistent, is a fundamental aspect of change. Introducing new methods carries benefits and drawbacks, and perfect solutions rarely emerge. Instead, the outcome typically unfolds gradually through exploration, discovery, and experimentation.[277]

Substantial achievement often results from a steady march of incremental progress. Consider any endeavor that requires prolonged and sustained effort and commitment, such as reshaping corporate culture, assembling a team to innovate a new product, launching a new business unit, or acquiring another company. These activities are akin to marathons rather than sprints. Substantial gains in skill, performance, talent, or innovation take time. They are the culmination of countless minor improvements over time. Each incremental advance contributes to a more significant, transformative outcome.

Teams that embrace incrementalism tend to exhibit the most significant overall improvement. Ideally, each individual or group concentrates on making small but consistent advancements. These cumulative efforts generate a compounding effect, resulting in substantial overall enhancement. Everyone becomes a valued contributor to the collective success.

The contagious nature of incremental gains encourages further contribution and progress. Moreover, focusing on small victories increases the likelihood that contributors will experience continuous, incremental successes, fostering a sense of fulfillment and accomplishment. This, in turn, fuels motivation to continue seeking and pursuing further improvement.[278]

While essential for growth, innovation, and staying competitive, change management is inherently challenging due to its disruption of established processes and the uncertainty it brings. Successful change requires careful planning, clear communication, and strong leadership to navigate the emotional and logistical obstacles, ensuring that both people and operations adapt and thrive in the new environment.

It's important to celebrate small wins to inspire positive momentum. Lead by example, demonstrating successful strategies for change. Show that updating old practices can be beneficial and enjoyable, improving worker satisfaction and safety. Encourage innovation by questioning outdated methods and embracing new ideas.

The secret of change is to focus all of your energy, not on fighting the old, but on building the new. —Socrates.

Evolution of Leadership

Workforces around the world are changing at a pace previously unseen. Diversity in all its forms, along with the rapid pace of technological advancement and economic globalization, creates complex challenges and dynamics at work. As a consequence, leaders must adapt to meet evolving challenges. Generational diversity will likely influence future leadership, impacting leadership style, priorities, and preferences.

Baby Boomers (born from 1946 to 1964) are either retiring, approaching retirement, or choosing to delay retirement. Gen-Xers (born from 1965 to 1981) are currently about one-third the size of the Baby Boomer population, which means there are not enough Gen-Xers to fill the population void that Baby Boomers are leaving behind as they depart the workforce. Leadership ranks are now transitioning from Baby Boomers to Gen-Xers and Millennials (born from 1982 to 2002).

A significant challenge we face is the potential shortage of leadership personnel in C-Suites and boardrooms in the coming years if we fail to adequately prepare the next generation of leaders. While hiring experienced Gen-Xers provides a short-term solution, developing Millennial leaders today is crucial to ensure a sustainable supply for the future. To achieve this goal, leadership training programs must evolve to reflect the changing leadership styles embraced by the new generation.

While generalizations should be approached cautiously, studies have shown distinct leadership styles among different generations. Baby Boomers often lead from the top down, employing directional, process-oriented, and structured techniques. Conversely, Gen-Xers tend to lead from the side, demonstrating independence, delegation-oriented approaches, and entrepreneurial spirit. Millennials prefer leading from the middle, avoiding micromanagement and delegation downward. They prioritize collaboration and value input from all team members.

Engaging millennials deeply and empowering their participation in preparing the training curriculum is essential to train them effectively. Training should not be top-down or forced upon them. Listening to their challenges and gathering feedback on their training preferences is critical. Millennials prefer a faster training pace, and their ability to grasp new information quickly should be recognized as an asset. They seek respect for their individuality and embrace the change they bring.[279]

A recent survey of millennial managers revealed that, like earlier generations of leaders, they prioritize new products, business growth, and achieving corporate goals. They place significant importance on fostering a positive and nurturing workplace culture and seek meaningful work that integrates with their personal lives. Having grown up in the internet era, they value transparency and autonomy more than previous generations and expect rapid career advancement. However, they may lack the patience to achieve it. Millennial leaders appreciate job seekers who display eagerness to learn beyond relevant skills. They generally prefer managing Gen-Xers over other colleagues and may resist managing baby boomers.[280]

Workplace and leadership trends are likely to add a difficulty factor for leaders in the future. We've already experienced the complicating factor of social media in how we communicate with and engage each other and run our businesses. The recent Covid pandemic has also forced us to rethink and even accelerate our implementation of remote working. While predicting the future is impossible, we can extrapolate from recent trends with reasonable confidence.

The urgency to address climate change and global warming drives innovation and a renewed focus on sustainable growth. Companies are under pressure to behave responsibly and ethically, driven by the demands of the latest generation of workers. These workers seek jobs with ample learning opportunities, flexible policies, remote work options, and growth opportunities that avoid burnout. They also demand diversity, inclusion, acceptance, and *real* accountability from their leaders. In response, organizations are flattening structures, hiring diverse teams, and advocating for meaningful change in government policies. There's a growing recognition that truth, facts, and actions matter, particularly among younger generations, paving the way for real progress and change.

Companies recognize the importance of imagination and creativity in staying competitive and retaining customers. They prioritize speed and shorter cycle times, aiming to be customer-obsessed, purpose-driven, and highly networked. Embedding analytics in processes accelerates innovation and enhances customer experiences. Forward-thinking leaders prioritize sustainability, understanding its positive impact on their bottom lines. They prioritize employee welfare, mental health, and community engagement. These leaders inspire risk-taking and innovation, fostering environments where employees can learn and grow without fear of repercussions for failures.[281]

As companies transition to flatter organizational structures, managers and leaders face greater responsibilities managing larger, more complex, and often remote teams. With reduced hierarchy, responsibility becomes more diffuse across the organization, requiring leaders to navigate intricate relationships and decentralized decision-making processes. This shift demands enhanced communication skills, adaptability, and a deeper understanding of team dynamics to foster collaboration and drive performance effectively.

In today's workplace, managers need to understand how their teams use bots, software, and various communication tools in addition to the traditional tools and processes used in their daily work. This can make their workers' jobs more difficult to visualize and track, placing more burden on the rank and file to self-manage. When staffing challenges and shortages are at an all-time high, managers find themselves taking on the work of others in addition to their management tasks until their recruiting efforts pay off. Managing large and remote teams requires expertise in communications and outreach. Delegating, communicating, and collaborating remotely are critical skills for managers in digital and hybrid workplaces. Companies prioritizing management and leadership development are best equipped to thrive in this evolving landscape.[282]

As we move into the future, leaders must prioritize adaptability, emotional intelligence, and inclusivity, focusing less on rigid hierarchies and more on collaboration and empathy. The rise of remote work and digital transformation will require leaders to foster strong cultures of trust and engagement, even across virtual teams. Future leadership will likely emphasize ethical decision-making, sustainability, and social impact, with leaders being called upon to guide organizations and address broader societal challenges.

> *The leader of the past was a person who knew how to tell. The leader of the future will be a person who knows how to ask.* —Peter F. Drucker, Austrian American management consultant, educator, and author.

AI and Future Managers

When we think of managers, we often emphasize the human aspect of their roles, including coaching, mentoring, and team leadership. However, a significant portion of a manager's responsibilities involves administrative tasks such as writing personnel reviews, budgeting, and approving expense reports and procurement requests. These duties can consume considerable time, leaving less opportunity for management's more creative and impactful aspects. As administrative burdens increase, managers may experience overload and exhaustion, unable to consistently make quality decisions on the things that matter most.

The concept of an "AI manager" aims to automate mundane and repetitive managerial tasks, allowing managers to focus on more meaningful work. AI algorithms can handle various functions such as meeting scheduling, supply chain management, accounting, budgeting, and data analysis. Within finance, tasks like financial period closing, invoicing, and risk assessment can be managed by AI. AI can handle tasks like server rebooting, network monitoring, and cybersecurity in IT. It's conceivable that AI could eventually assist CEOs in decision-making and strategic planning by providing valuable insights and analysis.

The fear of AI replacing jobs is countered by the perspective that it can augment human capabilities and creativity. Just as calculators and computers have streamlined a multitude of tasks, AI can handle analytical tasks, allowing humans to focus on more creative endeavors that require emotional intelligence. With AI taking on routine tasks, individuals can allocate more time to mindful and innovative pursuits, potentially reducing stress and overwork. The symbiotic relationship between humans and AI suggests that automation can enhance productivity and creativity rather than entirely replace human effort.[283]

The advancement of AI holds promise in revolutionizing how we interact with technology. With AI-powered personal agents, tasks like writing emails, managing inboxes, scheduling, and handling routine communications can become more streamlined and intuitive. Users will be able to communicate with their personal agents using natural language, enabling smoother interactions and reducing the need for manual input. As AI technology evolves, its integration into various devices and platforms could significantly enhance productivity and efficiency.

As automation continues to reshape the workplace, future managers will likely experience a shift in their roles and responsibilities. With mundane management tasks increasingly handled by automation, managers can redirect their focus toward the more human aspects of leadership. This may involve spending less time on technical oversight and more time fostering creativity, ideation, and strategy within their teams. Additionally, managers may prioritize talent development by enhancing coaching, mentoring, and providing emotional support to their employees. As organizations evolve and flatten, managers will play a crucial role in nurturing and facilitating a culture of innovation, collaboration, and employee well-being. By serving as catalysts for positive change and guiding their teams toward success, future managers will be instrumental in navigating the complexities of an increasingly competitive business environment.[284]

The future of AI holds immense promise and potential for humanity, offering possibilities that were once only confined to the realms of science fiction. However, with this power comes the responsibility to deploy AI thoughtfully and ethically, mitigating potential risks while maximizing its benefits. While change often elicits doubt and fear, history has shown that technological advancements have ultimately improved the human condition. Embracing progress and adapting to new technologies is inevitable and essential for driving positive change and innovation in society.

> *Technology is nothing. What's important is that you have a faith in people, that they're good and smart, and if you give them tools, they'll do wonderful things with them.* —Steve Jobs.

Tomorrow's Leaders

What does the future hold for leadership in general? Can today's leaders maintain their traditional behaviors and succeed in the ever-evolving global and digital marketplace? Perhaps not. Digitalization, an ever-increasing competitive landscape, the evolving and diverse workforce, and the demand for breakneck speed and agility suggest a need for a fundamental evolution and reimagining of leadership. If companies are to succeed and excel well into the future, they'll need to be transformed, which means that their leaders must likewise adapt.[285]

> *When digital transformation is done right, it's like a caterpillar turning into a butterfly, but when done wrong, all you have is a really fast caterpillar.* —George Westerman, digital transformation researcher, lecturer, and author.

Transformative leadership teams are reimagining leadership in the new economy. Technology will shape the world of tomorrow in ways beyond our current imagination. Referred to as the "Fourth Industrial Revolution," this era demands leaders embrace digital transformation by discarding old technologies and adopting new systems and methodologies. These evolving tools will enable unprecedented opportunities that were unimaginable just a few years ago, fundamentally altering how we live and work in exciting and transformative ways.[286]

Progressive leaders recognize the vital importance of being digitally savvy. They embrace this evolution and foster skill development in using analytics to inform decision-making and leveraging machine learning in operations. In today's landscape, data literacy is no longer confined to a select few; it's a collective responsibility. Effective leaders must attain a certain level of proficiency to advocate for advanced tools across the organization. Embracing software is crucial for every company, as those who resist may encounter future challenges. Tomorrow's business leaders must grasp technology, just as technology leaders must comprehend business principles.

Change is the law of life and those who look only to the past or present are certain to miss the future. —John F. Kennedy, American politician, and 35th president of the United States.

Thus far, leaders are lagging in their transformative endeavors. A 2020 study of 1,984 large companies worldwide revealed that only 7% of surveyed executive teams and 17% of individual top management members were deemed digitally savvy. Less than a quarter of CEOs and only one-eighth of CFOs were considered digitally competent. Surprisingly, only 47% of CTOs and 45% of CIOs were viewed as digitally capable.

Tech companies boast the highest proportion of digitally savvy executives. At the same time, industries like construction, arts, entertainment, recreation, agriculture, forestry, fishing, and hunting have the fewest, with less than 1% possessing such expertise. Across the board, companies with digitally savvy teams experience 48% higher revenue growth and valuations and 15% higher net margins than others. For every 10% increase in top team digital savviness, there's a 0.4% increase in profitability and a 0.7% increase in revenue growth, surpassing industry averages. Pairing digitally savvy CEOs and CFOs yields premium performance.

Digitally savvy executives foster rapid learning cultures characterized by test-and-learn experimentation, minimum viable product releases, and evidence-based decision-making. They move away from traditional command-and-control leadership styles to embrace a coach-and-communicate approach. These leaders develop hypotheses and test them for early measures of success, which are correlated with financial performance.[287]

Modern leadership demands personal immersion and engagement in all forms of digital conversations to demonstrate relevance and currency. Relying solely on professional bloggers to speak on your behalf is no longer sufficient. Effective leaders must become fluent in AI, big data, and cloud technologies, as these tools are critical for present and future leadership.

Attracting and retaining tomorrow's multi-generational and diverse workforce necessitates reevaluating our recruitment strategies. Younger workers, in particular, anticipate having access to the same tools and environments in the workplace as they do at home or in college. If they can work while sitting on a sofa, they expect similar flexibility and comfort in the workplace. Gone are the days of standardizing workplace computer tools solely for financial reasons. Today's workers expect to be free to choose their preferred computer platform.

Tomorrow's leaders may need to reconsider the traditional concept of a stable workforce. Future workers might prefer a career that moves between short-term projects alongside other specialized freelancers. Many may never meet their managers or direct reports face-to-face. With the growing complexity of corporate operations and logistics, AI algorithms could manage mundane tasks like performance reviews, employee surveys, automated interviewing, candidate searches, scheduling, and expense reports. AI's speed and efficiency will enhance corporate productivity, enabling new policies that prioritize healthy work-life balance. Candidates will be evaluated based on their ability to foster cultures of transparency, accountability, and empathy, vital for motivating workers in an increasingly technology-driven and interconnected environment.[288]

> *We will need to learn new skills and behaviors to effectively collaborate with non-human teammates. Our identities and egos are likely to be stretched by this new kind of partnering. A leader with a background in evolutionary psychology and/or social sciences will help team members adapt their patterns, mindsets, and ways of working to productively connect with and find meaning from non-human relationships.*
> —Rodney Evans, entrepreneur, and change expert.

Fortunately, colleges are adapting their curricula to prepare tomorrow's leaders for the challenges of the digital age. Forward-thinking programs offer MBA students diverse courses, including AI, software development, game design, analytics, and biotech. These graduate students apply their classroom learning to business challenges through class projects and company internships. This combination of textbook and experiential learning, plus targeted humanities studies focusing on resilience, communication, EQ, collaboration, creativity, and empathy, prepares our future leaders with the versatility needed for success in the evolving landscape.[289]

When assessing your leadership team, it's important to examine whether it resembles a traditional, homogenous network that has retained control for years. Are the members predominantly similar in appearance and behavior, and do they exhibit unchanged tendencies from the past? Effective leaders recognize the importance of humility and acknowledge areas where they lack knowledge. They embrace the necessity for change and modernization, promptly seeking out team members with diverse and forward-thinking perspectives to foster innovation and growth.

Today's and tomorrow's leaders require a revamped playbook characterized by new behaviors, updated skills, modernized cultures, and growth mindsets. The era of top-down leadership is fading as individuals seek democratization in decision-making processes, empowering everyone to feel engaged and accountable. Ethical conduct, trustworthiness, and integrity remain critically important and must be consistently demonstrated. Additionally, digital savviness emerges as an indispensable leadership skill essential for navigating future challenges.

> *Transformation isn't a future event, it's a present day activity.* —Jillian Michaels, American personal trainer, businesswoman, author, and television personality.

CHAPTER 15

Conclusion: Embracing the Future

> ***Pessimism leads to weakness, optimism to power.*** —William James, American philosopher, historian, psychologist, and educator.

The last few years have undoubtedly been among the most distressing and stressful in recent memory. We've faced unprecedented political turmoil, rapid digital transformation, the looming threat of climate change, inflation, widespread layoffs and worker resignations, the devastating toll of the pandemic, attacks on voting rights and democracy, and efforts to undermine various personal and civil liberties and freedoms. The sheer pace and volume of challenges we're confronting can feel overwhelming and unprecedented.

The pace of change in our world has never been greater. We're witnessing a troubling rise in powerful voices and actions that seek to disrupt established norms, dispute settled science, oppose advanced education, reject life-saving vaccines, and roll back years of progress on crucial social issues. These actors thrive on spreading conspiracy theories and falsehoods, undermining our pursuit of truth.

In corporate America, entire industries are disappearing, leaving workers without jobs and struggling to adapt to rapidly changing circumstances. Meanwhile, emerging industries advance rapidly, demanding longer hours and contributing to increased worker stress and burnout. Economic inequality persists, with wealth accumulating disproportionately among the affluent while many in the lower and middle classes struggle to make ends meet.

But despite the challenges we face, there is much to be hopeful for. Life expectancy is at an all-time high. We enjoy the fruits of rapid healthcare advancement, which enables longer and healthier lives. The coronavirus, for all the deaths and sickness it has caused, will pose an opportunity for technological growth in various sectors. Thanks to the internet, enormous knowledge and wisdom are available at our fingertips that prior generations never experienced. Social networks and VR enable us to connect with others in increasingly meaningful and immersive ways. Investment in new technologies is at an all-time high, driving down costs for clean energy solutions and making sustainability goals more achievable than ever. And now, AI holds the potential to unlock unprecedented innovations, transforming the way we understand and address the world's most complex challenges.[290]

When we examine historical data, we find remarkable strides in life expectancy and overall human progress. Just over a century ago, babies born in England or Wales had a life expectancy of only 41 years, whereas today, they can expect to live well into their 80s. Similarly, a hundred years ago, impoverished people in Bombay or Delhi had little hope of surviving beyond their late 20s. Yet, today, the average life expectancy in India is around 70 years. These statistics underscore the incredible advancements in healthcare, sanitation, and quality of life over the past century, representing a remarkable measure of human progress.

CONCLUSION: EMBRACING THE FUTURE • 347

Many remarkable advancements and innovations often go unnoticed by the general public, unfolding quietly but significantly over time. Take, for instance, the eradication of smallpox, once a deadly infection that claimed countless lives, especially among children. Today, thanks to vaccines and advancements in healthcare, smallpox is no longer a threat. Similarly, simple skin scrapes no longer pose the risk of deadly bacterial infections, and access to clean drinking water has dramatically reduced the incidence of diseases like cholera. While these breakthroughs may have originated in the laboratories of scientists and engineers, their widespread implementation and impact were made possible by the collective efforts of activists, lawyers, politicians, and countless others who played vital roles in ideating, facilitating, and commercializing these advancements globally.

However, we must recognize the current risk posed by those seeking to reverse, degrade, or override the confidence we've come to embrace in our medical and scientific experts. Their efforts to undermine trust in established knowledge and advancement pose a significant risk to public health and progress. Now more than ever, we must remain vigilant in opposing such individuals and groups. We must continue to support and uphold the authority of our medical and scientific experts, resisting any attempts to reverse the hard-won progress and intellectual advancements that have brought us to where we are today.[291]

Despite the challenges posed by the shift to remote work and the disruptions caused by the pandemic, businesses are experiencing unprecedented levels of profitability and productivity. Many companies have seen remarkable gains due to their focus on technology and innovation. This highlights the resilience and adaptability of business in the face of adversity. While negative news dominates headlines, forward-thinking companies are seizing the opportunity to innovate and solve pressing challenges. This reaffirms that investing in innovation, rather than cost-cutting measures, is key to weathering storms and driving long-term success.

Maintaining a positive outlook can be challenging amidst a barrage of negativity, but it's important to remember the virtues of resilience and hope. These qualities can shape our lives, define our journeys, and guide us through dark times. With resilience and hope, we can overcome adversity, find meaning in hardship, and triumph when faced with uncertainty. They provide the strength and optimism to navigate life's challenges with courage and determination.

Resilience and hope are intertwined and reinforce each other. When we face challenges, whether at work or home, resilience enables us to develop a sense of self-efficacy and confidence. This, in turn, creates a sense of hope for a brighter future. Together, they form a positive feedback loop.[292]

> *I've missed more than 9,000 shots in my career. I've lost almost 300 games. 26 times, I've been trusted to take the game-winning shot and missed. I've failed over and over and over again in my life. And that is why I succeed.* —Michael Jordan, American businessman, and former professional basketball player.

As we contemplate the many challenges we face in our work and daily lives, it's important to make good choices and do the *right* things. Choices and decisions shape our identity, not solely based on their outcomes, but on the intentions behind them. For instance, lending your car to a trustworthy friend, even if they crash it, remains the right choice because of the trust and goodwill behind it. Similarly, even if it fails, starting a business fueled by passion is worthwhile because it aligns with your values and aspirations. Likewise, despite facing opposition, standing up to defend someone who was wronged is unequivocally the right thing to do. Our actions reflect our character and values, regardless of the external results.[293]

Our professional and personal lives are inextricably linked, and the behaviors, attitudes, and values we cultivate shape our careers and broader contributions to society. A positive, "can-do" attitude, unwavering ethical principles, and integrity set the foundation for long-term success. Embracing truth and facts, guided by the Golden Rule, ensures that our actions are not just effective but also just and honorable. We must strive to do the *right* things rather than merely what is possible, fostering a culture of morality and ethical decision-making.

Leading by example is more crucial than ever in our increasingly challenging global and digital marketplace. As leaders, we are responsible for inspiring greatness in our employees, nurturing their potential, and guiding them toward excellence. By embodying the principles of integrity, empathy, and resilience, we can create environments where individuals are motivated to innovate and excel.

Modernizing our tools and techniques in this digital age is not just an option but a necessity. Embracing artificial intelligence and other technological advancements can significantly enhance productivity and efficiency. However, the human element remains irreplaceable. By combining cutting-edge technology with our unique human capabilities—creativity, empathy, and ethical judgment—we can navigate the complexities of the modern workplace with agility and foresight.

Imagining new ways of shepherding our workers and companies into the future involves a commitment to continuous learning and adaptation. We must be open to new ideas, flexible in our approaches, and ready to seize the opportunities that lie ahead. The future holds endless possibilities, and our responsibility is to prepare ourselves and our teams to meet these challenges with optimism and energy.

As we look forward, let us embrace the promise of the future with confidence and integrity. By fostering a culture of ethical leadership, continuous growth, and innovation, we can build a world where individuals and organizations thrive. Together, we can create a future that is not only successful but also just, inspiring, and full of boundless potential. The journey ahead is bright, and with the right mindset and tools, we can achieve greatness beyond our wildest dreams.

Finally, success isn't about making money—it's about being happy with who you are. And who you are isn't about the outcome of your choices—it's about the reasons behind them. Rejoice in what you have. Cherish your friends, and love your family. So far as we know, we only have one life to live—so make the most of it!

> *Enjoy the game of life.* —Jack Nicklaus, American professional golfer, golf course designer, and philanthropist.

Looking Ahead: What's Next in Career Intelligence

As you reach the conclusion of *General Career Intelligence*, I hope you have found valuable insights and practical guidance to navigate your career journey. But this is just the beginning. The world of career development is vast and ever-evolving, and there is so much more to explore.

In my upcoming book, tentatively titled *Advanced Career Intelligence*, we will delve deeper into the complexities and nuances of professional and personal growth. This final installment will build on the foundational concepts you've learned, taking you into advanced territories that are crucial for thriving in today's dynamic work environment.

This next book will provide you with the tools and knowledge to elevate your career to new heights. Stay tuned for more updates, and thank you for embarking on this journey with me. Together, we will continue to unlock the full potential of your career intelligence.

Acknowledgements

Writing a book is often a journey fraught with sleepless nights, self-doubt, and the relentless challenge of turning a nebulous idea into a tangible reality. It's easy to get lost in the depths of our own thoughts, overwhelmed by the weight of our aspirations and the intricacies of our work.

In these moments, stepping back and seeking the support of trusted friends, colleagues, and family members becomes not just a comfort but a critical step toward clarity and success. Their insights, encouragement, and unwavering belief provide the perspective and strength needed to navigate the rough patches and bring our vision to life.

I am profoundly grateful to those involved with this book. The editing, organizing, restructuring and redacting that took place were influenced substantially by several individuals. Substantial discussion and behind the scenes effort influenced the scope, content, coverage, and graphic design. The individuals listed below were deeply supportive and influential:

My daughter and son. Cori and Kyler served as my inspiration for writing this book, and provided the persistent encouragement that fueled my multi-year venture. They offered critical insights and advice on the content and cover design, and urged me onward whenever I needed a jump-start.

Michael Ainscow. My friend Michael provided substantial input and guidance on the cover design. His creativity, unique concepts and patient encouragement led me to the final design. Bravo!

MK Cornfield. Many thanks to MK for her publishing expertise and moral support.

Mike Eneboe. My "Best Man," Mike provided shrewd advise on book content, and consistently counseled me on the value of brevity as I marshalled through multiple phases of redactions, first with a machete, and finally a scalpel. Every piece of advice that Mike provided was spot-on, although it often took me time and contemplation to expose and recognize his genius.

Guy Kawasaki. Tech titan Guy took a chance on me, when he returned an email request for publishing advice. Since our first phone call, he has expertly advised and mentored me on publishing strategy, cover design, title, and scope of content. His willingness to provide a "Foreword" to my book was a testament to his faith in my writing and commitment to helping others. Most importantly, our relationship has expanded beyond this project. The entire day that we spent in my woodshop, crafting his custom surfboard balance-trainer, is a memory I'll never forget. Guy is truly "Remarkable", in every sense of the word.

My wife. Elaine has been central to my ability to pursue this project. While her direct influence on book content and cover design was invaluable, the patience she exhibited as a writer's "widow" for several years enabled this book in the most fundamental sense. Words are not enough, but thank you Elaine for supporting my passion—I love you, and owe you big time!

About the Author

Ray Blasing is a recently retired engineering technologist, innovator, inventor, serial entrepreneur, and engineering consultant. His expansive career charts a course from spacecraft antenna engineering to spearheading the development of the now-ubiquitous millimeter wave full-body scanner, a recognizable security fixture at airports worldwide. An inventor with more than 40 patents to his name, Ray's expertise in founding and leading tech startups, mentoring and coaching diverse teams, and navigating the intricacies of space, military, commercial, and consumer electronics provides him with profound insights into the domains of engineering innovation, product development, and high-tech leadership.

Notes

Introduction

[1] **Adding to this upheaval**: David Brooks. How America Got Mean. https://www.theatlantic.com/magazine/archive/2023/09/us-culture-moral-education-formation/674765/ (accessed 7/30/2024).
[2] **Amid these changes**: Simone Stolzoff. In Praise of the Meandering Career. https://every.to/p/in-praise-of-the-meandering-career (accessed 12/28/2023).
[3] **So, how do you navigate**: Jay Fulcher. https://www.linkedin.com/in/jayfulcher/detail/recent-activity/ (accessed 7/19/2020).

Education and Learning

[4] **Education, in the most**: Michael Bloomberg. Mike Bloomberg at the 2019 NAACP Convention: Education Holds the Key to Our Biggest Challenges. https://www.bloomberg.org/blog/follow-data-podcast-mike-bloomberg-110th-naacp-annual-convention-remarks/ (accessed 9/12/2019)
[5] **On the other hand**: Mareo McCracken. The 10 Most Impactful Books To Read in 2019 (+ listed in the order they should be read). https://www.linkedin.com/pulse/10-most-impactful-books-read-2019-listed-order-should-mareo-mccracken (accessed 1/1/2019).
[6] **Science has shown**: Jessica Stillman. This is How Reading Rewires Your Brain, According to Neuroscience. https://www.inc.com/jessica-stillman/reading-books-brain-chemistry.html (accessed 2/22/2021).
[7] **Investing in yourself**: Taylor Locke. Mark Cuban on the 'best investment' he ever made: 'Most people don't put in the time' to do it. https://www.msn.com/en-us/money/personalfinance/mark-cuban-on-the-best-investment-he-ever-made-most-people-dont-put-in-the-time-to-do-it/ar-BB19INvZ (accessed 1/25/2021).
[8] **Given the societal**: Ayelet Haimson Lushkov. Underfunding classics and humanities is dangerous. https://thehill.com/opinion/education/540804-underfunding-classics-and-humanities-is-dangerous (accessed 2/27/2021).
[9] **Female students are**: Jeroo Billimoria. Is STEM education all it's cracked up to be? https://medium.com/world-economic-forum/is-stem-education-all-its-cracked-up-to-be-d73d3364b8dd (accessed 6/25/2020).
[10] **While a nationwide**: John Murawski. An argument against emphasis on STEM education. https://www.charlotteobserver.com/entertainment/books/article73350382.html (accessed 6/25/2020).
[11] **These days, there's**: Bill Gates. We need more Rogers. https://www.gatesnotes.com/Books/Range (accessed 12/27/2020).
[12] **Successful companies leverage**: 2U. To future-proof your career, start by embracing cross-disciplinary thinking. https://qz.com/1589490/to-future-proof-your-career-start-by-embracing-cross-disciplinary-thinking/ (accessed 5/7/2020).

[13] **Companies highly value:** Vikram Mansharamani. Harvard lecturer: 'No specific skill will get you ahead in the future'—but this 'way of thinking' will. https://www.msn.com/en-us/money/careersandeducation/harvard-lecturer-no-specific-skill-will-get-you-ahead-in-the-future-but-this-way-of-thinking-will/ar-BB15vFE6 (accessed 4/23/2021).

[14] **Often, we emphasize:** Matt Krupnick. After decades of pushing bachelor's degrees, U.S. needs more tradespeople. https://www.pbs.org/newshour/education/decades-pushing-bachelors-degrees-u-s-needs-tradespeople (accessed 11/4/2019).

[15] **These days, students:** Glenn Adamson. Making The Nation. https://www.smithsonianmag.com/arts-culture/state-american-craft-never-been-stronger-180976483/ (accessed 1/28/2021).

[16] **Apple's Tim Cook:** Tim Cook Discusses Apple's Future in China I Fortune. https://www.youtube.com/watch?v=_ng8xQ-SNGc (accessed 2/2/2023).

[17] **And yet, we're seeing:** Max Taves. Why do Republicans keep attacking higher education? There's a sinister reason. https://www.charlotteobserver.com/opinion/article285745351.html (accessed 11/27/2024).

[18] **Regardless of political agendas:** George D. Kuh. Why Skills Training Can't Replace Higher Education. https://hbr.org/2019/10/why-skills-training-cant-replace-higher-education (accessed 9/8/2022).

[19] **Unfortunately, while community:** James Sullivan. As community college students return to class, let's help them graduate. https://www.msn.com/en-us/news/politics/as-community-college-students-return-to-class-lets-help-them-graduate/ar-AAOT436 (accessed 9/27/2021).

[20] **Arizona recently passed:** Laurie Roberts. Allowing Arizona's' community colleges to offer bachelor's degrees? Now, that's smart. https://www.azcentral.com/story/opinion/op-ed/laurieroberts/2021/05/04/arizona-community-colleges-can-now-offer-bachelor-degrees-smart/4945997001/ (accessed 5/6/2021).

[21] **Google is working:** The Latest from the Talent Tech Industry. https://tatech.org/ta-tech-business-newz-18/ (accessed 4/1/2022).

[22] **Half of the U.S.:** LaShana Lewis. How tech's outdated reliance on college degrees hinders workplace DEI. https://www.fastcompany.com/90943937/how-techs-outdated-reliance-on-college-degrees-hinders-workplace-dei (accessed 9/11/2023).

[23] **While educators are:** Armstrong Williams. Too few good men and women. https://thehill.com/opinion/finance/532058-too-few-good-men-and-women (accessed 12/31/2020).

[24] **Successful companies often:** Lifelong learning is key to success for Infosys. https://brand-studio.fortune.com/infosys/why-investing-in-diverse-talent-is-a-business-imperative/?prx_t=aJsGAc4NLAovEQA (accessed 4/18/2021).

[25] **In the current job market:** Andrew Hermalyn. Adapting higher education for the lifelong learner. https://brand-studio.fortune.com/2u/adapting-higher-ed-for-lifelong-learner/? (accessed 6/30/2021).

[26] **The recent pandemic:** David G. Collings and John McMackin. The Practices That Set Learning Organizations Apart. https://sloanreview.mit.edu/article/the-practices-that-set-learning-organizations-apart/ (accessed 2/6/2022).

[27] **Pursuing intellectual knowledge:** Edric Huang, Jenny Dorsey, Claire Mosteller, Emily Chen. Understanding Anti-Intellectualism in the U.S. https://www.studioatao.org/post/understanding-anti-intellectualism-in-the-u-s (accessed 1/5/2022).

[28] **Leaders, educators:** Monica Potts. Why Being Anti-Science is now Part Of Many Rural Americans' Identity. https://fivethirtyeight.com/features/why-being-anti-science-is-now-part-of-many-rural-americans-identity/ (accessed 4/25/2022).

Foundational Character Traits

[29] **While character and:** Hokuma Karimova. Personality & Character Traits: The Good, The Bad, and the Ugly. https://positivepsychology.com/character-traits/ (accessed 4/10/2022).

[30] **As I reflect on:** Carolyn Everson. Facebook's Carolyn Everson: Why enlightened leadership is effective leadership. https://fortune.com/2021/02/10/facebook-enlightened-leadership-empathy-effective-management/ (accessed 4/15/2021).

[31] **Self-confidence is a common:** Michele Molitor. 5 Ways to Rewire Your Brain and Reboot Your Confidence. https://www.nectarconsulting.com/5-ways-to-rewire-your-brain-reboot-your-confidence/ (accessed 10/4/2020).

[32] **As epigenetic experts:** Michele Molitor. 5 Ways to Rewire Your Brain and Reboot Your Confidence. https://www.nectarconsulting.com/5-ways-to-rewire-your-brain-reboot-your-confidence/ (accessed 10/4/2020).

[33] **Over the past decade:** Camille Gaines. How to Rewire Your Brain for Success—The Missing Step. https://retirecertain.com/how-to-rewire-your-brain-for-success/ (accessed 10/2/2020).

[34] **Some additional ways to develop:** Andrew Thomas. 10 Habits of the Most Confident People. https://www.inc.com/andrew-thomas/10-ways-extremely-confident-people-train-their-minds-every-day.html (accessed 5/25/2021).

[35] **As a manager, consistently:** Wanda Thilbodeaux. 4 Signs Your Employees need More encouragement From You. https://www.inc.com/wanda-thibodeaux/4-signs-your-employees-need-more-encouragement-from-you.html (accessed 4/8/2020).

[36] **Accomplishment and advancement :** Benjamin Hardy. 10 Things Unstoppable People Do That Average People Don't. https://www.inc.com/benjamin-p-hardy/10-things-unstoppable-people-do-that-average-people-dont.html (accessed 11/5/2019).

[37] **Recent research has found that we are particularly:** Dan Jones. How curiosity can supercharge your brain and boost your success. https://www.newscientist.com/article/mg25634080-200-how-curiosity-can-supercharge-your-brain-and-boost-your-success/ (accessed 10/20/2022).

[38] **Productive curiosity requires:** Jony Ive. Jony Ive on What He Misses Most About Steve Jobs. https://www.wsj.com/articles/jony-ive-steve-jobs-memories-10th-anniversary-11633354769 (accessed 10/4/2021).

[39] **"Intelligent curiosity" is:** Lisa Patrick. Want Influence? Use Intelligent Curiosity. https://www.entrepreneur.com/article/356014 (accessed 12/4/2020).

[40] **Our egos can prevent:** Tim Denning. How To Have more Humility So You Don't Screw Up Any Success You Have. Better Marketing. https://medium.com/better-marketing/how-to-have-more-humility-so-you-dont-screw-up-any-success-you-have-4ccf4f8cb2ef (accessed 9/15/2019).

[41] **In business leadership:** Dan Cable. How Humble Leadership Really Works. https://hbr.org/2018/04/how-humble-leadership-really-works (accessed 11/29/2019).
[42] **Plenty of brilliant:** Jeff Haden. When Jeff Bezos Made His Grandmother Cry, His Grandfather Stopped the Car to Teach Him a Powerful Lesson About Kindness. https://www.inc.com/jeff-haden/when-jeff-bezos-made-his-grandmother-cry-his-grandfather-stopped-car-to-teach-him-a-powerful-lesson-on-kindness.html (accessed 11/10/2019).
[43] **Being kind doesn't:** Jessica Stillman. Want to Be a Great Leader? Stop Being Nice and Start Being Kind. https://www.inc.com/jessica-stillman/kindness-leadership-ethics-santa-clara-university.html (accessed 5/4/2021).
[44] **If you spend your:** Vanessa Wasche. Being 'nice' can actually hurt your career. Do these three things instead. https://www.fastcompany.com/90632277/being-nice-can-actually-hurt-your-career-do-these-three-things-instead (accessed 5/15/2021).
[45] **While kindness and decency:** Jessica Stillman. To Be More Successful, Follow Elon Musk's Advice and Redefine the Word 'Rude'. https://www.inc.com/jessica-stillman/to-be-more-successful-follow-elon-musks-advice-redefine-word-rude.html (accessed 4/14/2021).
[46] **Leadership is a privilege:** Jessi Hempel. Satya Nadella on growth mindsets: "The learn-it-all does better than the know-it-all." https://www.linkedin.com/pulse/satya-nadella-growth-mindsets-learn-it-all-does-better-jessi-hempel (accessed 12/11/2019).
[47] **Empathy and sympathy:** Bill Murphy Jr. People Who Use These 3 Beautiful Words Have Very High Emotional Intelligence. https://www.inc.com/bill-murphy-jr/people-who-use-these-3-beautiful-words-have-very-high-emotional-intelligence.html (accessed 5/22/2021).
[48] **Empathy and listening:** Brigette Hyacinth. Listening is the Most Important skill a Leader can have. https://brigettehyacinth.com/listening-is-the-most-important-skill-a-leader-can-have-2/ (accessed 2/1/2021).
[49] **Empathy plays a critical:** Jason Aten. Microsoft's CEO, Satya Nadella, Says This 1 Trait Is More Important than Talent or Experience. It's Something Anyone Can Learn. https://www.inc.com/jason-aten/microsofts-ceo-satya-nadella-says-this-1-trait-is-more-important-than-talent-or-experience.html (accessed 11/13/2021).
[50] **A recent study found that early:** Tim Herrera. How Early-Career Setbacks Can Set You Up for Success. https://www.nytimes.com/2019/10/27/smarter-living/career-advice-overcome-setback.html (accessed 10/30/2019).
[51] **Another recent study**: Do Optimistic People Live Longer? https://skinnynews.com/2020/04/do-optimistic-people-live-longer/ (accessed 4/18/2024).
[52] **Humanity is a virtue:** Wikipedia. Humanity (virtue). https://en.wikipedia.org/wiki/Humanity_(virtue)(accessed 4/10/2022).
[53] **Our humanity inspires:** Lawrence. R. Samuel. The 10 Universal Human Traits. https://www.psychologytoday.com/us/blog/boomers-30/202012/the-10-universal-human-traits (accessed 4/10/2022).

Ethical Principles and Integrity

[54] **Integrity is an exceptional:** Susan M. Heathfield. What is Integrity? https://www.liveabout.com/what-is-integrity-really-1917676 (accessed 10/24/2022).

[55] **Integrity requires consistent:** Brigette Hyacinth. Integrity is everything! https://brigettehyacinth.com/integrity-is-everything/ (accessed 11/8/2019).

[56] **We all deserve:** Spencer Huang. How you treat people speaks volumes about your character. It boils down to respect. https://www.linkedin.com/pulse/how-you-treat-people-speaks-volumes-your-character-boils-huang/ (accessed 10/6/2019).

[57] **Reframe the question:** Matt Abrahams. How to Handle a Question You Don't Want to Answer. https://www.gsb.stanford.edu/insights/how-handle-question-you-dont-want-answer (accessed 2/17/2021).

[58] **Dishonesty takes various:** Lottie Miles, M.A. 5 Signs of Intellectual Dishonesty and How to Beat It. https://www.learning-mind.com/intellectual-dishonesty-signs/ (accessed 5/16/2020).

[59] **While we may at first:** Big Think. Marcelo Gleiser. Does science tell the truth? https://bigthink.com/13-8/science-what-is-truth/ (accessed 4/22/2021).

[60] **How might we endeavor:** CW Headley. Scientists discovered how to spot liars using a 3-step process. https://www.theladders.com/career-advice/scientists-discovered-how-to-spot-liars-using-a-3-step-process (accessed 4/22/2021).

[61] **A recent poll has found:** Leonardo Blair. Majority of young Americans say there is no absolute truth, challenging Bible: poll. https://www.christianpost.com/news/majority-of-young-americans-say-there-is-no-absolute-truth-poll.html (accessed 11/3/2022).

[62] **For those who reject:** B.J. Rudell. America must come to grips with the difference between truth and belief. https://www.msn.com/en-us/news/politics/america-must-come-to-grips-with-the-difference-between-truth-and-belief/ar-BB1cyHff (accessed 1/7/2021).

[63] **Peter Wehner, an:** Lee Moran. Ex-Bush Aide Gives Chilling Reality Check About Continued GOP Capitulation To Trump. https://www.huffpost.com/entry/peter-wehner-donald-trump-gop-violence_n_60a8cf82e4b0a24c4f7c4f0dm (accessed 5/22/2021).

[64] **The importance of truth:** Laura Hazard Owen. Yes, it's worth arguing with science deniers—and here are some techniques you can use. https://www.niemanlab.org/2019/06/yes-its-worth-arguing-with-science-deniers-and-here-are-some-techniques-you-can-use/ (accessed 6/20/2020).

[65] **Moral virtues overlap:** Kate Douglas. The Roots of Morality. https://freelibrary.overdrive.com/media/9434810 (accessed 3/11/2023).

[66] **Warren Buffet describes:** Marcel Schwantes. Warren Buffett Has a Simple Test for Living Your Best Life. Here's How it Works. https://www.inc.com/marcel-schwantes/warren-buffetts-simple-test-for-living-your-best-life.html (accessed 4/23/2020).

[67] **Every leadership decision carries:** Jason Aten. Tim Cook Says This Is the 1 Question Every Leader Should Ask. https://www.inc.com/jason-aten/tim-cook-says-this-is-1-question-every-leader-should-ask.html (accessed 2/7/2021).

Inner Strength and Personal Growth

[68] **Courage is a *foundational*:** Jim Detert and Evan Bruno. The Courage to Be Candid. https://sloanreview.mit.edu/article/the-courage-to-be-candid/ (accessed 2/6/2022).

[69] **Steve Jobs described how:** Marcel Schwantes. Inc. Steve Jobs Says There Is 1 Simple Habit That Separates the Doers from the Dreamers (and Leads to Great Success). https://www.inc.com/marcel-schwantes/steve-jobs-says-there-is-1-simple-habit-that-separates-doers-from-dreamers-and-leads-to-great-success.html (accessed 10/6/2019).

[70] **Many struggle to initiate:** Alexander Young. What Isaac Newton and Richard Branson Can Teach You About Overcoming Fear and Getting Started on Your Goals. https://www.entrepreneur.com/article/371596 (accessed 7/4/2021).

[71] **Research indicates that mental:** Scott Mautz. Jeff Bezos Says to Build a Life You're Proud of, Ask These 12 Questions. https://scottmautz.com/jeff-bezos-says-to-build-a-life-youre-proud-of-ask-these-12-questions/ (accessed 4/20/20).

[72] **As an entrepreneur:** Monel Amin. Making of the Entrepreneurial You. https://diligently.azurewebsites.net/entrepreneurial-journey-as-a-teacher/ (accessed 7/31/2019).

[73] **There's an important:** Dividend Mantra Team. The Three P's of Life—Patience, Persistence, Perseverance. https://www.dividendmantra.com/2013/03/the-three-ps-patience-persistence/ (accessed 2/19/2021).

[74] **Success in one's career:** Mary Juetten. The Importance of Perseverance. https://www.forbes.com/sites/maryjuetten/2020/01/23/the-importance-of-perseverance/?sh=7747a57728a5 (accessed 2/19/2021).

[75] **While we persevere:** An excerpt from Option B with a new foreword on resilience during COVID-19. https://optionb.org/bookexcerpt (accessed 2/19/2021).

[76] **Studies indicate that alongside:** Jeff Haden. If You Can Rate Yourself a 5 on These 6 Questions, You're Likely to Accomplish Huge Goals. https://www.inc.com/jeff-haden/if-you-can-consistently-rate-yourself-a-5-on-these-six-questions-science-says-youre-much-more-likely-to-accomplish-huge-goals.html (accessed 3/26/2021).

[77] **The key to resilience:** Shawn Achor and Michelle Gielan. Resilience Is About How You Recharge, Not How You Endure. https://hbr.org/2016/06/resilience-is-about-how-you-recharge-not-how-you-endure (accessed 1/2/2022).

[78] **Fear of failure is a universal:** Arthur C. Brooks. Go Ahead and Fail. https://arthurbrooks.com/article/go-ahead-and-fail/ (accessed 2/25/2021).

[79] **Elon Musk, for example:** Jessica Stillman. 3 Billionaires' Best Advice for Getting Over Your Fear of Failure. https://www.inc.com/jessica-stillman/elon-musk-richard-branson-sara-blakely-failure-advice.html (accessed 12/7/2020).

[80] **I like to reflect:** Richard Koch. How Steve Jobs Turned Setbacks Into Success. https://www.entrepreneur.com/article/362293 (accessed 1/15/2021).

[81] **To be present:** Sherrie Hurd. 7 Ernest Hemingway Quotes That Offer Deep Insights Into Life. https://www.learning-mind.com/ernest-hemingway-quotes/ (accessed 6/2/2020).

[82] **If you've done or said:** Nichole Kelly. The 5 trigger phrases every leader should stop using. https://www.fastcompany.com/90607928/the-5-trigger-phrases-every-leader-should-stop-using (accessed 4/4/2021).

[83] **Consider the pervasive:** Kate Gibson. CEOs rake in 940% more than 40 years ago, while average workers earn 12% more. https://www.cbsnews.com/news/ceo-pay-in-940-more-than-40-years-ago-workers-make-12-more/ (accessed 8/20/2019).

Emotional and Psychological Management

[84] **Every manager should know:** Alison Green. How to Recover After Yelling at an Employee. https://www.inc.com/alison-green/how-to-recover-after-yelling-at-an-employee.html (accessed 5/5/2021).

[85] **When someone wrongs you:** Sherrie Hurd. 7 Ernest Hemingway Quotes That Offer Deep Insights Into Life. https://www.learning-mind.com/ernest-hemingway-quotes/ (accessed 6/2/2020).

[86] **Similarly, when faced:** Valerie Soleil. 10 Traits of Genuinely Smart People (That Have Nothing to Do With Intelligence). https://www.learning-mind.com/traits-genuinely-smart-people/ (accessed 6/25/2020).

[87] **Elon Musk and the late:** Justin Bariso. Why Intelligent Minds Like Elon Musk and Steve Jobs Embrace the Rule of Awkward Silence. https://www.inc.com/justin-bariso/why-intelligent-minds-like-elon-musk-steve-jobs-embrace-rule-of-awkward-silence.html (accessed 6/24/2020).

[88] **Some individuals who:** David Vallance. The key to defeating imposter syndrome. https://blog.dropbox.com/topics/work-culture/imposter-syndrome (accessed 3/8/2020).

[89] **Surrounding yourself with friends:** Ruth Gotian Ed.D., M.S. 10 Ways to Overcome Imposter Syndrome. https://www.psychologytoday.com/intl/blog/optimizing-success/202206/10-ways-overcome-imposter-syndrome (accessed 6/5/2022).

[90] **As ego expands:** Rasmussen Hougaard, Jacqueline Carr. Ego is the Enemy of Good Leadership. https://hbr.org/2018/11/ego-is-the-enemy-of-good-leadership (accessed 11/10/2020).

[91] **Research indicates that people are:** Tomas Chamorro-Premuzic and Amy Edmondson. How to spot the warning signs of an insecure leader (and how to work with one). https://www.fastcompany.com/90656628/how-to-spot-the-warning-signs-of-an-insecure-leader-and-how-to-work-with-one (accessed 7/23/2021).

Influences and External Factors

[92] **Social and behavioral:** Surbhi S. Difference Between Attitude and Behavior. https://keydifferences.com/difference-between-attitude-and-behavior.html (accessed 10/15/2022).

[93] **In many ways, we have:** Betsy Mikel. Stanford Professor: These 3 Small Actions Make You a Magnet for Attracting Luck. https://www.inc.com/betsy-mikel/a-stanford-professors-simple-3-step-formula-to-make-your-own-luck.html (accessed 5/8/2020).

[94] **Money and success tend:** Christopher Ryan. Why Are Rich People So Mean? Wired. https://www.wired.com/story/why-are-rich-people-so-mean/. (accessed 10/15/2019).

[95] **Building and maintaining:** The Oracles. 9 habits that can instantly destroy your reputation, according to these self-made millionaires. https://www.cnbc.com/2020/01/17/9-habits-that-will-instantly-destroy-your-reputation-according-to-self-made-millionaires.html (accessed 1/19/2020).

Professional Conduct and Behaviors

[96] **There's a lot to be:** Melody Wilding. How to Turn Sensitivity Into a Superpower, According to a Human Behavior Professor. https://www.inc.com/melody-wilding/trust-yourself-sensitive-striver-leader-intuition-confidence.html (accessed 5/7/2021).

[97] **Even one person:** Nicholas W. Eyrich, Robert E. Quinn, David P. Fessell. How One Person Can Change the Conscience of an Organization. https://hbr.org/2019/12/how-one-person-can-change-the-conscience-of-an-organization (accessed 6/6/2021).

[98] **Setting boundaries and:** Kathomi Gatwiri, Lynne PcPherson. The power of no: Simone Biles, Naomi Osaka and Black women's resistance. https://theconversation.com/the-power-of-no-simone-biles-naomi-osaka-and-black-womens-resistance-165318 (accessed 7/30/2021).

[99] **For example, when:** Jing Pan. 'Who dreams this crap up?': Kevin O'Leary slams new rule that allows employees to ignore their bosses after hours. https://finance.yahoo.com/news/dreams-crap-kevin-oleary-slams-110400900.html (accessed 9/3/2024).

[100] **As leaders, it's essential:** Scott Mautz. 8 Defining Moments When You Should Push Back on Your Boss. https://www.inc.com/scott-mautz/8-defining-moments-when-you-should-push-back-on-your-boss.html (accessed 3/9/2021).

[101] **Adopting a can-do:** Jeff Haden. 7 Things Steve Jobs Said That You Should Say Every Single Day. https://www.inc.com/jeff-haden/7-things-steve-jobs-said-that-you-should-say-every-single-day.html (accessed 12/9/2019).

[102] **Gossip, often synonymous:** Deborah Grayson Riegel. Stop Complaining About Your Colleagues Behind Their Backs. https://hbr.org/2018/10/stop-complaining-about-your-colleagues-behind-their-backs (accessed 1/7/2020).

[103] **Stop gossip as:** Deborah Grayson Riegel. Stop Complaining About Your Colleagues Behind Their Backs. https://hbr.org/2018/10/stop-complaining-about-your-colleagues-behind-their-backs (accessed 1/7/2020).

[104] **Recent studies have also:** Richard Jenkins. Scientists discover that swearing helps us tolerate pain by up to a third. https://www.swnsdigital.com/2019/07/scientists-discover-that-swearing-helps-us-tolerate-pain-by-up-to-a-third/ (accessed 6/16/2020).

[105] **Nonetheless, there are:** Breanna Robinson. The most offensive American swear words ranked. https://www.indy100.com/viral/us-worst-swear-words-ranked-b1827546-2656995131 (accessed 3/20/2022).

[106] **That said, escalating:** Dana Brownlee. What To Do When Leadership Is In Denial: Try These 3 Techniques. https://www.forbes.com/sites/danabrownlee/2020/04/05/what-to-do-when-leadership-is-in-denial-try-these-3-techniques/ (accessed 4/5/2020).

[107] **These days, the landscape:** Don Reisinger. Companies Should Learn Elon Musk's 'Chain of Command' Rule. https://www.inc.com/don-reisinger/companies-should-learn-elon-musks-chain-of-command-rule.html (accessed 7/18/2020).

Skill Building

[108] **In the current economy:** Dan Schawbel. Are You Ready For The Age Of Career Diversification? https://www.forbes.com/sites/danschawbel/2014/01/10/are-you-ready-for-the-age-of-career-diversification/?sh=742de1bd54ca (accessed 3/9/2023).
[109] **Demonstrating an ability:** Nina Bowman. How to Demonstrate Your Strategic Thinking Skills. https://hbr.org/2019/09/how-to-demonstrate-your-strategic-thinking-skills (accessed 3/25/2020).
[110] **Recent research that analyzed:** Gene Hammett. 6 Signs Your Teammates Aren't on the Same Page. https://www.inc.com/gene-hammett/6-signs-your-teammates-arent-on-same-page.html (accessed 4/22/2021).
[111] **Generally, when you:** Matt Abrahams. Three Questions You Should Always Ask. http://www.nofreakingspeaking.com/wp-content/uploads/2017/08/Three_Questions_You_Should_Always_Ask_GSB_Article_07_28_17.pdf (accessed 5/27/2020).
[112] **Mastering the art:** Ellevate. 8 Game-Changing Strategies to Become More Influential at Work. https://www.entrepreneur.com/article/309103 (accessed 3/8/2021).
[113] **In sales and marketing, I:** Spencer Huang. Rap Music Taught Me How To Listen. https://www.linkedin.com/pulse/why-rap-artists-so-successful-conducting-work-meetings-spencer-huang (accessed 11/4/2019).
[114] **Writers today can benefit:** Bryan M Wolfe. Best AI writers of 2024. https://www.techradar.com/best/ai-writer (accessed 1/15/2024).
[115] **AI writing tools can also:** Viesturs Abelis. 10 productive ways how to use ChatGPT at work (your boss won't mind). https://desktime.com/blog/how-to-use-chatgpt-at-work (accessed 1/16/2023).
[116] **Conversation is an act:** Bedros Keuilian. Why Mastering the Art of Conversation Will Make You More Money. https://www.entrepreneur.com/article/326280 (accessed 12/3/2019).
[117] **Initiating a conversation:** Joe Keohane. How to Become a Master at Talking to Strangers. https://www.entrepreneur.com/starting-a-business/how-to-become-a-master-at-talking-to-strangers/375641 (accessed 7/13/2022).
[118] **Effective conversations begin with:** Minda Zetlin. How Bill Gates Has a Conversation and So Should You. https://www.inc.com/minda-zetlin/how-bill-gates-has-a-conversation-so-should-you.html?cid=search (accessed 3/16/2020).
[119] **Giving a speech to an audience:** Scott Mautz. How to Nail Every Presentation, According to TED's Top Speaking Coach. https://scottmautz.com/how-to-nail-every-presentation-according-to-teds-top-speaking-coach/ (accessed 11/6/2019).
[120] **Most people seek:** Scott Mautz. Bill Gates Accidentally Learned the Key to Public Speaking By Giving a Talk to Warren Buffett And Friends. https://www.inc.com/scott-mautz/bill-gates-accidentally-learned-key-to-public-speaking-by-giving-a-talk-to-warren-buffett-friends.html (accessed 11/18/2019).
[121] **Psychologists have determined:** Matt Abrahams. Five Common Communication Mistakes (And How to Fix Them). https://www.gsb.stanford.edu/insights/five-common-communication-mistakes-how-fix-them (accessed 5/22/2020).
[122] **Various studies have found:** Kasia Wezowski. 6 Ways to Look More Confident During a Presentation. https://hbr.org/2017/04/6-ways-to-look-more-confident-during-a-presentation (accessed 12/27/2019).

[123] **Neuroscientist Andrew:** Jessica Stillman. 3 Ways to Hack Your Brain to Conquer Your Nerves, According to a Stanford Neuroscientist. https://www.inc.com/jessica-stillman/stress-public-speaking-stanford-brain-hacks.html (accessed 6/1/2021).

[124] **It's OK to embrace:** Monica Torres. HuffPost. How to Calm Your Nerves Before Public Speaking at Work. https://www.huffpost.com/entry/public-speaking-tips-work_l_5d5aeb3fe4b04e1e14deb4bc (accessed 8/24/2019).

[125] **The primary goal of a slide:** Jason Aten. Please Stop Reading Off Your PowerPoint Slides. Here's What to Do Instead. https://www.inc.com/jason-aten/please-stop-reading-off-your-powerpoint-slides-heres-what-to-do-instead.html (accessed 3/9/2020).

[126] **Some advocate for:** Geoffrey James. The Real Reason Steve Jobs Hated PowerPoint. https://www.inc.com/geoffrey-james/steve-jobs-hated-powerpoint-you-should-too-heres-what-to-use-instead.html (accessed 2/7/2020).

[127] **Jeff Bezos, CEO:** Geoffrey James. Jeff Bezos Banned PowerPoint and It's Arguably the Smartest Management Move He's Ever Made. https://www.inc.com/geoffrey-james/jeff-bezos-banned-powerpoint-its-arguably-smartest-management-move-that-hes-ever-made.html (accessed 7/6/2020).

[128] **Instead, communicate:** David Ogilvy. Use smaller words. https://www.briankurtz.net/use-smaller-words/ (accessed 5/23/2020).

[129] **The ancient Greeks:** Bryan Clark. What Makes People Charismatic, and How You Can Be, Too. https://www.nytimes.com/2019/08/15/smarter-living/what-makes-people-charismatic-and-how-you-can-be-too.html (accessed 1/12/2021).

[130] **In business, leaders:** Matthew Hutson. The Charisma Effect. https://www.theatlantic.com/magazine/archive/2016/09/the-charisma-effect/492740/ (accessed 2/5/2021).

[131] **Maintaining consistent eye:** Ryan Shea. 8 ways smart people always start conversations. https://www.theladders.com/career-advice/8-ways-smart-people-always-start-conversations (accessed 1/27/2021).

[132] **According to research, participants:** Scott Olster. Embarrassment boosts creativity, why crying at work helps us all, and more top insights. https://www.linkedin.com/pulse/embarrassment-boosts-creativity-why-crying-work-helps-rundown-us-/ (accessed 10/5/2019).

[133] **What's most important is your story:** Paul Smith. 10 Stories Great Leaders Tell. https://www.linkedin.com/pulse/10-stories-great-leaders-tell-paul-andrew-smith/. (accessed 8/1/2019).

Unlocking Soft Skills

[134] **By some estimates:** Jessica Stillman. Why Success Depends More on personality Than Intelligence. https://www.inc.com/jessica-stillman/success-depends-more-on-personality-than-intelligence-new-study-shows.html (accessed 5/19/2021).

[135] **Intelligence is a term:** Difference Between IQ and Intelligence. http://www.differencebetween.net/science/difference-between-iq-and-intelligence/ (accessed 10/11/2021).

[136] **While there are several:** Jeff Haden. Steve Jobs Said This Is the Ultimate Sign of High Intelligence. But There Is a Catch. https://www.inc.com/jeff-haden/steve-jobs-said-this-is-ultimate-sign-of-high-intelligence-but-there-is-one-catch.html (accessed 3/6/2021).

[137] **In general, people who possess:** Bruno Campello de Zouza. What are behavioral signs that someone has an IQ above 140 (it doesn't matter if in a public or private atmosphere)? https://www.quora.com/What-are-behavioural-signs-that-someone-has-an-IQ-above-140-it-doesn-t-matter-if-in-a-public-or-private-atmosphere (accessed 3/19/2020).

[138] **They often exhibit active:** Michael Ealey. What is the best way to quickly detect high-IQ people? https://www.quora.com/What-is-the-best-way-to-quickly-detect-high-IQ-people?share=1 (accessed 3/18/2021).

[139] **Our intellectual capacity:** Jessica Stillman. How to Think Like a Genius, According to Nobel Laureate Richard Feynman. https://www.inc.com/jessica-stillman/richard-feynman-genius-intelligence-advice.html (accessed 2/20/2021).

[140] **Years of research have revealed:** Norman Murray. 11 Signs you Lack Emotional Intelligence! https://www.linkedin.com/pulse/11-signs-you-lack-emotional-intelligence-norman-murray (accessed 4/16/2020).

[141] **This finding challenges:** Fernando Teixeira and Izabela Cardozo. The 'lone genius' myth: Why even great minds collaborate. https://www.bbc.com/worklife/article/20210308-the-lone-genius-myth-why-even-great-minds-collaborate (accessed 4/4/2021).

[142] **Emotional Intelligence (EI):** Shawn Andrews. EQ vs EI Revisited. https://www.drshawnandrews.com/blogs/eq-vs-ei-revisited (accessed 2/9/2022).

[143] **EQ can be further:** Daniel Goleman, Richard E. Boyatzis. Emotional Intelligence Has 12 Elements. Which Do You Need to Work On? https://hbr.org/2017/02/emotional-intelligence-has-12-elements-which-do-you-need-to-work-on (accessed 5/16/2021).

[144] **EQ is what helps:** Marcus a. wright. What is Leadership Emotional Intelligence? http://marcusawright.com/emotional-intelligence/ (accessed 6/24/2020).

[145] **If you are deficient:** Travis Murray. 11 Signs You Lack Emotional Intelligence! https://www.entrepreneur.com/growing-a-business/11-signs-that-you-lack-emotional-intelligence/299452 (accessed 1/6/2019).

[146] **Abraham Lincoln's legacy:** Adi Ignatius. Real Leaders: Abraham Lincoln and the Power of Emotional Discipline. https://hbr.org/podcast/2020/03/real-leaders-abraham-lincoln-and-the-power-of-emotional-discipline (accessed 3/19/2020).

[147] **Studies reveal the profound:** What is Optimism? https://www.psychologytoday.com/us/basics/optimism (accessed 10/26/2022).

[148] **Among the most:** Why good leaders learn it's not about the next step, but taking a step back. https://federalnewsnetwork.com/federal-insights/2021/02/why-good-leaders-learn-its-not-about-the-next-step-but-taking-a-step-back/ (accessed 2/17/2021).

[149] **Studies have confirmed that practicing:** Nicole Lanctot. How to lead-and succeed-with emotional intelligence. https://www.fastcompany.com/90604305/how-to-lead-and-succeed-with-emotional-intelligence (accessed 2/20/2021).

Cognition and Bias

[150] **Bias is a fundamental:** Maria Popova. The Benjamin Franklin Effect: The Surprising Psychology of How to Handle Haters. https://www.brainpickings.org/2014/02/20/the-benjamin-franklin-effect-mcraney/ (accessed 7/26/2020).
[151] **I've seen many:** Carey Morewedge. How to stop cognitive bias from affecting our decisions. https://thehill.com/opinion/finance/467892-how-to-stop-cognitive-bias-from-affecting-our-decisions (accessed 10/29/2019).
[152] **Authority Bias:** Marcus Lu. 50 Cognitive Biases in the Modern World. https://www.visualcapitalist.com/50-cognitive-biases-in-the-modern-world/ (accessed 3/15/2021).
[153] **Sunken-cost Fallacy:** Jessica Stillman. 6 Cognitive Biases That Are Messing Up Your Decision Making. https://www.inc.com/jessica-stillman/6-cognitive-biases-that-are-messing-up-your-decision-making.html (accessed 7/5/2020).
[154] **This phenomenon, known:** Elliot Aronson and Carol Tavris. The Role of Cognitive Dissonance in the Pandemic. https://www.theatlantic.com/ideas/archive/2020/07/role-cognitive-dissonance-pandemic/614074/ (accessed 7/15/2020).

Decisions and Problem-Solving

[155] **Warren Buffett exemplifies:** Wanda Thibodeaux. There Are 2 Types of Leaders: Water and Rock. Here's Why Both Are Important. https://www.inc.com/wanda-thibodeaux/there-are-2-types-of-leaders-water-rock-heres-why-both-are-important.html (accessed 3/30/2020).
[156] **Effective decision-making often:** Cheryl Strauss Einhorn. 11 Myths About Decision-Making. https://hbr.org/2021/04/11-myths-about-decision-making (accessed 5/12/2022).
[157] **Jeff Bezos claims:** Jeff Haden. Billionaire Jeff Bezos: People who are 'right a lot' make decisions differently than everyone else—here's how. https://www.cnbc.com/2019/03/12/amazon-billionaire-jeff-bezos-explains-why-the-smartest-people-change-their-minds-often.html (accessed 3/3/2020).
[158] **While much has been written:** Joseph L. Badaracco. How to Tackle Your Toughest Decisions. https://hbr.org/2016/09/how-to-tackle-your-toughest-decisions (accessed 8/23/2024).
[159] **Reflecting on that:** David Maxfield. How to Get People to Accept a Tough Decision. https://hbr.org/2018/04/how-to-get-people-to-accept-a-tough-decision (accessed 12/27/2019).
[160] **However, the reality is something:** Jeff Haden. How Do Great Leaders Solve Problems? By Asking 1 Question, Then Shutting the (Heck) Up. https://www.inc.com/jeff-haden/how-do-great-leaders-solve-problems-by-asking-1-question-then-shutting-heck-up.html (accessed 1/29/2021).
[161] **Bill Gates is an excellent:** Chris Williams. I worked closely with Bill Gates for 8 years as an executive at Microsoft. Here are the 3 lessons he taught me that I'll never forget. https://www.entrepreneur.com/business-news/bill-gates-is-always-right-3-lessons-from-ex-microsoft-vp/450844 (accessed 5/10/2023).
[162] **The World Economic:** Want better strategies? Become a bulletproof problem solver. https://www.mckinsey.com/business-functions/strategy-and-corporate-finance/our-insights/want-better-strategies-become-a-bulletproof-problem-solver (accessed 7/5/2021).

[163] **Define the problem:** Sellingsherpa. Bulletproof problem-Solving (Book Summary). https://sellingsherpa.com/index.php/2020/08/30/bulletproof-problem-solving-book-summary/ (accessed 8/6/2022).
[164] **Ideally, while decisions**: Marcel Schwantes. Jeff Bezos Says Your Most Important Decisions in Life Should Always Be Made This Way (but It Will Make Many Uncomfortable). https://www.inc.com/marcel-schwantes/jeff-bezos-says-your-most-important-decisions-in-life-should-always-be-made-this-way-but-it-will-make-many-uncomfortable.html (accessed 3/1/2020).
[165] **Your intuition can be considered:** Stacey Hagen. Using your intuition in business can be powerful. https://www.createcoachingconsulting.com/how-to-use-your-intuition-in-business/ (accessed 11/6/2022).

Transitioning Jobs

[166] **According to the Bureau:** Amy Blaschka. The 3 Best Ways To Embrace Your Non-Linear Career. https://www.forbes.com/sites/amyblaschka/2023/06/10/the-3-best-ways-to-embrace-your-non-linear-career/ (accessed 8/29/2024).
[167] **A non-linear career path:** Caroline Castrillon. Why Non-Linear Career Paths Are The Future. https://www.forbes.com/sites/carolinecastrillon/2023/02/26/why-non-linear-career-paths-are-the-future/ (accessed 8/29/2024).
[168] **Workers who remain:** Vivian Giang. You Should Plan On Switching Jobs Every Three Years For the Rest Of Your Life. https://www.fastcompany.com/3055035/you-should-plan-on-switching-jobs-every-three-years-for-the-rest-of-your-?__twitter_impression=true (accessed 1/15/2021).
[169] **It's common to see:** Ron Martinsen. Lessons Learned after 25 Years At Microsoft. https://www.linkedin.com/pulse/lessons-learned-after-25-years-microsoft-ron-martinsen/ (accessed 10/17/2019).
[170] **A recent study:** New DDI Research: 57 Percent of Employees Quit Because of Their Boss. https://www.prnewswire.com/news-releases/new-ddi-research-57-percent-of-employees-quit-because-of-their-boss-300971506.html (accessed 2/2/2020).
[171] **Despite the fear:** Brigette Hyacinth. Work for someone who appreciates your ideas, loyalty and hard work. https://brigettehyacinth.com/work-for-someone-who-appreciates-your-ideas-loyalty-and-hard-work-2/ (accessed 11/8/2019).
[172] **When you decide:** J. T. O'Donnell. Quitting your job? A hiring manager says these are the 6 worst ways to do it. https://www.cnbc.com/2019/01/22/6-common-mistakes-to-avoid-when-quitting-your-job.html (accessed 1/19/2020).
[173] **Submitting a resignation:** Allison Pohle. How to Quit Your Job Gracefully. https://www.wsj.com/articles/how-to-quit-your-job-gracefully-11623600002 (accessed 6/13/2021).
[174] **Career change often involves:** Herminia Ibarra. Reinventing Your Career in the Time of Coronavirus. https://herminiaibarra.com/reinventing-your-career-in-the-time-of-coronavirus/ (accessed 12/14/2020).
[175] **Sometimes, it takes:** Maddy Savage. Has the meaning of work changed forever? https://www.bbc.com/worklife/article/20201112-has-the-meaning-of-work-changed-forever (accessed 12/9/2020).

Job Search Strategies

[176] **The interview is an opportunity:** Peter Economy. 5 Simple Ways to Reveal a Toxic Company Culture in a Job Interview. https://www.inc.com/peter-economy/5-simple-ways-to-learn-about-toxic-company-culture-in-a-job-interview.html (accessed 1/26/2020).

[177] **Critically assess each target:** Amy Elisa Jackson. These are the 7 types of companies that you should stay away from. https://www.fastcompany.com/90439288/these-are-the-7-types-of-companies-that-you-should-stay-away-from?ref=hvper.com (accessed 3/25/2021).

[178] **In today's rapidly:** Schwabjobs. "Technology is changing, and the world is evolving. I believe that networking gives you the ability to connect with people, build relationships, have conversations, and ask questions." https://jobs.schwabjobs.com/6-tips-on-networking-and-how-to-make-connections (accessed 8/23/2021).

[179] **Interestingly, networking with:** Llana Gershon. "A Friend of a Friend" Is No Longer the Best Way to Find a Job. https://hbr.org/2017/06/a-friend-of-a-friend-is-no-longer-the-best-way-to-find-a-job (accessed 1/4/2020).

[180] **Don't rely solely:** Charlotte Cowles. How to Get Back Into the Job Market. https://www.nytimes.com/2021/04/24/travel/job-market-tips.html (accessed 5/15/2021).

[181] **Your résumé should be:** Scott Mautz. The CEO of a Major Headhunting Firm Says the Best Resume He's Ever Seen Had These 6 Things. https://www.inc.com/scott-mautz/the-ceo-of-a-major-headhunting-firm-says-best-resume-hes-ever-seen-had-these-6-things.html (accessed 4/22/2020).

[182] **Customize: Tailor your:** Korn Ferry Advance. Five Common Resume Mistakes to Avoid. https://www.kfadvance.com/articles/5-common-resume-mistakes-to-avoid (accessed 5/20/2021).

[183] **Contact info: Include:** Kyle Schnitzer. If your resume is missing this number, you can kiss the job away. https://www.theladders.com/career-advice/resume-missing-this-number-goes-in-trash (accessed 4/30/2021).

[184] **Remote-specific skills:** Jared Lindzon. 5 ways your résumé should look different post-pandemic. https://www.fastcompany.com/90656448/5-ways-your-resume-should-look-different-post-pandemic (accessed 7/24/2021).

[185] **Objective: Some recruiters:** Melanie Curtin. 5 Things to Leave Off Your Resume, According to Recruiters. https://www.inc.com/melanie-curtin/5-things-recruiters-wish-youd-leave-off-your-resume.html (accessed 3/3/2020).

[186] **Exaggerating: For recent:** Courtney Connley. Suzy Welch: 3 words every recent grad should remove from their resume 'right this minute'. https://www.msn.com/en-us/money/careersandeducation/suzy-welch-3-words-every-recent-grad-should-remove-from-their-resume-right-this-minute/ar-BBZGbOL (accessed 2/5/2020).

[187] **Clarity: Strive to:** Tim Denning. After 4 months and 50+ Rejections, I finally Landed My Dream Gig. https://www.linkedin.com/pulse/after-4-months-50-rejections-i-finally-landed-my-dream-tim-denning/ (accessed 10/8/2019).

[188] **Maintaining an active:** Dustin McKissen. Here's an example of the perfect LinkedIn profile summary, according to Harvard career experts. https://www.cnbc.com/2019/09/25/example-template-of-perfect-linkedin-profile-according-to-harvard-career-experts.html (accessed 1/16/2021).

[189] **Your online profile picture:** Peter Economy. LinkedIn Career Expert Says to Get Your Next Job, Your LinkedIn Profile Should Have These 7 Simple Things. https://www.inc.com/peter-economy/linkedin-career-expert-says-to-get-your-next-job-your-linkedin-profile-should-have-these-7-simple-things.html (accessed 2/26/2020).

[190] **Artificial intelligence, bots:** Cara Heilmann. Artificial Intelligence And Recruiting: A Candidate's Perspective. https://www.forbes.com/sites/forbescoachescouncil/2018/06/22/artificial-intelligence-and-recruiting-a-candidates-perspective/#3cd32c997a88 (accessed 10/2/2020).

[191] **However, researchers ultimately:** John Sullivan. 7 Rules for Job Interview Questions That Result in Great Hires. https://hbr.org/2016/02/7-rules-for-job-interview-questions-that-result-in-great-hires (accessed 2/15/2020).

[192] **If you're struggling to land:** Rosa Elizabeth Vargas. Is Your Lack Of Confidence Holding Your Job Search Back? https://www.workitdaily.com/job-search-confidence (accessed 10/2/2020).

[193] **A recent survey of 1,000:** Shalene Gupta. This is how many rejections it takes before job seekers lose confidence. https://www.fastcompany.com/90763477/survey-how-many-rejections-job-seekers-lose-confidence-joblist (accessed 6/29/2022).

[194] **Courage, confidence:** Tim Denning. After 4 months and 50+ Rejections, I finally Landed My Dream Gig. https://www.linkedin.com/pulse/after-4-months-50-rejections-i-finally-landed-my-dream-tim-denning/ (accessed 10/8/2019).

[195] **Don't overlook job postings:** Art Markman. You Don't Need to Meet Every Qualification to Apply for a Job. https://hbr.org/2019/05/you-dont-need-to-meet-every-qualification-to-apply-for-a-job (accessed 1/17/2021).

[196] **Job seekers should believe:** Brigette Hyacinth. You Get the Talent that You Pay for! https://brigettehyacinth.com/you-get-the-talent-that-you-pay-for/ (accessed 11/8/2019).

[197] **Your "personal brand" is an:** Catherine Cote. Personal Branding: What It Is & Why It Matters. https://online.hbs.edu/blog/post/personal-branding-at-work (accessed 7/16/2024).

[198] **When evolving your personal:** Rachel Montañez. How to Define, Develop, and Communicate Your Personal Brand. https://hbr.org/2023/09/how-to-define-develop-and-communicate-your-personal-brand (accessed 7/16/2024).

[199] **It's important to dress:** Elizabeth C. Tippett. Pants or no pants? Tips for virtual job interviews from home. https://theconversation.com/pants-or-no-pants-tips-for-virtual-job-interviews-from-home-137552 (accessed 5/4/2020).

[200] **Every candidate should:** Christine Schoenwald. 3 Things People Immediately Judge You On When You First Meet Them. https://www.yourtango.com/self/what-people-judge-you-on-first-impression (accessed 8/26/2021).

[201] **Be honest, and don't:** Rachel Feintzeig. The Lies We Tell During Job Interviews. https://www.wsj.com/articles/the-lies-we-tell-during-job-interviews-11610326800 (accessed 1/15/2021).

[202] **Ask questions freely:** Betsy Mikel. Barbara Corcoran: Avoid Asking 3 Questions in a Job Interview at All Cost. It'll Cost You the Job. https://www.inc.com/betsy-mikel/the-3-worst-questions-you-could-ask-in-any-job-interview-according-to-barbara-corcoran.html (accessed 12/1/2019).

[203] **Failures: When asked:** Korn Ferry Advance. How To Tackle 5 Trick Interview Questions. https://www.kfadvance.com/articles/how-to-tackle-5-interview-trap-questions (accessed 5/20/2020).

[204] **Teamwork: When responding:** Nicholas Hawkins. Your ultimate guide to ace the most common interview questions. https://www.fastcompany.com/90756503/your-ultimate-guide-to-ace-the-most-common-interview-questions (accessed 6/2/2022).

[205] **"Tell me about yourself:** Kent Aldershof. What is the best answer to the interview question 'Tell me something about yourself'? https://www.quora.com/What-is-the-best-answer-to-the-interview-question-Tell-me-something-about-yourself/answer/Kent-Aldershof (accessed 7/10/2020).

[206] **Pride: If you're asked:** KForce. 5 Behavioral Interview Questions to Know. https://www.kforce.com/articles/common-behavioral-interview-questions/ (accessed 3/4/2021).

[207] **While you must impress:** Skip Freeman. Is the Hiring Process Really a 'Game'? Yes, it is! https://www.personalbrandingblog.com/is-the-hiring-process-really-a-game-yes-it-is/ (accessed 2/4/2020).

[208] **Ageism remains:** 4 Telltale Signs of Ageism in the Workforce. https://www.leclerclaw.com/blog/2020/07/4-telltale-signs-of-ageism-in-the-workplace/ (accessed 1/8/2021).

[209] **Age bias can vary:** Clare Ansberry. Worried About Ageism? Where You Live Matters. https://www.wsj.com/articles/worried-about-ageism-where-you-live-matters-11612198542 (accessed 2/4/2021).

[210] **However, a recent study examining:** Jeff Haden. A Study of 2.7 Million Startups Found the Ideal Age to Start a Business (and It's Much Older Than You Think). https://www.inc.com/jeff-haden/a-study-of-27-million-startups-found-ideal-age-to-start-a-business-and-its-much-older-than-you-think.html (accessed 2/2/2019).

[211] **It's interesting how human:** Katherine Ellen Foley. Scientifically, this is the best age for you to lead. https://qz.com/work/1614701/the-best-age-to-lead-is-probably-in-your-50s (accessed 06/12/2019).

[212] **Further, age does not:** Rich Karlgaard. It's never too late to Start a Brilliant Career. The Wall Street Journal. https://www.wsj.com/articles/its-never-too-late-to-start-a-brilliant-career-11556896617 (accessed 10/6/2019).

[213] **If you're encountering:** Beth Jensen. Explain Career Gaps and Transitions on Your Resume. https://www.gsb.stanford.edu/insights/explain-career-gaps-transitions-your-resume (accessed 5/22/2020).

[214] **When you first receive:** Gary Burnison. The Biggest Mistakes to Avoid in Salary Negotiation. https://www.kfadvance.com/articles/the-biggest-mistakes-to-avoid-in-salary-negotiation (accessed 5/20/2020).

[215] **When negotiating, refrain:** Amy Elisa Jackson. Nine Words And Phrases to Avoid When You're Negotiating A Salary. https://www.fastcompany.com/3068323/nine-words-and-phrases-to-avoid-when-youre-negotiating-a-salary (accessed 1/13/2021).

[216] **Is this the job:** Gwen Moran. 5 essential questions to ask before you accept any job offer. https://www.fastcompany.com/90419934/5-essential-questions-to-ask-before-you-accept-any-job-offer (accessed 11/15/2019).

[217] **If faced with a:** J.T. O'Donnell. Never do these 2 things after getting a lowball salary offer, says career expert—a 'perfect example' of how to respond. https://www.cnbc.com/2021/04/08/example-of-how-to-respond-to-lowball-job-salary-offer-and-2-things-you-should-never-do.html (accessed 4/8/2021).

Management and Leadership

[218] **Most successful leaders are characterized:** Sylvia Lafair. Here's Why Ineffective Bosses Are So Hard to Fire, According to Warren Buffett. https://www.inc.com/sylvia-lafair/heres-why-ineffective-bosses-are-hard-to-fire-according-to-warren-buffett.html (accessed 4/26/2020).

[219] **The distinction between:** Rose Johnson. What Are the Essential Differences Between Being an Effective Manager & an Effective Leader? https://smallbusiness.chron.com/essential-differences-between-being-effective-manager-effective-leader-32963.html (accessed 10/18/2020).

[220] **The difference between managing:** Liz Brunner. Managers create circles of power. Leaders create circles of influence. https://ceoworld.biz/2022/01/08/managers-create-circles-of-power-leaders-create-circles-of-influence/ (accessed 12/3/2022).

[221] **Not everyone excels at:** John P. Kotter. What Leaders Really Do. https://enterprisersproject.com/sites/default/files/What%20Leaders%20Really%20Do.pdf (accessed 12/14/2019).

[222] **Managers and leaders complement:** Ron Ashkenas and Brook Manville. You Don't Have to Be CEO to Be a Visionary Leader. https://hbr.org/2019/04/you-dont-have-to-be-ceo-to-be-a-visionary-leader (accessed 3/8/2021).

[223] **Affiliative: Affiliative leaders:** David Vallance. Stop trusting your gut and lead with intent. https://blog.dropbox.com/topics/work-culture/leading-with-intent (accessed 12/16/2019).

[224] **Amiable: Amiable leaders:** 4 Personality Types that all Leaders Should Learn to Recognize. https://crestcom.com/blog/2015/11/24/4-personality-types-that-all-leaders-should-learn-to-recognize/ (accessed 3/20/2021).

[225] **Harmonizing: Harmonizing leaders:** Marcel Schwantes. 5 Personality Traits You Must Learn, Based on The Most Successful Leaders. https://www.inc.com/marcel-schwantes/5-personality-traits-you-must-learn-based-on-most-successful-leaders.html (accessed 12/20/2019).

[226] **Producer: These:** Marcel Schwantes. 5 Personality Traits You Must Learn, Based on The Most Successful Leaders. https://www.inc.com/marcel-schwantes/5-personality-traits-you-must-learn-based-on-most-successful-leaders.html (accessed 12/20/2019).

[227] **While many leaders employ:** Marcel Schwantes. Want to Be a Great Leader? The Smartest Ones Start by Doing These 4 Rare Things. https://www.inc.com/marcel-schwantes/want-to-be-a-great-leader-smartest-ones-start-by-doing-these-4-rare-things.html (accessed 12/3/2019).

[228] **Beyond leadership style:** Dennis C. Miller. Nonprofit Leadership Styles and Skills for Success. https://dennismiller.com/blog/nonprofit-leadership-styles-and-skills-for-success (accessed 5/10/2021).

[229] **As teams and businesses:** Julie Zhuo. As Your Team Gets Bigger, Your Leadership Style Has to Adapt. https://hbr.org/2019/03/as-your-team-gets-bigger-your-leadership-style-has-to-adapt (accessed 1/4/2020).

[230] **As a leader, creating:** Peter Bregman. To Develop Leadership Skills, Practice in a Low-Risk Environment. https://hbr.org/2019/04/to-develop-leadership-skills-practice-in-a-low-risk-environment (accessed 1/6/2020).

[231] **Many managers still rely:** Marcel Schwantes. 7 Harsh Truths That Will Improve Your Leadership Skills Overnight. https://www.inc.com/marcel-schwantes/7-brutal-truths-every-smart-leader-needs-to-constantly-revisit.html (accessed 11/24/2019).

[232] **The saying "Actions:** Maya Hu-Chan. Why Words Can Speak Louder Than Actions in Leadership. https://www.inc.com/maya-hu-chan/why-words-can-speak-louder-than-actions-in-leadership.html (accessed 2/4/2021).

[233] **Avoid using contractions:** Jeff Boss. The Leadership Guide To Choosing The Right Words. https://www.forbes.com/sites/jeffboss/2015/10/02/the-leadership-guide-to-choosing-the-right-words/?sh=4af9a67f2618 (accessed 12/5/2022).

[234] **Plenty of managers thrive:** Steve Strauss. Why You Shouldn't Always Tell Your Employees What to Do. https://gusto.com/blog/people-management/employee-empowerment-defined (accessed 11/2/2019).

[235] **Management and leadership proficiency:** Quora. How to Avoid the Most Common Mistakes Leaders Make. https://www.inc.com/quora/how-to-avoid-most-common-mistakes-leaders-make.html (accessed 4/21/2020).

[236] **Gates, for example**: Sydney Lake. Bill Gates 'didn't believe in vacations' and worked on the weekends while building Microsoft—but regretted it. Here are his 3 tips for success. https://finance.yahoo.com/news/bill-gates-didn-t-believe-173907060.html (accessed 4/6/2024).

[237] **Wise leaders continually:** Rhett Power. 5 Life Lessons That Will Make You a Better Leader. https://www.inc.com/rhett-power/5-life-lessons-that-will-make-you-a-better-leader.html (accessed 3/21/2020).

[238] **Creating a culture of:** David Robson. Why it's so hard to work with a creative genius. https://www.bbc.com/worklife/article/20210507-why-its-so-hard-to-work-with-a-creative-genius (accessed 5/18/2021).

[239] **Superstars often exhibit:** Stephen Denny. 5 Rules for Managing Superstars (and Their Egos). https://www.inc.com/stephen-denny/5-rules-for-managing-superstars-and-their-egos-in-your-small-business.html (accessed 6/24/2020).

[240] **Micromanagement is generally:** Brigette Hyacinth. Micromanagement make Best People Quit. https://www.linkedin.com/pulse/micromanagement-make-best-people-quit-brigette-hyacinth/ (accessed 8/15/2020).

[241] **Executives are not :** Jeff Meade. If You're the Lifeblood of Your Business, Then You've Doomed It to Failure. https://www.entrepreneur.com/article/367240 (accessed 4/14/2021).

[242] **If you work for:** Sandeep Kahyap. Managing a Micromanaging Boss. https://www.linkedin.com/pulse/managing-micromanaging-boss-sandeep-kashyap/. (accessed 10/15/2019).

[243] **I've observed that weak**: Jeannine Mancini. Warren Buffett Warns Watch Out—'There Is Seldom Just One Cockroach In The Kitchen'. https://www.benzinga.com/personal-finance/24/02/37072933/warren-buffett-warns-watch-out-there-is-seldom-just-one-cockroach-in-the-kitchen (accessed 2/12/2024).

[244] **Receiving recognition from:** Tim Denning. The Power of Acknowledging Other People's Success. https://medium.com/swlh/the-power-of-acknowledging-other-peoples-success-94bd1b94cceb (accessed 8/24/2019).

[245] **Show your commitment:** Melissa Raffoni. How to Get Noticed by Your Boss's Boss. https://hbr.org/2019/10/how-to-get-noticed-by-your-bosss-boss (accessed 10/20/2019).

[246] **Research indicates that employees thrive:** Brigette Hyacinth. A person who feels appreciated will always do more than what is expected. https://brigettehyacinth.com/good-bosses-appreciate-their-employees-2/ (accessed 11/8/2019).

[247] **"Do what you say:** Cory Dobbs. Leadership Principle #1: Do What You Say You Will Do. http://accessathletes.com/blog/blogdisplay.cfm?/Leadership-Principle--Do-What-You-Say-You-Will-Do-815 (accessed 12/29/2019).
[248] **Taking ownership of mistakes:** Benjamin Hardy. 10 Things Unstoppable People Do That Average People Don't. https://www.inc.com/benjamin-p-hardy/10-things-unstoppable-people-do-that-average-people-dont.html (accessed 11/5/2019).
[249] **We all make mistakes:** Jim Schleckser. How to Say You're Sorry. https://www.inc.com/jim-schleckser/how-to-say-youre-sorry.html (accessed 12/4/2020).
[250] **Owning up necessitates:** Mark Chussil. 4 Ways to Put Your Employees on a Fast Track Out the Door. https://www.entrepreneur.com/article/328089 (accessed 4/15/2021).
[251] **Despite its importance**: Steve Crabtree. Worldwide, 13% of Employees Are Engaged at Work. https://news.gallup.com/poll/165269/worldwide-employees-engaged-work.aspx (accessed 4/20/2024).
[252] **Motivation isn't something:** Ron Carucci. What Not to Do When You're Trying to Motivate Your Team. https://hbr.org/2018/07/what-not-to-do-when-youre-trying-to-motivate-your-team (accessed 12/13/2019).
[253] **Motivated employees thrive:** Alex Liu. Making Joy a Priority at Work. https://hbr.org/2019/07/making-joy-a-priority-at-work (accessed 12/28/2019).
[254] **Fear-based managers may:** Liz Ryan. The Five Characteristics Of Fear-Based Leaders. https://www.forbes.com/sites/lizryan/2015/11/25/the-five-characteristics-of-fear-based-leaders/?sh=32c9cf658a96 (accessed 12/12/2022)
[255] **They provide autonomy:** Workopolis. 5 ways to inspire and motivate your employees. https://hiring.workopolis.com/article/5-ways-inspire-motivate-employees/ (accessed 12/12/2022).
[256] **Psychological studies consistently:** Benjamin Hardy. 10 Things Unstoppable People Do That Average People Don't. https://www.inc.com/benjamin-p-hardy/10-things-unstoppable-people-do-that-average-people-dont.html (accessed 11/5/2019).
[257] **Some adhere to the Three:** Scott Mautz. Google Identifies Its Very Best Leaders Using These 13 Questions. https://www.inc.com/scott-mautz/google-identifies-their-very-best-leaders-using-these-13-questions.html (accessed 2/1/2020).
[258] **Setting priorities and daily:** Marcel Schwantes. Steve Jobs' Advice on Becoming More Productive Is Quite Brilliant. https://www.inc.com/marcel-schwantes/steve-jobs-advice-on-becoming-more-productive-is-quite-brilliant.html (accessed 4/16/2020)
[259] **An Exceptional relationship:** Deborah Lynn Bumberg. How to Build Better Relationships. https://www.gsb.stanford.edu/insights/how-build-better-relationships (accessed 1/29/2021).
[260] **Managing across generations:** Emma Waldman. How to Manage a Multi-Generational Team. https://hbr.org/2021/08/how-to-manage-a-multi-generational-team (accessed 9/20/2021).
[261] **Words carry consequences:** Gillian Zoe Segal. Warren Buffett calls this 'indispensable' life advice: 'You can always tell someone to go to hell tomorrow'. https://www.cnbc.com/2020/01/09/billionaire-warren-buffett-shares-indispensable-life-advice-he-learned-more-than-40-years-ago.html (accessed 4/27/2021).
[262] **Humor has the potential:** Richard Branson. Humour is a human Resource. https://fb.watch/ixx8hkwJYj/ (accessed 8/11/2019).

[263] **Numerous studies have:** Alison Beard. Leading with Humor. https://hbr.org/2014/05/leading-with-humor (accessed 4/20/2021).

[264] **"Follow your passion" is:** Jon M. Jachimomicz. 3 Reasons It's So hard to "Follow Your Passion". https://hbr.org/2019/10/3-reasons-its-so-hard-to-follow-your-passion (accessed 10/20/2019).

[265] **Many individuals follow:** Bill Murphy Jr. Warren Buffett: People Who Ignore These 13 Words of Advice will Probably Make Bad Decisions. https://www.inc.com/bill-murphy-jr/warren-buffett-people-who-ignore-these-13-words-of-advice-will-probably-make-bad-decisions.html (accessed 3/16/2021).

[266] **Discovering passion in our work:** Gene Marks. Why Veteran Entrepreneurs Laugh at You for Following Your 'Passion'. https://www.entrepreneur.com/article/308022 (accessed 10/25/2021).

[267] **Employers play an essential:** Lori Goler, Janelle Gale, Brynne Harrington, Adam Grant. Why People Really Quit their Job. https://hbr.org/2018/01/why-people-really-quit-their-jobs (accessed 7/26/2019).

[268] **Effective managers delegate:** Whitney Johnson. Why Talented People Don't Use Their Strengths. https://hbr.org/2018/05/why-talented-people-dont-use-their-strengths (accessed 1/27/2021).

[269] **Of course, the hack:** Phil Watson. Letting go just a little bit: Small projects can lead to great things. https://www.linkedin.com/pulse/letting-go-just-little-bit-small-projects-can-lead-great-phil-watson/ (accessed 8/8/2020).

[270] **When managers become:** Kevin Oakes. Let Your Top Performers Move Around the Company. https://hbr.org/2021/08/let-your-top-performers-move-around-the-company (accessed 9/1/2021).

[271] **"Groupthink" is characterized by:** Psychology Today Staff. Groupthink. https://www.psychologytoday.com/us/basics/groupthink (accessed 12/18/2022).

[272] **Workforce silence often:** Patricia Omoqui. The real reason your team won't give you honest feedback. https://www.atlassian.com/blog/leadership/team-feedback (accessed 4/22/2021).

[273] **Managing up is more:** Katie Taylor. The fine art of managing up. https://www.atlassian.com/blog/leadership/managing-up (accessed 6/6/2021).

[274] **Sleep is widely recognized:** Matt Haber. Why Sleep May Be the Secret Key to Your Success. https://www.inc.com/matt-haber/sleep-research-productivity-leadership-immune-system.html (accessed 7/21/2020).

[275] **Other research revealed:** Marco Hafner, Martin Stepanek, Jirka Taylor, Wendy M. Troxel, Christian Van Stolk. Why sleep matters—the economic costs of insufficient sleep. https://www.rand.org/pubs/research_reports/RR1791.html (accessed 12/1/2020).

[276] **Recent research by the American:** John Boitnott. Why Science Says 6 Hours of Sleep Isn't Enough for Entrepreneurs. https://www.entrepreneur.com/article/344178 (accessed 2/20/2020).

[277] **Change success hinges:** Freek Vermeulen. Many Strategies Fail Because They're Not Actually Strategies. https://hbr.org/2017/11/many-strategies-fail-because-theyre-not-actually-strategies (accessed 1/7/2020).

[278] **Substantial achievement often:** Jeff Haden. Why Brilliant Leadership Minds Embrace the Rule of 1 Percent. https://www.inc.com/jeff-haden/why-brilliant-leadership-minds-embrace-rule-of-1-percent.html (accessed 3/13/2021).

[279] **Baby Boomers (born from:** Gabrielle Bosché. How Millennials Lead: 4 Steps To Prepare Them For Leadership Today. https://www.appreciationatwork.com/blog/how-millennials-lead-4-steps-to-prepare-them-for-leadership-today/ (accessed 4/27/2021).

[280] **A recent survey of millennial:** Yasmin Gagne. How millennial bosses lead. https://www.fastcompany.com/90265053/how-millennial-bosses-lead (accessed 3/11/2020).

[281] **The urgency to address:** Douglas A. Ready. Leadership Mindsets for the New Economy. https://sloanreview.mit.edu/article/leadership-mindsets-for-the-new-economy/ (accessed 11/6/2019).

[282] **As companies transition:** Michael Schneider. Being a Leader Is More Difficult Than Ever Before Thanks to These 5 Workplace Trends. https://www.inc.com/michael-schneider/being-a-leader-is-more-difficult-than-ever-before-thanks-to-these-5-workplace-trends.html (accessed 12/17/2019).

[283] **When we think of managers:** Citrix x Quartz Creative. What if AI could manage better than your manager? https://qz.com/1917008/what-if-ai-could-manage-better-than-your-manager/ (accessed 12/6/2020).

[284] **As automation continues:** Kathryn Dill. Your Next Boss: More Harmony, Less Authority. https://www.wsj.com/articles/your-next-boss-may-be-more-of-a-coach-than-a-dictator-11610467280 (accessed 1/15/2021).

[285] **What does the future:** Douglas A. Ready, Carol Cohen, David Kiron, and Benjamin Pring. The New Leadership Playbook for the Digital Age. https://sloanreview.mit.edu/projects/the-new-leadership-playbook-for-the-digital-age/ (accessed 12/26/20).

[286] **Technology will shape:** Fortune + Lumen. The new digital DNA. https://view.ceros.com/fortune-magazine/lumen-art1/p/1 (accessed 1/29/2021).

[287] **Thus far, leaders are:** Peter Weill, Stephanie L. Woerner, Aman M. Shah. Does Your C-Suite Have Enough Digital Smarts? https://sloanreview.mit.edu/article/does-your-c-suite-have-enough-digital-smarts/ (accessed 2/6/2022).

[288] **Tomorrow's leaders may need:** Citrix X Quartz Creative. Welcome to the new frontier of WX. https://cms.qz.com/wp-content/uploads/2021/01/CitrixReport-PDF.pdf (accessed 1/8/2021).

[289] **Fortunately, colleges are:** Tom Connor. The skills of tomorrow's leaders. http://sponsored.bostonglobe.com/damore-mckim/business-skills-for-the-future/ (accessed 4/22/2021).

Conclusion: Embracing the Future

[290] **But despite the challenges:** Invesco. Four charts that show the power of investing in innovation. https://qz.com/1963048/four-charts-that-show-the-power-of-investing-in-innovation/ (accessed 3/14/2021).

[291] **When we examine historical:** Steven Johnson. How Humanity Gave Itself an Extra Life. https://www.nytimes.com/2021/04/27/magazine/global-life-span.html?smid=url-share (accessed 5/27/2021).

[292] **Maintaining a positive outlook:** Resilience and Hope. Focus on Wellness—Winter/Spring 2024. Dominican Hospital Foundation.

[293] **As we contemplate the many challenges:** Kareem Abdul-Jabbar. Kareem's daily Quote. https://kareem.substack.com/p/musks-latest-moral-meltdown-and-a (accessed 12/12/2023).